Cambridge Readings
in
Dante's *Comedy*

Cambridge Readings
in
Dante's *Comedy*

edited by
KENELM FOSTER and PATRICK BOYDE

Cambridge University Press

Cambridge

London   New York   New Rochelle

Melbourne   Sydney

Published by the Press Syndicate of the University of Cambridge
The Pitt Building, Trumpington Street, Cambridge CB2 1RP
32 East 57th Street, New York, NY 10022, USA
296 Beaconsfield Parade, Middle Park, Melbourne 3206, Australia

First published 1981

Printed in Great Britain at the Pitman Press, Bath

Library of Congress catalogue card number: 81-3861

British Library cataloguing in publication data
Cambridge readings in Dante's Comedy.
1. Dante Alighieri. Divina commedia – Addresses,
essays, lectures
I. Foster, Kenelm   II. Boyde, Patrick
851'.1   PQ4390
ISBN 0 521 24140 5

For

Uberto Limentani

Professor of Italian in the University of Cambridge

1962–1981

Contents

Contributor	Present Appointment	Date of 'lectura'
PIERO BOITANI	Professor of English, Perugia	11 March 1974
PATRICK BOYDE	Serena Professor of Italian, Cambridge	11 February 1974
JOSEPH CREMONA	Lecturer in Romance Philology, Cambridge	9 March 1981
JUDITH DAVIES	Lecturer in Italian, Cambridge	4 March 1974
PETER DRONKE	Reader in Medieval Latin, Cambridge	3 March 1975
KENELM FOSTER	Emeritus Reader in Italian, Cambridge	10 March 1980
ROBIN KIRKPATRICK	Lecturer in Italian, Cambridge	19 February 1979
UBERTO LIMENTANI	Emeritus Professor of Italian, Cambridge	8 February 1971
PHILIP McNAIR	Serena Professor of Italian, Birmingham	26 January 1970
PRUDENCE SHAW	Lecturer in Italian, Bedford College, London	1 March 1971

Preface

This book is called 'Readings' because the ten studies in it all started life as lectures given at Cambridge between 1970 and 1981, and given more or less in the manner of the traditional Italian *Lectura Dantis*, that is to say a commentary on one canto out of the hundred in the *Comedy*, followed by a reading aloud of the canto in full. For the purpose of this book the final canto-reading has been omitted, most of the text of each canto being included in the lecture, accompanied by a plain translation provided by the lecturer. The original lectures have of course been revised. Basically and recognisably, however, all the ten contributions remain lectures, and lectures very definitely intended – as they were in their original form – for non-specialists.

The idea itself of putting on a series of such lectures for the general public at Cambridge was the result of the warm reception accorded to a series of public lectures on Dante given in 1965 by the Department of Italian in the University to commemorate the seventh centenary of the poet's birth (these were subsequently edited by Professor Limentani and published by the Cambridge University Press under the title *The Mind of Dante*). The *lecturae* began in the Lent Term 1969 with eight selected cantos from the *Inferno*. The audience was provided with texts and literal translations and each speaker set out to weave an indispensable minimum of background information, paraphrase and the elucidation of obscurities into a connected critical account of the canto's style, structure, narrative technique, imagery, symbolism and thought. The formula proved a good one and the Department organised two further series of eight readings from the *Purgatorio* and *Paradiso* in 1970 and 1971. Three such cycles have now been completed, making a total of seventy-two lectures; and we believe that the ten readings selected represent a fair cross-section. Of the contributors to this volume nine are past or present members of the Italian Department at Cambridge, while the tenth, Mr Dronke, is Reader in Medieval Latin and has contributed to eight of the nine series.

The volume is offered, with affection and gratitude, to Uberto Limentani to mark his retirement from the Chair of Italian in 1981. Having made his way to England as a refugee from Fascism in 1939, he came to Cambridge as lector in 1945 and then rose through the ranks to succeed E. R. Vincent as Professor of Italian in 1962. In his various roles as lecturer, supervisor, scholar, editor, administrator and examiner he has made an inestimable contribution to the health and development of Italian Studies in Cambridge and in the British Isles. He has always been generous with encouragement and practical help, and everyone who has had dealings with him will know his courtesy and personal kindness. Although he would not regard himself as a Dantist, the *lecturae* have been his brain-child and especial concern and could never have taken place without his initiative and wise guidance. We therefore hope that the volume will prove an appropriate gift, and we are particularly glad that we have been able to include one of his own readings.

As interpretations of Dante the essays do not necessarily agree at all points. It was hardly to be expected that they would. It will be evident, for example, that Mr Dronke and Dr Foster offer rather different interpretations of some of the symbols used by Dante in the last cantos of the *Purgatorio*. Nor again is it to be assumed that the views of each and every contributor have remained entirely unchanged since the composition of his or her original *lectura*. The *lecturae* have been revised for publication in this collection, but the need for brevity has in some cases prevented a more nuanced exposition or the fuller development and documentation of a particular line of thought. It is partly with this in mind that we have given a list of the contributors, showing their present appointments and the dates of their original *lecturae*.

KENELM FOSTER
PATRICK BOYDE

Inferno XIII

PATRICK BOYDE

It has been said that any great narrative must contain passages of great drama, and there could hardly be a more striking instance of this truism than the thirteenth canto of the *Inferno*. A scene is set where acts of violence succeed each other in an atmosphere of mystery and suspense. Six actors reveal themselves in the sharply characterised words they are given to speak (almost two thirds of the canto being cast in the form of direct speech). The plot advances through the interaction of these six characters as they misunderstand and hurt each other, interrupt, taunt, plead for sympathy, or suffer pain and remorse. And the chief actor in the drama rewards study as an almost perfect example of the tragic hero as described by Aristotle in the *Poetics*.

It is not the first such play within the story of the *Comedy*, and the reader has been prepared for some of its more striking features in earlier cantos, notably the fifth and the tenth. We have already learnt that the protagonist of the poem – Dante himself, of course – does not remain a passive spectator as he passes through the vast, subterranean prison of Hell. He has been portrayed, with remarkable candour and detachment, as an impulsive, passionate and fallible man who is still all too preoccupied with the transient scandals, politics and often questionable ethical values of his own times. In the 'open prison' described in Canto v, the protagonist Dante was reduced to a dazed silence as he listened to the adulteress Francesca (murdered by her husband some fifteen years earlier) while she defended and exalted her guilty passion, using arguments and words that sound like a paraphrase of some of Dante's own love-poems. And he fainted when he heard how she had been seduced through the agency of one of the Arthurian romances he himself had so greatly admired. Later, in Canto x, in

1

the first block of the 'high security prison', he was goaded to anger and drawn into a brief but acrimonious exchange of insults by the inflexible and aggressively condescending attitude of Farinata degli Uberti, who had been the political and military leader of the Florentine Ghibellines in the years immediately before Dante's birth: a conversation that began with an appeal to their native city degenerated for a time into a quarrel that showed both men as incapable of distinguishing their *patria* from their *parte*. Here, in Canto XIII, Dante the character will suffer even more painful emotions and gain a deeper insight into the nature of right and wrong as he is confronted with another near contemporary who had been known throughout Italy in his lifetime, and whose career, writings and misfortunes anticipated those of the historical Dante.

Our canto differs from its predecessors, however, in one very important respect. Dante the poet has now given his readers some warning of what to expect. In Canto XI he interrupted the headlong thrust of his narrative by giving Virgil a long speech in which he explains the classification of sins that underlies the physical shape and the moral structure of Hell. The element of suspense in earlier cantos was of the relatively simple kind that results from a total ignorance of what to expect on the part of reader and protagonist alike. Thereafter it will be assumed that both the protagonist and the reader are in possession of a rough 'plan' or 'sketch' of the physical and moral geography of the Underworld. And the narrator creates suspense of a more subtle kind by modifying or frustrating the expectations set up by that plan.

We have learnt that the offences that bring a soul to Hell may be divided into two main classes, which correspond well enough for our present purposes with the distinction we still make between 'sins' and 'crimes'. Actions in the first category – the lesser offences punished in Upper Hell, as in the case of Francesca – resulted from weakness and a lack of self-control. They include the consequences of chronic idleness, outbursts of anger, excessive preoccupation with food, excessive indulgence in alcohol, the reckless satisfaction of sexual desire and the delusory pursuit of material possessions. Most people are familiar with the misery and the sheer waste of human potential that may follow from such causes. We deplore such behaviour – at least in others. And whatever the nature of our religious beliefs, we may still find it appropriate to speak not only of 'vices' but of 'sins'. However, we do not punish the offenders at law, if only because we recognise that the chief victims of these sins of weakness or incontinence are none other than the agents themselves.

The majority of the misdeeds punished in Lower Hell, on the other hand, are still regarded as 'crimes' even today. The sinners who suffer within the walled fortress of the City of Dis are punished for precisely the same reasons that criminals are punished in every human society. They acted with malice (*malizia*); they deliberately caused suffering to other people (Dante's verb is *contristare*); they did them an *ingiuria* (a word that in Dante's usage seems to hover between 'injustice' and 'injury'). Their actions are said to be 'displeasing to God' and 'hated in Heaven'. But they are also found displeasing and hated by men here on earth.

The sins of malice are subdivided into those involving violence or force, used deliberately but openly as in the case of an attack by a wild animal, and those that are performed stealthily or fraudulently with conscious deception of the victim. Unlike many modern English judges, who deal with muggers more severely than with confidence tricksters, Dante regards the crimes committed *con frode* as worse than those committed *con forza*. Such crimes destroy the ties of trust and love that should bind all men together, and they require the use or abuse of man's distinctive faculty, the God-given and godlike faculty of reason. Accordingly they are described as '*most* hateful to God', and they are punished in the eighth and ninth circles of Hell, which are the scene of the next three readings in this volume. The lesser sins of violence are dealt with in the seventh circle, which is where we find ourselves at the beginning of Canto XIII.

Most people have no difficulty in grasping the concepts of *incontinenza*, *malizia*, *forza* and *frode*, and no difficulty either in giving their general assent to the validity of the classification entailed. But many people are troubled both conceptually and emotionally by Virgil's further subdivision of the sins of violence. Highwaymen and tyrants obviously use open violence, and obviously deserve punishment. But what are money-lenders doing in Hell? What is the connection between blasphemy and

3

homosexuality? And why are profligates and suicides linked so closely together?

Reduced to its essentials, Virgil's reasoning goes something like this. Christ enjoined us to love God, ourselves and our fellow human beings, and these are the three 'persons' to whom we do violence ('si fa forza a tre persone / . . . . a Dio, a sé, al prossimo': *Inf.* XI, 29 and 31). In the most familiar case, that of violence to our fellows, we may hurt them directly, *in se*, by killing them or causing them grievous bodily harm, or we may hurt them indirectly, *in re*, by damaging, destroying or removing their possessions ('si pòne / far forza, dico, in loro ed in lor cose': 32). The same distinction may be introduced, however, in the analysis of the other main kinds of violence. We may attack God directly, through blasphemy, or indirectly, by committing offences against nature (which for Dante include the sins of Sodom and Cahors, sodomy and usury). We may hurt ourselves *in re*, by squandering our possessions, or *in se*, by killing ourselves. Hence we must expect to find prodigality and suicide punished together in the second of the three concentric rings or *gironi* that make up the seventh circle of Hell. The following table summarises the information that the reader is assumed to possess (Canto XI, 28–51).

				Canto
	al prossimo	in loro	Thugs	
		in lor cose	Robbers	XII
Malizia con FORZA	a sé	in sé	Suicides	
		ne' suoi beni	Squanderers	XIII
	a Dio	bestemmiando . . .	.Blasphemers	XIV
		spregiando . . .	Homosexuals	XV
			Usurers	XVI

It will be seen that, strictly speaking, only the last two of the seven sins of violence may be properly described as sins 'against nature'. But Dante believed that our love for God, ourselves, and our fellows is innate and natural, and that the attempt to hurt any of these three 'persons' is therefore *un*natural. And so he deliberately chose to dwell at length on the unnaturalness of the setting and the inhabitants in the seventh circle. The guardian who confronts the two poets as they scramble down a scree to enter the circle is the Minotaur, half man, half bull. The custodians of the first *girone* are centaurs, half horses and half men; and this *girone*, which is reserved for the violent-against-others, is filled with a river – of boiling blood. The ground of the third *girone* will prove to be a sterile waste of sand (an 'orribil sabbione'), where the 'sky' above will rain down flakes of fire. And at the beginning of our canto, having forded the river of blood in the company of one of the centaurs, Nessus, the travellers find themselves in a pathless wood, which is the negation in every possible way of the forest that Dante will enter in the Garden of Eden on the summit of Mount Purgatory. The simple negatives in lines 1 and 3 give way to a triple antithesis ('non . . . ma') driven home by the harsh-sounding words, especially the words in rhyme; while the negative form of the third sentence reminds us that, for Dante, the word 'savage' (*selvaggio*) derives from 'forest' (*selva*; cf. *Inf.* I, 5), which is in turn the enemy of cultivation or culture ('i luoghi colti').

> Non era ancor di là Nesso arrivato,
> quando noi ci mettemmo per un bosco
> che da neun sentiero era segnato.
> Non fronda verde, ma di color fosco;
> non rami schietti, ma nodosi e 'nvolti;
> non pomi v'eran, ma stecchi con tòsco.
> Non han sì aspri sterpi né sì folti
> quelle fiere selvagge che 'n odio hanno
> tra Cecina e Corneto i luoghi cólti. (1–9)

(Nessus had still to reach the other side, when we set off into a wood that was unmarked by any path. The leaves were not green but black; the branches not straight but gnarled and intertwined; and there was no fruit, only poisonous thorns. The thickets were even harsher and denser than in the area between Cècina and Corneto where the wild beasts shun all cultivation.)

The forest in the Garden of Eden will be gladdened by the song of birds. Here the nesting is done by the monstrous Harpies, who had spoken to Aeneas's men only to prophesy misfortune, and whose utterances now are not songs but lamentations:

> Quivi le brutte Arpie lor nidi fanno,
> che cacciar de le Strofade i Troiani
> con tristo annunzio di futuro danno.
> Ali hanno late, e colli e visi umani,
> piè con artigli, e pennuto 'l gran ventre;
> fanno lamenti in su li alberi strani. (10–15)

(This is where the Harpies make their nests – the loathsome creatures who drove the Trojans from the Strophades with a cruel prophecy of disasters to come. Their wings are broad, but they have the necks and faces of men. Their feet have claws, and their great bellies are covered in feathers. They utter lamentations on the unearthly trees.)

The grand manner of this last terzina, with its poetic word order, its strong caesurae, and the syntactic isolation of each line, gives way abruptly to direct speech in which the colloquial structures flow easily over the metrical boundaries. But the relaxation of the style is only illusory. Virgil's remarks are intended to heighten the suspense, not to explain it away:

> E 'l buon maestro: 'Prima che più entre,
> sappi che se' nel secondo girone',
> mi cominciò a dire, 'e sarai mentre
> che tu verrai ne l'orribil sabbione.
> Però riguarda ben; sì vederai
> cose che torrien fede al mio sermone.'　　(16–21)

(And my good master began: 'Before you go any further, you must realise that you're now in the second ring, and you'll remain there until you reach the Desert of Horror. So keep your eyes open. You'll see things that would rob my words of any credibility.')

Dante would have rejected any explanation by Virgil as beyond belief until he had gained direct experience through his senses. In the event, however, the senses of sight and hearing proved to be of no help, because they provided contradictory information: the protagonist could hear human beings crying in pain but could see no one. The banal explanation would have been that the voices were coming from people who were playing hide-and-seek behind the trees; and this is the thought that Virgil assumed he could read in his pupil's mind. Or, rather, this is what the narrator now ventures to assume that Virgil assumed, but at this point nothing is certain, and nothing can be affirmed with perfect confidence. At any rate, Virgil then encouraged Dante to resort to his sense of touch and to snap off a twig from one of the trees.

> Io sentia d'ogne parte trarre guai
> e non vedea persona che 'l facesse;
> per ch'io tutto smarrito m'arrestai.
> Cred' ïo ch'ei credette ch'io credesse
> che tante voci uscisser, tra quei bronchi,
> da gente che per noi si nascondesse.

6

Però disse 'l maestro: 'Se tu tronchi
qualche fraschetta d'una d'este piante,
li pensier c'hai si faran tutti monchi.'   (22–30)

(I could hear howls and sobs on all sides but could not see anyone who
uttered them, so I halted in confusion. I think he thought I thought that
all these voices were issuing among the trees from people who were
hiding from us. So he said: 'If you break off any small branch from one
of these trees, those thoughts of yours will all be cut short too.')

Hesitantly and unwillingly, Dante does as he is told. He
stretches out a hand just a little ('un poco'), and he plucks – not
'breaks' – the smallest of branches ('un ramicel'). But he has done
violence. A scream of pain issues from the offended tree itself.
There is a sinister pause while the trunk is stained with blood, for
this is not a gash but a wound. Then the tree hisses more words of
pain, reproach and rancour. Only now do we discover the grim
secret of the infernal forest. And in retrospect the half-human
monsters or the river flowing with boiling blood come to seem
almost natural as we realise that the gnarled, poisonous thorn-
trees in the pathless wood had all once been men.

Allor porsi la mano un poco avante
e colsi un ramicel da un gran pruno;
e 'l tronco suo gridò: 'Perché mi schiante?'
Da che fatto fu poi di sangue bruno,
ricominciò a dir: 'Perché mi scerpi?
non hai tu spirto di pietade alcuno?
Uomini fummo, e or siam fatti sterpi:
ben dovrebb' esser la tua man più pia,
se state fossimo anime di serpi.'   (31–9)

(Then I reached forward a little with my hand and plucked a twig from a
huge tree. And its trunk cried out: 'Why are you tearing me?' Then when
it had grown dark with blood, it continued: 'Why do you lacerate me?
Have you no spirit of pity? We used to be men; now we have become
thorn-trees. Your hand would have shown more pity if we had been the
souls of snakes!')

The situation itself is incredible, as we shall be told in line 50.
But Dante the poet works hard to make us suspend our disbelief
by concentrating our attention on one detail, and making it
comprehensible through a simile that has always been admired for
its precision. The blood and the words issue simultaneously from
the wounded trunk. How can this be? Well, it is no different in

principle from the bubbles of sap and hissing air that are expelled together from one end of a piece of green wood when the other end is put into a fire.

> Come d'un stizzo verde ch'arso sia
> da l'un de' capi, che da l'altro geme
> e cigola per vento che va via,
>   sì de la scheggia rotta usciva insieme
> parole e sangue; ond' io lasciai la cima
> cadere, e stetti come l'uom che teme.   (40–5)

(When a green log is burning at one end, it will weep at the other and whistle with the escaping wind; just so words and blood came out together from the broken branch. So I let the tip fall, and I stood stock-still like a man in fear.)

Virgil now expresses some remorse at his part in the affair (51), and yet excuses himself by implying that Dante ought to have been willing to believe the account that he, Virgil, might have given (46, 48; cf. 21). Dante the character is said to know the whole *Aeneid* by heart (*Inf.* xx, 114). He must therefore have remembered the haunting episode at the beginning of Book III, which occurred shortly before the Trojans had their unpleasant brush with the Harpies. Aeneas had landed in Thrace with a view to founding his new city. In preparing for a sacrifice, he tried to uproot several shoots from a clump of myrtle. There too the tree had shed drops of dark blood, and finally a voice had called from the foot of the clump: 'Aeneas, why do you lacerate me?' ('quid me, Aenea, laceras?'). The voice proved to be that of the murdered Polydorus, a son of Priam, who had been killed for his gold by his Thracian host; and the saplings that grow up from his body resemble the spears used by his assassins. Dante had read all this in Virgil's poem (48). But he behaved like the apostle Thomas, refusing to believe until he had 'stretched out his hand' (49; cf. John 20.27), and had placed it, so to speak, in the tree's bleeding side. The character has been painfully reminded of the scholastics' tag: *oportet addiscentem credere* ('a pupil must take things on trust'). And the reader is probably intended to meditate on Christ's final words to his doubting disciple: 'Blessed are they that have not seen, and yet have believed'.

A closer comparison of Dante's free imitation with the Virgilian original would reveal a great deal about his narrative art, for it is wholly characteristic of him that he should find inspiration in the work of a classical poet – especially in his *autore* – and that he should totally transform his source by his powers of compression, assimilation and adaptation to a new context. Everything that really matters in the scene we have read comes from Dante himself. The words and the blood flow together from the wound inflicted. The act of violence is so slight. It is done at the instigation of another, as part of a very subtle developing relationship between the doubting disciple and a fallible master, who is still perhaps slightly piqued at his pupil's evident lack of confidence (cf. *Inf.* IX, 1–30). The tree in this case *is* the man; he or it is part of a whole forest of men become trees by an act of God. And we shall see that 'arborification' is not a casual punishment, not interchangeable with that visited on other sinners, but very revealing of Dante's attitude to the sin of violence against the self.

Virgil now tries to 'make amends' by inviting the 'wounded soul' to say who he was so that Dante may 'refresh his memory in the world above' (46–54). And his sweet words prove to be an irresistible 'lure' and 'lime' in which the soul willingly allows himself to be caught (the verb *adescare* is from *esca*, 'a lure'; while *inveschiare* is from *vischio*, 'bird-lime'). He does not name himself: it is enough to say that he was secretary and right-hand man of Frederick.

> E 'l tronco: 'Sì col dolce dir m'adeschi,
> ch'i' non posso tacere; e voi non gravi
> perch' ïo un poco a ragionar m'inveschi.
> Io son colui che tenni ambo le chiavi
> del cor di Federigo . . .'   (55–9)

(And the trunk replied: 'You lure me so effectively with your sweet words, that I cannot be silent; do not be offended if I am inveigled into conversation for a time. I am the man who held both keys to the heart of Frederick . . .')

Just as the name Victoria when used on its own today can only refer to a queen who has been dead for nearly eighty years, so the name Frederick in 1300 could only refer to the Emperor Frederick II who had died in 1250, fifteen years before Dante was born. He had been one of the most powerful and remarkable men in Europe. Born in 1194, he was grandson of the Emperor Frederick Barbarossa and overlord of what is now Germany and

Austria. More important, he had inherited the throne of Sicily and Southern Italy from his mother, Constance. Apart from his skills as a ruler, military leader and negotiator, he was a gifted linguist, a poet, a keen amateur in philosophy and science, an authority on falconry, the keeper of a harem, and, for most of his life, an excommunicate and open enemy of the Church because his political ambitions kept him in permanent conflict with the Papacy. For Dante, he was an *illustris heros* who had sought to live like a man, who had pursued nobility and right-eousness, and who had attracted many like minds to his court (*Dve* I, xii, 4); he was a heretic, condemned in the sixth circle of Hell (*Inf.* x, 119); and he was the last true Emperor, the last man who had tried to 'sit in the saddle' and bring peace and unity to Italy under the just rule of the Empire (*Con.* IV, iii, 6; ix, 10; cf. *Purg.* VI, 92).

Frederick's right-hand man – the wounded soul who is also the tree – was called Pier della Vigna ('Peter of the Vineyard', presumably with reference to his humble origins). He is known to history as a diplomat (he was in England in the 1230s), as the author of many Latin letters in which he waged a propaganda war on the Emperor's behalf, as one of the leading poets in the court circle and as the power behind the throne. At the height of his influence, in 1249, he was charged with treason, thrown into prison and blinded. And there in prison, as we can deduce from our knowledge that he is in the second *girone* of the seventh circle, he had taken his life in despair.

Dante's Piero now tells a story that will remind English readers of Thomas Becket, Cardinal Wolsey or Thomas Cromwell. He was Frederick's private secretary, taking all decisions to act or not to act, and cutting off all others from access to the Emperor. He was devoted and loyal, sacrificing his health and repose to the great office. But his position excited envy; the envious courtiers aroused Frederick's suspicions; and he fell into disgrace.

> 'Io son colui che tenni ambo le chiavi
>   del cor di Federigo, e che le volsi,
>   serrando e diserrando, sì soavi,
>   che dal secreto suo quasi ogn' uom tolsi;
>   fede portai al glorïoso offizio,
>   tanto ch'i' ne perde' li sonni e ' polsi.

> La meretrice che mai da l'ospizio
> di Cesare non torse li occhi putti,
> morte comune e de le corti vizio,
>   infiammò contra me li animi tutti;
> e li 'nfiammati infiammar sì Augusto,
> che ' lieti onor tornaro in tristi lutti.'   (58–69)

('I am the man who held both keys to the heart of Frederick. I turned them so smoothly as I locked and unlocked that I shut almost everybody out from his secret affairs. I brought fidelity to the glorious office, so much so that I lost my sleep and health. But the whore who never turns her shameless eyes from Caesar's household – the common death and the special vice of courts – she set all men's minds ablaze against me; and their blaze in turn set Augustus ablaze, so that the glad honours changed to dismal mourning.')

Disdaining the disdain in which he was now held, he sought to escape through suicide. He was thereby guilty of an act of injustice or *ingiuria* against himself, but he had been guiltless and just in his dealings with the Emperor. He had never broken faith. And he begs his aggressor to set the record straight in the world of men.

> 'L'animo mio, per disdegnoso gusto,
> credendo col morir fuggir disdegno,
> ingiusto fece me contra me giusto.
>   Per le nove radici d'esto legno
> vi giuro che già mai non ruppi fede
> al mio segnor, che fu d'onor sì degno.
>   E se di voi alcun nel mondo riede,
> conforti la memoria mia, che giace
> ancor del colpo che 'nvidia le diede.'   (70–8)

('My mind was of a scornful cast, and believing that it could flee from scorn through death, it made me act unjustly against myself, although my cause was just. By the still recent roots of this tree, I swear to you that I never broke faith with my lord, who was so worthy of honour. And if one of you is to return to the world, let him restore my good name, which still lies prostrate under the blow that envy gave.')

It will be seen that Dante's Piero is too 'disdainful' to call a spade a spade. His whole speech is a most elaborate circumlocution, which serves to define himself and the manner of his death; and every phrase he utters is consciously lifted above ordinary discourse by the free use of rhetorical artifice. After the opening alliteration ('sì col dolce dir m'adeschi') and the extremely precious verb-metaphors in rhyme ('m'adeschi' and 'm'inveschi'), he

11

goes on to develop the noun-metaphor of the two keys and the personification of Envy as a brazen harlot (both images having a biblical flavour). The half-German, half-Norman king of Sicily is dignified with the Roman titles of Caesar and Augustus. Then the language grows ever more mannered and involute with the adnominations on *infiammare* and *disdegno* (67–8, 70–1) and the elaborate double antithesis of 'lieti onor' and 'tristi lutti' (69, coming after the simple pairing of 'sonni' and 'polsi': 63; and the simple antithesis of 'serrando' and 'diserrando': 60; or 'morte' and 'vizio': 66). And the high point of this verbal elaboration is reached with the paradox of line 72, which incorporates repetition, antithesis and chiasmus, thus:

Piero's use of rhetoric, moreover, is not limited to figures and tropes. His speech is an exercise in the art of persuasion, a masterpiece of special pleading. Everything is subordinate to his main purpose – to 'refresh' and 'comfort' his memory on earth; and the repetitions that really matter are those of lines 62 and 74: '*fede* portai . . .', and 'non ruppi *fede* al mio segnor . . .' Dante has provided a brilliant pastiche of the style he found in the poems and letters of the historical Piero, and he has also borne out the characterisation of Piero given by his master, Brunetto Latini. In his work called *La rettorica italiana*, Brunetto had defined rhetoric as 'the science by which we may speak or write ornately (*ornatamente*)'. He then cited 'maestro Pier dalle Vigne' as his sole example of the good *parlatore* and *dittatore*; and he indicated that it was through the mastery of rhetoric that Piero had become 'the secretary of Frederick II, Emperor of Rome, and completely master of him and of the Empire (*e tutto sire di lui e dello 'mperio*)'.

Although it is necessary nowadays to dwell at some length on the presence of rhetoric in Piero's speech, it would be wrong to suggest, as De Sanctis did, that Dante the poet has been unable to reveal the man behind the words, to throw light on his psychology or to establish a link between his temperament and the sin for which he is condemned. Piero emerges as a lonely man, with no life outside his work, wrapped up in himself, contemptuous of others, jealous and still intensely proud of his exclusive power over Frederick's heart. He is unable to grasp that his conduct (61) must necessarily have made all men his enemies. And there is more than a hint of paranoia in the way he presents himself as a victim of the abstract force of Envy (64, 78). It is probably significant, too, that he speaks of himself with the name of a part, as an *animo*, that is, as a mind or reasoning faculty, and not as an *anima*, which denotes the vital principle of a whole man. It was his *animo* (70) with its perverse logic that drove him to commit suicide, as if in an attempt to disprove Aristotle's dictum that 'no man can be unjust to himself' ('nullus sibi ipsi facit iniustum'). Far from refuting that 'glorious philosopher', as Dante had called him, his story confirms the truth of Aristotle's relatively unsympathetic analysis of the causes and moral worth of suicide. Hated by others, Piero sought to flee from life. His personality had become divided: in Aristotle's phrase, it had entered into a 'state of contention against itself' ('in quadam *contentione contra* seipsam'). And long before Dante the character came to lacerate him (*scerpere*), his soul had been 'dragged in various directions and been in discord with itself' ('*anima* eius in diversas partes *discerperetur* et *contra seipsam discreparet*'). As Aristotle made clear, laying hands upon himself ('sibi ipsi manus iniciens') in order to flee from disgrace ('*fugiendo malum* tristabile'; cf. line 71) was a sign not of fortitude but of weakness or softness ('quaedam *mollities animi*').[1]

We can throw further light on Piero's shortcomings as a man, and on Dante's attitude to his suicide, if we compare him with Boethius, another distinguished man of letters who had risen high in the service of a 'German' emperor more than seven hundred years before. Boethius, too, was imprisoned on a charge of treason. But he did not commit suicide. While he was awaiting execution (A.D. 524) he composed the *Consolation of Philosophy* in which he described how he was visited in his cell by Lady Philosophy, and how he was helped to find the strength to endure the external blows of fortune by discovering a spiritual serenity founded on contemplation of the truth. The book had a decisive influence on Dante when he was seeking comfort for his grief at the death of Beatrice (*Con.* II, xii). And it is Boethius, not Piero, that he holds up for our admiration, describing his death as a 'martyrdom', and placing him with gratitude among the souls of the wise in the Heaven of the Sun (*Par.* x, 124–9).

As an Aristotelian, Dante felt that Piero's suicide sprang from a want of courage or fortitude, which is one of the four cardinal virtues known and practised by the pagans of antiquity. As a Christian, he knew that Piero had taken his life because he lacked the theological virtue of hope. Christian hope rests on faith – faith in God, in the Redemption, in personal immortality and in the possibility of enjoying for all eternity the 'Emperor who reigns on high' (*Inf.* i, 124; *Par.* xii, 40). Piero had *fede*, but his *fede* was placed in a mortal, heretical emperor; and it led not to hope, but despair. The only kind of immortality that concerned him was his 'memory' on earth. He tried to destroy himself, but all he could achieve was to separate prematurely his immortal soul from the body, and to cut himself off from God for ever.

Of course, Dante the poet has given Piero back something of his good name and assured him a kind of immortality. And it is not difficult to understand Dante's compassion for the tragic figure of Piero when we remember that he himself had been unjustly disgraced and exiled from Florence on pain of death, and that he would put his pen at the service of a new Emperor, Henry VII of Luxembourg. But although Dante had suffered humiliation and despair, he found renewed consolation in philosophy and in the Psalms, he kept his faith, and so he never abandoned hope. Indeed, he will make Beatrice say that 'no son of the Church Militant could equal him in hope' ('La Chiesa militante alcun figliuolo / non ha con più speranza . . .': *Par.* xxv, 52–3). That is the difference between the 'tree' and the living man.

Dante the character simultaneously reveals his profound compassion for Piero and his renewed trust in Virgil's power to read his thoughts by asking his guide to formulate the question that he cannot bring himself to put into words (79–84). And so Virgil gently but insistently requests the 'incarcerated spirit' to clarify two further points. First, how is it that a human soul can enter into a compound with the knotty trunk and twisted branches of a thorn-tree? (In this regard we must remember that, for a

14

Christian Aristotelian like Dante, the soul is the 'form' or 'structure' that makes a man 'what he is': a tree 'body' with a human
'form' is as impossible as sulphuric acid with the formula of H_2O.)
Secondly, will any of the souls ever be released from these
arboreal 'limbs', that is, what will happen on the Day of Judgement when the souls of the blessed and the damned alike will be
'reclothed' in the body?

> '. . . ancor ti piaccia
> di dirne come l'anima si lega
> in questi nocchi; e dinne, se tu puoi,
> s'alcuna mai di tai membra si spiega'. (87–90)

('. . . be so kind as to tell us, further, how the soul is fused with these
"knots"; and tell us, if you can, whether any soul ever extricates itself
from such "limbs"'.)

Hissing laboriously (91), the tree replies. When a soul has
'uprooted' itself from the body (the ironic metaphor matches
Virgil's reference to the 'limbs' of the tree), it appears before the
judgement seat of Minos (cf. *Inf.* v, 4–15). Minos sends it hurtling
down to the seventh circle. It has no predetermined place. It is not
imprisoned in an existing tree, nor is it transformed into a tree
immediately. In a grim parody of the processes of human gestation, which will be described at length in *Purgatorio* xxv, it
germinates and becomes successively a sapling and a tree. The
Harpies tear open the bark as they feed and thereby produce an
outlet for the expression of the pain they cause. (This is the
explanation of the 'guai' heard by Dante in line 22, and for a
moment the rhythms and syntax echo those of the description at
the beginning of the canto.)

> 'Quando si parte l'anima feroce
> dal corpo ond' ella stessa s'è disvelta,
> Minòs la manda a la settima foce.
> Cade in la selva, e non l'è parte scelta;
> ma là dove fortuna la balestra,
> quivi germoglia come gran di spelta.
> Surge in vermena e in pianta silvestra:
> l'Arpie, pascendo poi de le sue foglie,
> fanno dolore, e al dolor fenestra.' (94–102)

('When the cruel soul quits the body from which it uprooted itself,
Minos sends it down to the seventh gullet. It falls in the wood, and its

site is not chosen; but wherever chance has flung it, it sprouts like a grain of millet. It springs up as a shoot and then as a monstrous tree. As the harpies feed on its leaves they cause pain and an outlet for that pain.')

So much for the answer to the first question; but the worst is yet to come. On the Day of Judgement the souls of the suicides will go to the Valley of Jehoshaphat (cf. *Inf.* x, 10–12) like all the others. Unlike the others, however, they will not be 'reclothed' in their resurrected bodies. Instead they will drag their bodies down to Hell and hang them for ever on the branches of the trees. It is an appalling vision, expressed with the utmost simplicity, restraint and resignation.

> 'Come l'altre verrem per nostre spoglie,
> ma non però ch'alcuna sen rivesta,
> ché non è giusto aver ciò ch'om si toglie.
>   Qui le strascineremo, e per la mesta
> selva saranno i nostri corpi appesi,
> ciascuno al prun de l'ombra sua molesta.' (103–8)

('Like the other souls we shall come for our remains, but not to put them on again. It is not just that a man should have what he has rejected. We shall drag them here, and our bodies will be hung throughout the desolate forest, each on the tree of the soul that did it violence.')

Neither of these two related acts of judgement – those of Minos and the Son of Man – is derived from the Bible; and Dante's early commentators were disturbed by the heretical proposition that the souls of the suicides would not be reclothed in their bodies: as Boccaccio says, this is 'dirittamente contrario alla verità cattolica'. We may reasonably infer, therefore, that Dante's attitude to the sin of suicide was both complex and personal in its emphases. As we have seen, he seems to have accepted Aristotle's view that suicide is normally the result of weakness rather than of ·a superhuman triumph of the will over the blind instinct to survive at all costs (the case of Cato in *Purgatorio* I is the exception that proves the rule). There are no grounds for supposing that he dissented from the mainstream of Catholic orthodoxy, which treated suicide as a sin against God, who gave the gift of life, and as a special case of murder, all the more grave because it was born of despair (a sin against the Spirit) and all the more dangerous because it automatically deprived the 'murderer' of any opportunity to feel remorse, to seek forgiveness and to make expiation (cf.

Summa Theol. 2*a*–2*ae*, 64, 5). In his last speech Piero reminds us of Virgil's discourse in Canto XI by dwelling on the 'violence' (the soul is 'feroce' and 'molesta') which is the common denominator of all the sins punished in the 'settima foce'. And we may reflect that just as love is greater than hope (I Corinthians 13.13), so hate is worse than despair. The suicide is guilty not only of despair but of hating himself in defiance of the self-love (*amor sui, amor proprius*) that is natural to all beings, which Dante had called the 'foundation of all other loves' ('lo proprio amore di me medesimo, lo quale è principio di tutti li altri': *Con.* III, i, 5; cf. I, ii, 5; IV, xxii, 5).

All these strands of thought seem to be present in the canto, but the nature of the punishment suggests that Dante condemned suicide above all as an offence against the body, or better, as an offence against the union or unity of soul and body that constitutes a human person. Dante was not immune from the dualism that would oppose spirit to matter, and soul to body, as light is opposed to dark, and good to evil. But when he is most fully himself, he will consistently deny all validity to such oppositions. All matter was created in the beginning by God and must therefore be good. Every species exists to play a distinct part in the workings of the cosmos, a part for which it is fitted by its nature or form; and the human form, no less than the form of minerals, plants and animals, can exist only in matter. Moreover, the union of soul and body in man is the result of a direct intervention by God in the formation of each human individual in time. In *Purgatorio* XXV we learn that the human foetus is indeed fashioned in the womb by a power inherent in the father's seed, but that it does not become fully human – rational, free and immortal – until God himself has joyfully breathed into the foetus a new spirit, which draws up into itself all the existing powers of vegetative and sensitive life to become a single human soul – 'un'alma *sola*' (*Purg.* XXV, 66–75).[2] Man is a 'whole' – what Aristotle called a *synolon*, or *simul totum* of matter and form. He cannot live a human existence or fulfil his human purpose without the organs of the body. Furthermore, any doubts that may have attached to the goodness of the human body after the Fall were dispelled at the moment of the Incarnation, when God took on human flesh. And Christ's resurrection contains the promise that we shall all be resurrected from the dead (I Corinthians 15.12). Anyone who finds it easy to think of death as the 'release' of the soul from its bondage to matter may find it correspondingly difficult to accept the doctrine of resurrection. But Dante's intellectual difficulties were connected with the problem of how the human soul could go on existing as a disembodied form. For him the resurrection of the body to make the 'human person entire again' is a glorious certainty, which he will celebrate in some of the most radiant lines in the whole poem (*Par.* XIV, 37–60). And it is to these lines we must refer if we want to understand the 'positive pole' in Dante's conception of the relationship between the soul and its body, and to grasp why he should have devised this particular punishment for the suicides in the 'forest of negation'.

We must now return to the drama and meet the three minor characters who complete the cast list. But before we leave Dante's thought, we ought to remind ourselves that violence may be done *in re* as well as *in se*, and that we have been warned to expect that the souls of the squanderers or the prodigal will be punished in the same *girone* as the suicides. The prodigal man is not simply careless or extravagant with his money. He wilfully runs through his whole fortune and casts it away. Aristotle, paraphrased by Aquinas, defined the vice as consisting in the 'reckless destruction or consumption of one's own substance or wealth' ('in indebita corruptione vel consumptione substantiae, idest propriarum divitiarum'). And the word *prodigus* was thought to be related semantically to *perditus*, because 'the man who destroys the wealth that should preserve his life would seem to destroy his own being' ('homo corrumpendo proprias divitias per quas vivere debet, *videtur suum esse destruere* quod per divitias conservatur').[3]

While Dante and Virgil remain with their attention fixed on the 'tree', they are surprised by a noise of charging animals and breaking branches such as might be heard by a hunter when the wild boar is driven towards his post (107–14). Suddenly two figures burst into view from the left, their naked bodies scratched by the thorn-bushes through which they force their way in the speed of their flight (115–17). As he runs, the leader is imploring Death to overtake him and come to his aid (118)! The other is falling behind. He finds just enough breath, however, to hurl an

18

insult after his companion, whom he names as Lano. He mocks Lano for showing a much cleaner pair of heels now than he did on the day when he met his death while trying to run away from a minor battle – the soul ironically calls it a 'joust' – at a ford near Arezzo. Then, winded by his exertion and his taunt, the second soul tries to escape his pursuers by taking refuge behind a bush (119–23). But there is no escape in Hell, and retribution is exacted in six expressive lines. The first terzina is cast in the imperfect tense and fills the wide screen with the hounds of Hell, making an effective use of enjambement ('piena /di nere cagne'), and switching to a plunging dactylic rhythm in the third line:

> Di rietro a loro era la selva piena
> di nere cagne, bramose e correnti
> come veltri ch'uscisser di catena.   (124–6)

(Behind them the wood was full of black bitches, ravenous and swift like greyhounds who have just been slipped from the chain.)

The second terzina shows us a close-up of the kill and dismemberment. Each line is chopped off at the end and is cut in the middle by a strong caesura following a verb in the past definite. There is only one word signifying violence ('dilaceraro'), but its meaning seems to re-echo with its sound in the following 'a brano a brano'; and the cumulative effect of sense, rhythm, vowels and consonants is one of violence made audible. And yet one may feel that the most expressive word in the context is the apparently colourless demonstrative *quello*: repeated in each line, it thrusts the action before our eyes and reduces the human being to a mere object, a rag doll torn to pieces by an angry child.

> In quel che s'appiattò miser li denti,
> e quel dilaceraro a brano a brano;
> poi sen portar quelle membra dolenti.   (127–9)

(They sank their teeth into the one who huddled on the ground. They tore him apart lump by lump. Then they carried off the tortured pieces.)

After the disappearance of the hunt Dante and Virgil remain on stage, apparently alone. But the silence is broken by more words of pain. The dismembered prodigal – now named as Jacopo da Santo Andrea – was not the only victim of the bitches' savagery. The bush or *cespuglio* behind which Jacopo had sought refuge was

19

badly damaged in the attack. And like all the other *piante silvestre* in the *mesta selva* the bush is also the 'body' of a suicide. The bitches caused 'dolore, e al dolor fenestra', just as the Harpies do, and just as Dante did to Piero. The difference is that the *cespuglio* suffered a much greater violence. Its branches lie scattered on the ground, and it 'puffs out blood and lamentation' not from one gash but from many bleeding holes ('rotture *sanguinenti*': 132; '*tante* punte': 137). The lament is vain (132; cf. xi, 42), but it is full of pathos – especially in the soul's request that Virgil and Dante should gather up his branches (how naturally he says 'le *mie* fronde'), and place them at the foot of his bush. And we are in any case touched by the way in which Dante the character and his guide have drawn closer together after the failure of trust on Dante's part and Virgil's perhaps excessive reaction. The quiet gesture of line 130 is to be understood as a sign of reconciliation.

> Presemi allor la mia scorta per mano,
> e menommi al cespuglio che piangea
> per le rotture sanguinenti in vano.
>   'O Iacopo', dicea, 'da Santo Andrea,
> che t'è giovato di me fare schermo?
> che colpa ho io de la tua vita rea?'
>   Quando 'l maestro fu sovr' esso fermo,
> disse: 'Chi fosti, che per tante punte
> soffi con sangue doloroso sermo?'
>   Ed elli a noi: 'O anime che giunte
> siete a veder lo strazio disonesto
> c'ha le mie fronde sì da me disgiunte,
>   raccoglietele al piè del tristo cesto.'   (130–42)

(My guide then took me by the hand and led me to the bush, which was lamenting through its bleeding gashes, in vain. 'Oh Jacopo da Santo Andrea', it was saying, 'What good did it do you to make a shield of me? Was I to blame for your life of sin?' When my master stood beside the bush, he said, 'Who were you, who bleed and utter words of pain through so many wounds?' And he said to us, 'Oh souls who chanced to witness the shameful torture that has scattered my branches far and wide, gather them up at the foot of my tormented bush.')

In the closing lines of the canto the bush answers Virgil's question by means of a circumlocution (143–51), which indicates that he was a Florentine who had hanged himself in his own house. The circumlocution is worded to remind us that Florence was perpetually plagued by *violenza* in all its forms, which are here imaged as assaults by Mars who had been the city's protector before it adopted John the Baptist as its patron saint. The soul seems to suggest that the change of patron had been a mistake, and he alludes to the common superstition that the city would have been utterly destroyed centuries before if it had not managed to preserve a mutilated statue of the Roman god of war! More importantly, however, his words also contain (150) an un-acknowledged allusion to the opening of Psalm 127, through which Dante the poet reveals his own thoughts on the matter. The psalm begins: 'Except the Lord build the house, they labour in vain that build it: *except the LORD keep the city*, the watchman waketh but in vain.'

The true cause of Florence's sufferings – to paraphrase the opening of the very next psalm – was that its citizens neither feared the Lord nor walked in His ways. Dante regarded himself as an innocent victim of the never-ceasing political struggle that we may think of here as Florence's corporate act of violence against herself. His terrifying descriptions of what he is about to call the 'horrible art of God's justice' ('di giustizia orribil arte': XIV, 6; cf. 16–18) were intended to inculcate 'fear of the LORD' as the 'beginning of wisdom'. But the last brief scene in the drama enacted in the Unnatural Wood puts before our eyes a gesture born of natural compassion. Moved by love of his native or 'natural' place, Dante the character gathers together the branches of his now exhausted compatriot and restores them to their owner. These lines come at the beginning of the next canto, but they form the only possible conclusion to a *lectura* in which I have tried above all to bring out the many different qualities that make Dante one of the greatest dramatists never to have written a play:

> Poi che la carità del natio loco
> mi strinse, raunai le fronde sparte
> e rende'le a colui, ch'era già fioco.   (XIV, 1–3)

Notes

1 See *Nicomachean Ethics* III, 7, 1116a 10–16; V, 11, 1138a 5–1138b 14; IX, 4, 1166b 1–30. The Latin quotations in the text are from the paraphrase by Aquinas that Dante is known to have used (§§ 557, 1094, 1098, 1815, 1817 in the edition of R. M. Spiazzi in the collected works published by Marietti, Rome).

2 See chapter 11 ('The Makings of a Man') in my *Dante Philomythes and Philosopher: Man in the Cosmos* (Cambridge, 1981). The whole book constitutes an introduction to the full exposition of *Purg.* XXV, 37–78 in this last chapter.
3 See *Nicomachean Ethics* IV, 1, 1119*b* 28–1120*a* 5 and Aquinas's commentary *ad loc.*, ed. cit. § 656).

Inferno XXV

ROBIN KIRKPATRICK

The twenty-fifth canto of the *Inferno* is the second to depict the punishment of theft. The scene of the punishment is established in Canto XXIV; there, too, the sinner who speaks at the opening of Canto XXV – Vanni Fucci – makes his first appearance.

The thieves are punished in the seventh ditch of a series of ten, which Dante names the 'Malebolge'. On arriving at the seventh *bolgia*, Dante and Virgil at first see nothing; the ditch is too dark for the eye to penetrate (*Inf.* XXIV, 70–1). Drawing, however, as close as they dare, they see that the *bolgia* is swarming with reptiles. The thieves run naked in this throng. Yet exposure to the serpents is merely a part of their punishment. So, as Dante gazes, a snake springs up and transfixes the windpipe of one of the sinners. The sinner is Vanni Fucci. At the bite of the snake he disintegrates into dust and ashes, only to have his remains restored inexorably to their former shape:

> e poi che fu a terra sì distrutto,
> la polver si raccolse per sé stessa
> e 'n quel medesmo ritornò di butto.
>
> (*Inf.* XXIV, 103–5)

(And so lying destroyed upon the ground, his dust of its own accord drew itself together again, returning on the instant to its self-same shape.)

The *contrappasso* of theft has, then, two aspects. The first involves the action of the serpent, the second a process of material transformation; and the notions essential to Dante's diagnosis of theft are expressed in the two-fold nature of its damnation.

First, in associating theft with the image of the serpent Dante draws attention to cunning and underhand cleverness as particular

23

characteristics of the thief. On which score, the thieves are rightly consigned to the Malebolge. All the sins punished in this region of Hell proceed from the knowing misuse of human rationality; all are sins of deceit (*Inf.* XI, 52–60; XVII, 7). Like their fellows in the other *bolge*, the thieves are intelligent men who have used their intelligence perversely in acts of malice.

The second aspect of their penalty, however – physical transformation – marks the thieves off from 'simile lordura'. For while other forms of punishment, especially in the Malebolge, do entail physical distortion, none is so extreme or concerned so emphatically with the process of transformation as that which the thieves undergo. The extremity of their suffering as well as its nature is of significance; and both are consequences of the fact – apparently a simple one – that thievery is inspired by greed. The especial feature of theft is that – subtle as its action may be – its crude motive is the wish to possess. And this suggests why the poet should be as vehement as he is against the sin. For greed or *cupiditas* – which throughout the *Comedy* appears under various guises – invariably does evoke from Dante a ferociously personal reaction. Thus in *Inf.* VI, 48 the punishment of greed is declared to be, if not the worst, then the most disgusting, in Hell, and a reasoned account of the poet's hatred for greed is contained in the first book of the *Monarchy*, where, in Chapter XI, Dante declares that 'the extreme contrary of Justice is cupidity'.

The reasoning of the *Monarchy* is reflected, as well as the poet's obsession, in the twenty-fifth canto. For possessions are safeguarded by the institutions of human justice; and the value of the laws of property is revealed to the thieves who in Hell are denied secure possession of the physical matter that constitutes their own bodies. The justice, however, that is demonstrated in the metamorphoses embodies also a metaphysical law of creation and this may be understood more fully in the light of a passage concerning avarice in *Inferno* VII, which at once provides the first sustained piece of doctrine in the *Comedy* and, equally, presents, as does Canto XXV, an image of continual change. This is the discussion of *Fortuna*.

The passage concentrates, first (73–81), on the ever-changing character of Fortune as an aspect of God's providential plan. In its immediate context, the function of this passage is to enforce the lesson of Boethius's *Consolatio*: Fortune is the law that God has set over the 'beni vani' of the physical world, so that things must continually change hands, in 'permutations' (*ibid.* 79 and 88) incomprehensible to men. It follows that to set one's mind upon such goods is sheer folly. If, however, such a consequence applies to sinners of intemperate impulse, then it must apply still more to those who, like thieves, are endowed with acute intelligence. In attempting to outwit the dispensations of Fortune – whose action is 'occulto come in erba l'angue' (*ibid.* 84) – the thief proves himself wilfully obtuse.

Dante's emphasis upon physical mutability does not exhaust the relevance of the *Fortuna* passage to the *bolgia* of the thieves. Dante's *Fortuna* is not identical with Boethius's and the especially Dantean suggestion of Canto VII (73–8) is that material things do possess a splendour of their own. To the philosophical eye, the changes of Fortune are wonderful, and the lucid poetry in the *Fortuna* passage is itself an expression of Dante's rational admiration.

But if 'things' have their splendour, possessions, too, may be legitimate, deriving their legitimacy from the providential interest that God, as Creator, takes in the brief contingencies of the lowest order of existence. The thieves, however – intelligent as they are – prefer rather to satisfy their greed than to pursue this truth. And the permutations that they suffer in Hell drive home to them the nature of the incalculable design of God, which is expressed in the agency of Fortune. That the punishment, moreover, should bear upon the physical shape of the human being is an indication that the material bodies of men are in a sense the direct creation of God. Thus by the gospel of the resurrection the human body is assured of its own eternal existence. In Canto VI (94–111) of the *Inferno*, even before the consideration of *Fortuna*, Dante has spoken of how each individual on the Day of Judgement will return again to his flesh and distinctive figure. And in Canto XXIV, the truth of the resurrection is expressed no less strongly than the truth of human transience in the punishment of Vanni; the sinner is reduced to dust and ashes by the snake-bite, but an equal part of his punishment is that his remains should return immediately to a vulnerable human form. Following from this, Canto XXV constitutes one of the most powerful expressions in the *Comedy* of Dante's belief in the resurrection of the body.

25

The canto opens with the last words and the last vicious acts of Vanni Fucci. Though God has revealed his power to him only moments ago, Fucci persists in defiance, directing heavenwards a notorious obscenity – the sign of the figs. In imitation of the sexual act, he projects his thumbs between clenched fingers and strikes his fists upwards. The action is as vigorously drawn as any in the *Inferno*. Yet the vigour of the sinner is equalled by that of the response it evokes. As instruments of divine revenge, two serpents seize upon Vanni to throttle him and bind his hands down:

> Al fine de le sue parole il ladro
> le mani alzò con amendue le fiche,
> gridando: 'Togli, Dio, ch'a te le squadro!'
>   Da indi in qua mi fuor le serpi amiche,
> perch' una li s'avvolse allora al collo,
> come dicesse 'Non vo' che più diche';
>   e un'altra a le braccia, e rilegollo,
> ribadendo sé stessa sì dinanzi,
> che non potea con esse dare un crollo.
>   Ahi Pistoia, Pistoia, ché non stanzi
> d'incenerarti sì che più non duri,
> poi che 'n mal fare il seme tuo avanzi?
>   Per tutt' i cerchi de lo 'nferno scuri
> non vidi spirto in Dio tanto superbo,
> non quel che cadde a Tebe giù da' muri.   (1–15)

(His words at an end, the thief hoisted both his hands aloft – in each of them the fig sign – yelling: 'God, that's for you; I'm aiming them at you!' From that point on the serpents were my friends. First, one of them wound itself around his neck, as if to say: 'I'll have you speak no more'; and then, at his arms, a second bound him tighter still, knotting itself about him so the sinner in its links could neither shake nor stir. Ah! Pistoia, Pistoia, why do you not resolve to burn yourself to ashes, and thus endure no longer; for you outdo in the wrong you do the seed you sprang from. Through all the murk of all the circles of Hell, I saw no spirit as arrogant as this one in the face of God, not even he who fell from the battlements headlong at Thebes.)

As the canto proceeds, the obscenity of Fucci's gesture and the blasphemous use to which he puts his tongue will contribute significantly to the poet's theme. However, two other features of the passage deserve immediate attention. First, while Vanni is referred to in the present canto only as 'the thief', it is not his thievery that Dante now emphasises but rather his pride; he has seen no prouder spirit in Hell (14). Secondly, the punishment of Fucci seems to hold for Dante a peculiar interest; he consents to it entirely and the serpents become his friends (4).

On the first count, one should note that the scheme of the *Inferno* allots no special place to pride. Yet men with the marks of pride upon them appear at regular intervals throughout the work. One such is Capaneo in Canto XIV – to whom Dante here (15) compares Vanni Fucci. Others include Farinata in Canto X and the giant Nimrod in Canto XXXI. These appearances are sufficiently punctual to suggest that all sin must involve an element of pride. And the case, in theft, is especially clear; the thief presumes to meddle with a dispensation in the physical world that derives its sanction from the providence of God.

Implicit, as we have seen, in Dante's judgement of theft, is all his hatred of avarice. Now Dante speaks of pride, the primal sin. And from this it is clear that the moral vision of Canto XXV, though never losing sight of the particular nature of theft, will penetrate far beyond the consideration of a single evil. The conjunction, indeed, of pride and avarice is one that Dante will observe in the sin of Satan himself. For as Vanni does in his squalid way, so Satan presumes in an act of perverse intelligence to desire of providence more than providence affords him:

> . . . 'l primo superbo,
> che fu la somma d'ogne creatura,
> per non aspettar lume, cadde acerbo.
>
> (*Par.* XIX, 46–8)

(. . . the first proud being fell, unripe and bitter, from the height of all creation; he would not wait for light.)

In keeping with the intensity of its moral theme, the imagery of the twenty-fifth canto possesses an exceptional resonance. The figure of the serpent itself recalls the occasion of original sin, while mutability – depicted here as metamorphosis – is the evident outcome of Paradise lost. Yet the force of the canto does not derive from its imagery alone, but rather from an interplay of primitive suggestion and moral fervour. And this may already be seen in the second aspect of the opening sequence.

For if no sinner in Hell is prouder than Vanni Fucci, then nowhere in *Inferno* does the poet envisage with such precision the moral order in eternity that renders pride ridiculous. Where Vanni's own gesture is vain and ineffectual, the snakes proceed with exact calculation to repress the flailing hands and the voice of the sinner. By voice and gesture Farinata and Capaneo have claimed and possibly won respect for human identity. But these means of expression are here systematically extinguished. Indeed the next figure who appears is hardly human at all.

For Vanni now exits pursued by a centaur:

> El si fuggì che non parlò più verbo;
> e io vidi un centauro pien di rabbia
> venir chiamando: 'Ov' è, ov' è l'acerbo?'
>   Maremma non cred' io che tante n'abbia,
> quante bisce elli avea su per la groppa
> infin ove comincia nostra labbia.
>   Sovra le spalle, dietro da la coppa,
> con l'ali aperte li giacea un draco;
> e quello affuoca qualunque s'intoppa.   (16–24)

(He fled; he spoke no further word. And then I saw a centaur, all enraged, who cried as he came: 'Where is he, then, where is the sour creature?' There cannot be, I think, in all the region of Maremma as many snakes as were around that centaur, upward from its animal haunch to the point at which the countenance of the human being begins. Over its shoulders, behind the nape, a dragon was lying, its wings outspread; whatever it strikes up against it sets on fire.)

The image of the centaur, who himself is a creature damned for theft, parallels the image of Fucci; his presence provides a further instance of the subjugation of man. For where Fucci's human attributes are extinguished by the snakes, so, too, the human component of the centaur is that which is especially made to suffer; snakes ride around him from his thorax to his lower lip.

In regard, however, to the manner of presentation, the centaur is not identical with the human sinner. While Fucci's outrageous actions are depicted in dramatic terms, the centaur – who is after all a mythical beast – provides a point of focus for a moral meditation. He is not exactly an allegorical figure; the poet's imagination, in conceiving him, has worked too vigorously to admit of that. Yet as soon as Virgil speaks, the moral scheme by which the thieves are damned begins to assert itself.

As Virgil tells us at line 25, the centaur is Cacus; and this identification itself is significant. For it links the sin of the seventh

28

bolgia to the frame of judgement that the Malebolge, as a whole, embodies. At the entry to the Malebolge, one has seen already an image of distorted humanity, comparable to that which Cacus offers – Gerione. Dante and Virgil descend to the Malebolge on the back of the monster Gerione – as the 'sozza imagine di frode' ('filthy image of fraud': *Inf.* xvii, 7) – who has the face of a just man and the lower parts of a reptile. The serpent imagery in Canto xvii is clearly compatible with that which one finds in Canto xxv. But the connection between Cacus and Gerione is a more particular one; both of these monsters were victims of the hero Hercules. Indeed, as King Evander relates in *Aeneid* viii, 184–279, the cattle that Cacus herded beneath the Aventine Hill were cattle that Hercules himself had won from King Geryon. Cacus in turn stole the herd from Hercules, who then took a just revenge, and cleansed the territory of Rome from the effects of Cacus's depredations. This is the vengeance that Virgil now recounts:

> Lo mio maestro disse: 'Questi è Caco,
> che, sotto 'l sasso di monte Aventino,
> di sangue fece spesse volte laco.
>   Non va co' suoi fratei per un cammino,
> per lo furto che frodolente fece
> del grande armento ch'elli ebbe a vicino;
>   onde cessar le sue opere biece
> sotto la mazza d'Ercule, che forse
> gliene diè cento, e non sentì le diece.' (25–33)

('That', my master said to me, 'is Cacus. Beneath the rock of the Aventine Hill, the blood that he spilled spread, time and time over, to a lake. He does not take the road that all his brethren take. For Cacus won the great herd that he guarded there by a wilful deceit. And, fittingly, his twisted career was brought up short on that account beneath the club of Hercules. Of, perhaps, a hundred blows that Hercules dealt him, he may have been aware of ten.')

The first effect of Virgil's speech is to emphasise that theft, like all the sins of deceit, desecrates the social order. Gerione has already been described as the beast 'che tutto 'l mondo appuzza' ('whose strength entirely pollutes the world': *Inf.* xvii, 2–3). The Malebolge at large, following from this, presents a coherent picture of a corrupt and self-divided civilisation; and theft is firmly associated with such corruption. For Cacus, as a thief, pollutes the sacred realms of Rome. Yet Virgil's words also make clear that order must be and will be defended; Cacus, like Gerione, is overcome by Hercules.

Considering Hercules's relation to Gerione as well as Cacus, Dante's use of the figure is plainly systematic. And of several interpretations that the image of Hercules may commonly suggest, there are two that have a particular bearing on the twenty-fifth canto.

The first is suggested by Dante himself in his Seventh Epistle. Addressing the Emperor Henry VII, the poet pictures Tuscany as a pit of serpents, and pleads with the Emperor to restore order to the troubled realm. The example, however, that Dante holds before the Emperor is that, precisely, of the hero Hercules, who slew the reptilian Hydra (*Epist.* VII, 20).

The reference to Hercules in the canto confirms the suggestion that, parallel to the vision of theft, the poet intends to express an understanding of the power of justice. Latent, however, in the image of Hercules is a sense that Virgil, as a pagan, might not be supposed to recognise. For Hercules – who wins his divinity by his labours on earth – is an evident prefiguration of Christ himself. The interpretation is an established feature of late medieval iconography.[1] Dante himself suggests that he was aware of it in the epistle I have just cited. For there he lays before the Emperor the example not only of Hercules but also of 'the lamb of God' (*Epist.* VII, 10).

Thus the action of a just Emperor will reflect the labours both of Hercules and Christ. And in Canto XXV there is reason for the poet to invoke the Christian significance of Hercules. In Christ, as prefigured in Hercules, the truth against which the sinners have offended is itself declared. Man does indeed possess a two-fold nature, as Christ himself did, and the world is the arena in which men, like Christ, must labour. But the thief, working by guile and greed, travesties both political justice and the truth in creation that provides the pattern of his nature.

As we approach the central sequences of the canto, attention must turn from its themes to its poetic character. The theme – deriving from the poet's belief in the dignity of both the human mind and the human body – expresses a fundamental principle of his Christianity. Yet in a number of respects the poetry of the canto is not typical of the *Inferno*.

Most strikingly – in view of its subject – the narrative of the canto presents no human figure for the imagination to contemplate or criticise. Once Fucci and Cacus have disappeared no voice achieves more than fragmentary utterance, nor does any human figure appear for more than a moment in its normal lineaments. From line 33 Dante and Virgil themselves play no part in the action; Virgil propounds no explanation of the scene, and Dante, as *personaggio*, shows nothing of the emotion that marks in various ways his encounters with Francesca, Pier della Vigna, and the characters of the lower Malebolge.

In all of these respects, the twenty-fifth canto differs not only from better-known cantos of the *Inferno* but also from the canto that precedes it. In Canto XXIV, the treatment of Fucci is distinctly dramatic. But equally Dante and Virgil participate in the narrative; they are forced to climb from the sixth to the seventh *bolgia*. And their conversation, as they climb, mirrors some of the major themes of the theft-sequence. It is here, in fact – suiting word to action – that Virgil enunciates the ethic of Hercules, insisting upon the need for labour if men are to leave any mark upon the world (47–51); and his speech is clearly intended to bear a Christian interpretation. For he speaks at line 55 of the present effort as a preparation for the 'long stair' of Mount Purgatory – where men fulfil, in Christ, their proper natures.

Where is there, however, in Canto XXV, any comparable expression of the poet's theme? And what focus is there here for the sympathies or intellects of the reader? These questions concern the metamorphosis sequence. Yet their implications are dramatised by the sequence that follows the discussion of Cacus.

As the centaur runs by, Virgil is interrupted by the arrival of three more thieves:

> Mentre che sì parlava, ed el trascorse,
> e tre spiriti venner sotto noi,
> de' quai né io né 'l duca mio s'accorse,
>   se non quando gridar: 'Chi siete voi?';
> per che nostra novella si ristette,
> e intendemmo pur ad essi poi.

> Io non li conoscea; ma ei seguette,
> come suol seguitar per alcun caso,
> che l'un nomar un altro convenette,
>   dicendo: 'Cianfa dove fia rimaso?';
> per ch'io, acciò che 'l duca stesse attento,
> mi puosi 'l dito su dal mento al naso.   (34–45)

(The centaur, as Virgil was speaking, ran by and, beneath us, there came three spirits whom neither I nor my leader had noticed until they shouted out: 'So who are you?' Our talk was interrupted by this and we turned our attention solely on them. I did not know them. It happened, however, as commonly it will, that one of these three had to name another: 'Cianfa – where has he got to?' he said. At this, to make my leader pay heed, I held up my finger from chin to nose.)

At first, the action here is comprehensible, even banal. Nothing could be more normal than the questions that the spirits ask, or the comic impudence with which they break in upon Virgil. Natural, however, as these figures appear, their demeanour echoes the truculence of Vanni Fucci; like most of the spirits in the Malebolge, they illustrate humanity only in its most trivial aspect. And pitted against them is a power unaccountable in design and magnitude. Thus the everyday question, 'Where has Cianfa got to?' itself releases the first transformation. For Cianfa is the six-legged serpent who leaps now on the questioner:

> Com' io tenea levate in lor le ciglia,
> e un serpente con sei piè si lancia
>   dinanzi a l'uno, e tutto a lui s'appiglia.   (49–51)

(As, with straining eyes, I stared upon them, a six-footed serpent darts up in front of one of them, and grapples itself all around him.)

From now on, the reader has to contemplate not only the humiliation of the human figure but also an action that appears to contravene all schemes of thought that are natural to the human mind. Yet Dante has already acknowledged the problem that this poses. With a gesture of authority he presumes to silence Virgil; sensing that a mystery is to reveal itself, he seems to recognise the incapacity of the rational mind to comment upon it. At the same time, at line 46, he turns directly to the reader:

> Se tu se' or, lettore, a creder lento
> ciò ch'io dirò, non sarà maraviglia,
>   ché io che 'l vidi, a pena il mi consento.   (46–8)

(If you are slow at this point, reader, to credit what I tell you, it will not be remarkable. For I who observed it, can barely allow myself to believe.)

The twenty-fifth canto – untypical as otherwise it may be – touches here upon an essential characteristic of the *Inferno*. We are asked to believe – as we are throughout, though rarely with such intensity – the unbelievable. For Dante insists that he believed what he saw, and, though he excuses disbelief, his own example is offered as an encouragement to the reader to exert his own attentions.

Now it could be supposed that such a passage was a device, of the kind that any fiction might use, to ensure a willing suspension of disbelief. This view, however, would do little justice to the nature of Dante's fiction and certainly would detract from the force of the present canto. For it is an essential feature of Canto XXV – and of others to a lesser degree – that the reader, confronting, as Dante does himself, images of the utmost perversity, should seek to believe that good lies beyond them. Dante's intention from the first has been to 'treat of the good' that he found in Hell (*Inf.* I, 8). And certainly on an earlier occasion, when in Canto IX, 61–3 he addresses the reader directly, his purpose is to ensure that one should see beneath the confusion of Hell a display of providential goodness – a goodness expressed in the image of the 'Messo da Ciel', who secures the entry of Dante and Virgil to the City of Dis. The address in Canto XXV is, in some measure, comparable, enjoining an attitude of contemplation as the power of God displays itself. This certainly is the attitude that Dante, as protagonist, adopts and requires of Virgil.[2]

Yet it is possible to go further than this. For the belief that Dante requires of us is a belief not only in providence, but in our own identities as human beings. Conjuring images of perversity from the dark wood of his own imagination the poet tests the sanity of his reader's response. And in this regard a significant preparation for the address in Canto XXV occurs in Canto XX.

In Canto XX, the poet presents the punishment of the soothsayers, who walk through Hell with their heads reversed upon their shoulders. The sight of this moves Dante to tears and Virgil reproves him for his weeping. As we shall see, this reproof is the consequence of a misapprehension. But in Canto XX Dante has already appealed beyond the authority of Virgil, to the reader himself:

> Se Dio ti lasci, lettor, prender frutto
> di tua lezione, or pensa per te stesso
> com' io potea tener lo viso asciutto,
>   quando la nostra imagine di presso
> vidi sì torta, che 'l pianto de li occhi
> le natiche bagnava per lo fesso.

(Inf. xx, 19–24)

(So God may grant you, reader, that you gather fruit from your reading, now think for yourself whether I could have kept my countenance dry when I saw close at hand the image of humanity turned so askew that the tears of its eyes washed the buttocks at their cleft.)

Here again it appears that there is good or 'frutto' to be had from the vision of perversity. Yet the poet requires no cold assent. Dante weeps here, not for the sinners themselves, but rather for the perversion of the human form. And the reader is asked to display a natural sympathy for Dante's own distress. Between Dante and the reader, the community of normal emotion is affirmed. And those who, in their sympathy for Dante, discover in themselves a sense as strong as the poet's own for the value of the human form will arrive at the 'frutto' that the image contains.

Thus the image of perversion is a test, performed upon our normal emotions, of our trust in normality. And the test is hardly a fiction at all. To write – or even to read – such cantos as the twenty-fifth is to demonstrate how capable the mind can be of perversity. Yet to read – or write – the canto may produce, in revulsion, a *frutto* or *ben*. And Dante's own writing in Canto xxv offers in two ways a guarantee that such a test is one that can be passed.

The first will be found if one looks, in the moral plan of the *Comedy*, to the point where the 'fruit' of Dante's understanding should openly appear to us – the *Paradiso*. Here, in the Heaven of Justice, which has already supplied a parallel to the present sequence on the matter of pride, we find that the imagination of the poet has produced a thorough and detailed counterpoint. The souls of the just, like those of the thieves, participate in a process of transformation. But where Vanni is a self-confessed *mul* and the other thieves are soon to be transformed into serpents, the souls of the just come finally to rest before Dante's eyes in the form of an eagle – the emblem of both justice and love:

> e quïetata ciascuna in suo loco,
> la testa e 'l collo d'un'aguglia vidi
> rappresentare a quel distinto foco.
>
> (*Par.* xviii, 106–8)

(Each of them I saw now still within its place, depicted in the sharp-lined fire, the head and neck of an Eagle.)

The meaning of this parallel is clear: the thief is broken and passive before the word of God, the just move freely in the order of its creative mystery.[3] If Dante, however, continually discusses the theme of order, here he also enacts it. In the coherence of his own imagination, moving in the *Comedy* from point to point, he demonstrates the possibility of the mind's intrinsic poise. And this is true in a further respect of the twenty-fifth canto. For, while in the narrative no human form provides a focus for our ordinary expectations, there is after all a figure who does stand before us, to affirm the principle of justice. That figure, as in Canto xx, is Dante himself, not Dante as *personaggio* but Dante as poet.

In Canto xxv, the voice of the poet presents itself at every point with peculiar directness. One instance of this is his appeal to the reader at lines 46–8. Another and more remarkable illustration will occur at lines 94–102, where Dante – interrupting his account of metamorphosis – declares its superiority to similar passages in Lucan and Ovid. Yet if Dante calls attention here explicitly to his own poetic standing, then so he does from his first encounter with Fucci.

For Dante so fashions the opening sequence as to emphasise, first, the circumstances of his actual life. He then proceeds to reply to Fucci not simply as *personaggio* but as author of the *Comedy*.

Thus, at the end of Canto xxiv, Fucci is allowed to foretell the events that, in 1301, led to Dante's exile from Florence. His speech is conceived as an invidious attempt to deny the poet any pleasure that he might take in the sight of Fucci's damnation (xxiv, 140). The prophecy is accurate historically, as other prophecies have been earlier in the *Inferno*. Where, however, in

35

previous cantos, the poet clearly attributes his response to the *personaggio*, in the present case he delivers it from beyond the frame of the narrative. The denunciation of Pistoia at line 10 is the poet's riposte to Fucci.

Is this, however, to suggest that the poet directly enters a scene of political skirmishing? In part it is; to the exile, Dante, the *Comedy* was a potent weapon of self-justification; after all, the narrative shows the *personaggio* as a man acceptable to God, while, as an intellectual achievement, the *Comedy* demonstrates the adherence of the poet to certain essential principles of thought and conduct. It is precisely to emphasise the grounds on which his achievement rests that Dante permits a contrast between himself and Fucci.

This contrast revolves around three particular points, the first of which concerns justice and genealogy. For Pistoia, as Dante reminds us at line 12, is descended from the unwholesome seed of the Catiline conspirators. Dante, however – as a Florentine – would trace his own descent to the legitimate power of imperial Rome. And Virgil's account of the thief Cacus provides a model, in its mention of Hercules, for Dante's attack on the latter-day manifestation of the evil of theft. Yet Dante possesses a claim to justice greater than inheritance alone – a vehement impartiality. For the outcry against Pistoia is only one of a series of diatribes in the lower *Inferno*, which includes all the major cities of Tuscany. Indeed the five sinners who appear in Canto xxv after Fucci's departure are all Florentines; and Canto xxvi opens with an attack upon his own native city.

When Dante speaks of justice he speaks not as a partisan but as a prophet. And this is the second count on which he compares himself to Fucci. For accurate as Fucci's words are, the spirit that inspires his prophecy is blasphemous and divisive; Dante, in contrast, looks only to the absolute justice of God. Thus the culmination of the political diatribes that have their beginning in the Malebolge is found in the *Purgatorio*, where, lamenting the ills of the whole of 'serva Italia', he turns in expectation of a remedy to the 'abyss' of divine justice (*Purg.* vi, 121–3).

With this appears the third and most vital distinction between the poet and Vanni Fucci. For Fucci is proud. And so is Dante – especially, as we are yet to see, of the art he employs in Canto

xxv. Yet Fucci's pride, like Satan's, is impatient of delay or restraint, where Dante's pride is that of the just man, who waits on the word of God as the just souls do in Paradise. And waiting, they act and work. The poet, as soon as the transformations begin, makes clear what his work will be – what effort it will cost him – to express his understanding of evil.

A man has been assailed by a six-legged serpent:

> Co' piè di mezzo li avvinse la pancia
> e con li anterïor le braccia prese;
> poi li addentò e l'una e l'altra guancia;
>   li diretani a le cosce distese,
> e miseli la coda tra 'mbedue
> e dietro per le ren sù la ritese.
>   Ellera abbarbicata mai non fue
> ad alber sì, come l'orribil fiera
> per l'altrui membra avviticchiò le sue.
>   Poi s'appiccar, come di calda cera
> fossero stati, e mischiar lor colore,
> né l'un né l'altro già parea quel ch'era:
>   come procede innanzi da l'ardore,
> per lo papiro suso, un color bruno
> che non è nero ancora e 'l bianco more.   (52–66)

(With its middle feet it clasped the paunch; the arms were taken by those at the front. It sank its teeth into either cheek. Extending its hind-legs the length of each thigh, it now stuck its tail in between them, bending it up behind the loins. No growth of ivy, tangled in a tree, ever clung so tenaciously as that appalling monster, weaving its parts around and through the other like tendrils. And then, as if the two of them were heated wax, they stuck together; their colourings began to mix, and neither had the look of what, at first, he had been. So when a sheet of paper catches fire, a shadow precedes the spreading flame, not black and yet the whiteness dies.)

Implicitly, the closing lines of this passage convey how difficult – even perilous – the description that Dante here attempts must be. At lines 143–4 Dante will suggest that the novelty of his subject may well have confused his pen. The same possibility, however, is touched upon in the image of burning paper; the subject almost has the power to destroy the page on which the poet seeks to confine it. Yet language – as Dante also implies – is capable of containing within its bounds the most extreme abnormalities. For the image of the ivy is an allusion to Ovid's

Metamorphoses IV, 365, the image of melting wax an allusion to Lucan's *Pharsalia* IX, 782. And, while later Dante presumes to outdo both Ovid and Lucan, he relies here on his solidarity with the example of those who have gone before him in describing metamorphosis. Their language constitutes a model and a norm. Dante now enunciates a norm of his own, expressed in three aspects of the imagery that dominates the following transformations.

The first of these is number. As created order presents itself to the mind in the permutations of Fortune, so the adumbration of a greater truth appears in an unremitting play on the factors One, Two and Zero. Three sinners approached, yet the perfection symbolised by this number is destroyed as the serpent fuses, with its own six legs, the arms, cheeks and thighs of the single man. Nor is unity created by the fusion; the grotesque miscegenation produces only a negation of number:

> Li altri due 'l riguardavano, e ciascuno
> gridava: 'Omè, Agnel, come ti muti!
> Vedi che già non se' né due né uno.'   (67–9)

(The others looked on and each of them, dismayed, exclaimed: 'Agnello, how you change! Look, you are already neither two nor one.')

Yet the sense of number is not itself absent. For while the sinners themselves are passive in their recognition of it, the poet's own verse sustains the sense with the utmost vigour. This is especially evident in the handling of the caesura. Throughout the *Comedy*, the placing of the caesura is a vital feature of Dante's technique. And something of the subtlety he can attain by it is seen from the following lines, where the Christian philosophers celebrate, as the thieves cannot, the perfection of number in the Trinity, singing of:

> Quell'uno e due e tre che sempre vive
> e regna sempre in tre e 'n due e 'n uno.
>   (*Par.* XIV, 28–9)

(That one and two and three that lives for ever and reigns for ever in three and two and one.)

The fluency of such a passage is wholly lacking in Canto XXV. Here the pause is employed throughout to bring into relief the clash and contrast of number. Thus, not pausing to elaborate the pathetic cry of the sinners, the canto goes on, with its unremitting articulation:

> Già eran li due capi un divenuti
> quando n'apparver due figure miste
> in una faccia, ov' eran due perduti.
>   Fersi le braccia due di quattro liste;
> le cosce con le gambe e 'l ventre e 'l casso
> divenner membra che non fuor mai viste.
>   Ogne primaio aspetto ivi era casso:
> due e nessun l'imagine perversa
> parea; e tal sen gio con lento passo.   (70–8)

(The heads of the two by this time were one; and two having vanished, two profiles were seen mingling within one single face. Replacing four arm-lengths, two arms had appeared. And members were made – of a kind never seen – out of legs, out of thighs, out of stomach and chest. Now every original feature had been erased. A semblance it was of both two and none, that perverse image. And such as it was it then moved away at a slow pace.)

Important, however, as number is, there appear simultaneously two other groups of images to enforce its significance. The first derives from the natural world in its simplest aspect. Already the tangles of the snakes have been compared to ivy. And images of this kind, in the context of the cantos that precede and follow the twenty-fifth, have especial force. For both Canto xxiv and xxvi make emphatic reference to the natural world.

Thus Canto xxiv, 1–15 began with the great depiction of the peasant who – while eager to work – cannot do so until the sun has cleared a frost, which lies as thick on the ground as snow. The details of the winter landscape are given with the sharpest definition, and are matched in Canto xxvi, 24–30 by an equally fine description of a summer night and well-earned repose.

The force of these passages could hardly be clearer; to an eye stricken by the sights of Hell, the natural world – the sphere of man's natural labours – offers evidence of health and good order. And this certainly is the force of the image in the passage that follows:

> Come 'l ramarro sotto la gran fersa
> dei dì canicular, cangiando sepe,
> folgore par se la via attraversa,

39

sì pareva, venendo verso l'epe
de li altri due, un serpentello acceso,
livido e nero come gran di pepe;
   e quella parte onde prima è preso
nostro alimento, a l'un di lor trafisse;
poi cadde giuso innanzi lui disteso.
   Lo trafitto 'l mirò, ma nulla disse;
anzi, co' piè fermati, sbadigliava
pur come sonno o febbre l'assalisse.
   Elli 'l serpente e quei lui riguardava;
l'un per la piaga e l'altro per la bocca
fummavan forte, e 'l fummo si scontrava.   (79–93)

(As a lizard, cutting from hedgerow to hedgerow, beneath the great lash of the heat of high summer, is lightning, it seems, if it crosses your path, so likewise a serpent – small, keen and burning – as black as a grain of pepper, and livid, now struck at the guts of the other two. And one it transfixed at the point where our earliest nourishment enters. And then it fell back and stretched all its length before him. Transfixed he stared down; he said nothing at all. But stock-still he yawned as though hit by sleep or a fever. Eying the serpent, the serpent eyed him. The wound of the one and the mouth of the other gave out a dense smoke. The columns of smoke came together.)

Here with the utmost vigour and design the lizard is shown in its natural habitat; the heat of the summer day is evoked, the lines of the footpath are clearly defined by the movement of the lizard across them, and also by the emphasis that 'sepe' – 'hedgerow' – gives to its lateral limit. Such detail stands precisely in contradistinction to the details of the punishment. A sinister smoke replaces the clearness of the summer day, confusion replaces clarity, and passivity the agile movements of the lizard. In such a context, the lizard – unchanged – is the rare and strange.

With this one arrives at the last and most searching appeal to normality. For the transformations are presented throughout as a parody of sexual union.[4] It is here that Fucci's initial obscenity proves to have been no random outburst; the laws of creation that Fucci mocks in pride and blasphemy are laws that, rightly – if partially – express themselves in human sexuality. We are asked in Canto xxv to believe that, in spite of what the imagination might conjure up, these laws provide a pattern essential to our nature.

For a direct expression of Dante's own belief in this, we should have to turn to the twenty-fifth canto of the *Purgatorio*, where the poet, discussing conception and gestation, explains the union of soul and body – a union that Dante compares to that of the sun's heat and the liquor of the grape in wine (*Purg.* xxv, 77–8). But in this parallel canto of the *Inferno*, the truth must be grasped obliquely through a scene of birth, copulation and death. We have seen already the monstrous birth of the 'imagine perversa' that slouches off at line 77. We now see an act of penetration at the navel, 'the point where our earliest nourishment enters', which leads to nothing but the magical smoke and the sickly relaxation of the sinner's yawn.

It is at the climax of this unnatural scene that Dante expresses most acutely his awareness of his own poetic standing:

> Taccia Lucano omai là dov' e' tocca
> del misero Sabello e di Nasidio,
> e attenda a udir quel ch'or si scocca.
> Taccia di Cadmo e d'Aretusa Ovidio,
> ché se quello in serpente e quella in fonte
> converte poetando, io non lo 'nvidio;
> ché due nature mai a fronte a fronte
> non trasmutò sì ch'amendue le forme
> a cambiar lor matera fosser pronte.   (94–102)

(Let Lucan now fall silent when he comes to tell of wretched Sabellus and Nasidius, and pause to attend to what here shall be shot forth. Let Ovid be silent about Cadmus and Arethusa; for if, in writing his verses, he made a serpent of one and of one a well-spring, I feel no envy at all for that; for he never altered two natures, eye to eye, so that each distinctive form was quick to change its specific matter with another.)

The transformations that follow differ in a number of respects from the earlier set. Yet the stance of the author is consistent here with that which he has adopted from the opening of the canto. Against the primitive suggestions that his own images generate, the poet asserts the value of natural order. This assertion, however, requires of him the utmost sophistication in the exercise of his art. And to some degree that sophistication is drawn from the models of Latin literature; where Fucci's blasphemy is the flowering of the evil seed of Pistoia, so Dante's own art – at one with justice – has its roots in the example of the authors whom he now presumes to outdo. There is thus a conscious elevation of style not

41

only in allusions to the Latin poets but also in the form of the similes that Dante here employs. And at line 16 there occurred a conspicuous Latinism that suggests how such stylistic features may possess for Dante a moral significance. Thus as Vanni flees, the poet indicates that silence was forced upon Fucci, not with a simple 'parola', but the Latinate 'verbo':

> El si fuggì che non parlò più verbo.

The distance between the 'bestia' and the poet himself is enforced precisely by the elegance (not to mention the religious force) of the word that Dante chooses.

But how, then, is the poet distinguished from the Latin authorities? Even before lines 94–102 the art of the canto has asserted its independence. The strength of visual imagery and of rhythmic articulation are both characteristic of Dante. But he also draws throughout upon a harsh native lexicon. To describe the sights of Hell the poet needs 'rime aspre e chiocce' (*Inf.* XXXII, 1) and Canto XXV is distinguished not only by elevation of diction but also by words of such vernacular strength as 'epe' (82), 'ascelle' (112), 'muso' (123), and 'zavorra' (142).

With such locutions the canto acquires distinctness from the Latin model. Yet Dante, in his address to Lucan and Ovid, still insists upon the authority of his own text. And this insistence is compatible with an earlier feature of the canto, the silencing of Virgil himself.

Dante-*personaggio* silences Virgil at line 44. But Dante the poet does likewise in a sequence that appears to express the authority of the *Aeneid*, the description of Cacus. For the *Aeneid* has spoken of Cacus only as a *semihomo* (VIII, 194). Yet Dante has transformed the figure into a centaur, and doing so takes as his point of reference not Virgil's poem but his own *Comedy*. The centaurs have already appeared in Canto XII as the guardians of those who have sinned by violent greed. Virgil is made to emphasise this connection. However, the progressive vision of greed, robbery and theft reveals an understanding of these sins that only the Christian could comprehend. Virgil sees a social offence in Cacus's behaviour; the Christian observes a deformation in the greater law: man's mind is the custodian of his natural being, and sins of the mind must resonate throughout all aspects of his proper form.

When Dante wept in *Inferno* xx at the sight of the perversion of 'nostra imagine', Virgil upbraided him. The reproof, however, demonstrates the same limitation that Lucan and Ovid also display. For much as Virgil may value the moral nature of man, he cannot, as a pagan, be thought to comprehend the truth, essential to Christian belief, that the form of man is itself guaranteed in the eternal plan of creation. This is the truth that the resurrection declares. This is the truth that is borne upon Dante himself by the beauty and – for him the quite literal – immortality of Beatrice. And this, in the twenty-fifth canto, is the *ben* and *frutto* that the imagination of the reader must attempt to comprehend as Virgil cannot. That the author of the canto will himself do so is the point of distinction between his metamorphoses and those of Lucan and Ovid.

Consider, first, how Lucan treats the death of Sabellus. Bitten by a *seps*, his body begins to dissolve, revealing, sinew by sinew, bone by bone, the whole anatomy of human kind:

> Quidquid homo est, aperit pestis natura profana
> (*Pharsalia* ix, 779)

(The whole frame of man is revealed by the awful nature of that disease.)

The anatomy itself is a wonderful piece of work; and Dante scientifically would doubtless have admired it. Once revealed, however, the wonder is to Lucan that the work, reduced to a pool of corruption, should melt away like snow before the warm south wind:

> calido non ocius Austro
> Nix resoluta cadit nec solem cera sequetur.
> (*ibid.* 781–2)

(Snow does not melt and vanish more quickly before the warm south wind, nor will wax be affected faster by the sun.)

In Dante's transformations, on the other hand, the wonder is that nothing – or nothing proper to the body of man – is ever beyond recall. The ashes of Vanni Fucci return on the instant to their proper shape. And now, in the final transformations the punishment observes a similar, though more elaborate, economy.

Here 'man-shape' and snake-form are interchanged. Yet the rule that guides these changes is a rule of inverse progression; a

43

part that is cancelled in one of the creatures is produced simultaneously in the body of the other. And at no point does the penalty allow that any excess of matter should remain unaccounted for. Thus, while each of the sinners undergoes a total change in his identity, their punishment itself insists on the value of identity or distinctive shape:

> Insieme si rispuosero a tai norme
> che 'l serpente la coda in forca fesse,
> e 'l feruto ristrinse insieme l'orme.
>   Le gambe con le cosce seco stesse
> s'appiccar sì, che 'n poco la giuntura
> non facea segno alcun che si paresse.
>   Togliea la coda fessa la figura
> che si perdeva là, e la sua pelle
> si facea molle, e quella di là dura.
>   Io vidi intrar le braccia per l'ascelle,
> e i due piè de la fiera, ch'eran corti,
> tanto allungar quanto accorciavan quelle.
>   Poscia li piè di rietro, insieme attorti,
> diventaron lo membro che l'uom cela,
> e 'l misero del suo n'avea due porti.   (103–17)

(They answered in reciprocity to the rules of the change: the tail of the snake split open and it formed a fork; the footprints of the stricken man drew in upon themselves and met. Thigh closed on thigh, the legs adhering, shortly no trace at all was seen of the join between them. The form that, in one place, now disappeared, was taken in turn by the riven tail – the skin here grew soft as there it grew hard. I saw the arms shrink up towards the arm-pits; as these were shortened, the feet of the brute – mere stumps at first – both lengthened to the same extent. And then the part that a man keeps hidden was formed by the plaiting of the two hind-legs. The wretch from his member put forth a corresponding pair.)

In earlier sequences the imagination of the poet has affirmed the principles of motion and number; here the *frutto* beneath the horror is the truth that, in eternity, the individuality of men is guaranteed (*Inf.* VI, 97–8). Lucan, no less than the sinners who suffer its consequence, must be ignorant of this truth. And Ovid, too, will fall within the ban. For metamorphosis – to consider only the Cadmus episode – so far from being a punishment, is portrayed by Ovid as a fate that the wife of Cadmus knowingly chooses. Seeing her husband transformed into a serpent, she entreats the gods that she may become what he has become (*Metamorphoses* IV, 593–5). Such a desire, for Dante, would be not only a physical but a moral nonsense. Indeed, the human figure in Dante's thought is of such importance that the final *bolgia* contains men who have merely changed their shape by impersonating other men. The attitude, moreover, that Ovid adopts as he pictures the scene must appear no less repugnant. For the scene of change is surrounded by pathos and by a delicate, even erotic pleasure, as the two 'gentle' beasts move off, their coils intertwining:

> at illa
> lubrica permulcet cristati colla draconis,
> et subito duo sunt iunctoque volumine serpunt,
> donec in adpositi nemoris subiere latebras.
>
> (*ibid.* 598–601)

(But she only stroked the sleek neck of the crested dragon, and suddenly there were two serpents – intertwining their folds – which crawled away soon and hid in a nearby wood.)

Where Ovid's effect is pathetic, Dante's effect is harshly scientific; where Ovid finds sensuality, Dante finds perversity – translating into a parody of healthy love the images that Ovid's text may here have suggested to him.

Rejecting, however, the myths of Ovid, the poet affirms the *frutto* of his Christian understanding by a concentration in the following lines on two particular images, which convey, throughout the *Comedy*, his sense of the value of human form – the images of the eye and face.

Thus, the two creatures, as their muzzles change, fix upon each other the 'unholy lights' of their eyes:

> Mentre che 'l fummo l'uno e l'altro vela
> di color novo, e genera 'l pel suso
> per l'una parte e da l'altra il dipela,
> l'un si levò e l'altro cadde giuso,
> non torcendo però le lucerne empie,
> sotto le quai ciascun cambiava muso.
> Quel ch'era dritto, il trasse ver' le tempie,
> e di troppa matera ch'in là venne
> uscir li orecchi de le gote scempie;
> ciò che non corse in dietro e si ritenne
> di quel soverchio, fé naso a la faccia
> e le labbra ingrossò quanto convenne.　　　(118–29)

(With smoke casting over the one and the other a veil of strange new colour – causing in one place the hair to appear that it stripped away elsewhere – the one found his feet, the other fell prostrate. Neither averted, however, his unholy lights beneath which both were changing their snouts. He that was upright pulled his towards his temples; from excess of matter moving there, ears appeared upon naked cheeks. Of any surplus retained that did not run back, a nose was fashioned for that face, and the lips grew as thick as they needed to be.)

No reader of either the *Vita Nuova* or the *Paradiso* could fail to be offended by this. For the eyes and – finally – the smile of Beatrice make clear to Dante how beautiful the human person may be to God as well as to men. And when in *Paradiso* XXXIII Dante himself finally approaches God the encounter is one of face and eye. It is also an encounter that expresses the ultimate value of change. For, as Dante gazes on the being of God, his own self and the image of God are both transformed; God 'works' towards the responsive eye of Dante:

> una sola parvenza,
> mutandom' io, a me si travagliava
>
> (*Par.* XXXIII, 113–14)

(One sole appearance changed itself for me as I was changing.)

And the final act is that God should offer to Dante the face of His own humanity:

> mi parve pinta de la nostra effige   (*ibid.* 131)

(It appeared to me painted with our very image.)

The meeting of eyes in the *Paradiso* is a moment of pure activity; in *Inferno* XXV, the eyes of the sinners are empty and passive. But the eye of Dante the poet is not; endeavouring even here to discern and express a notion of order.

With which one reaches the final phase of the transformation. For the word of the poet, in counterpoint to the sufferings of the sinners, has provided in Canto XXV the only illustration of natural activity. And now the poet returns to the theme of language; as the canto began with a contrast between the poet's own virtuosity and the blasphemous obscenities of Fucci, so now it ends with a vision of the sinner's tongue, degraded and deformed. The newly-made serpent goes hissing across the floor of the *bolgia*; the newly-made man, when he opens his mouth, only spits and then utters words of sheer spite:

> Quel che giacëa, il muso innanzi caccia,
> e li orecchi ritira per la testa
> come face le corna la lumaccia;
>   e la lingua, ch'avëa unita e presta
> prima a parlar, si fende, e la forcuta
> ne l'altro si richiude; e 'l fummo resta.
>   L'anima ch'era fiera divenuta,
> suffolando si fugge per la valle,
> e l'altro dietro a lui parlando sputa.
>   Poscia li volse le novelle spalle,
> e disse a l'altro: 'I' vo' che Buoso corra,
> com' ho fatt' io, carpon per questo calle' . . .   (130–41)

(Laid flat, the other drove its muzzle outwards, then drew in its ears at its head like the horns of a snail. Its tongue had been whole once, and ready in speaking. Now it forked, while the fork of his counterpart healed. And then the smoke stopped. Changed now to the form of a brute the soul of the human ran hissing away down the valley floor; the other one spits as he speaks behind him. Turning his back – with its newly-made shoulders – 'I'll have Buoso scuttle', he said to the other, 'as I have, crabwise the length of this road' . . .)

The changes now are ended. They have been guided throughout by an apprehension of the order that resides in the power of God. Yet the point of resolution for the themes and images of Canto xxv lies in the *Purgatorio* and the *Paradiso*, and here we are not allowed to rest in contemplation of the patterns of truth. Nor does the force of the canto derive from design or pattern alone but rather from the effort that the poet, as he writes, must make to impose design upon his own gross imaginings. The effort is cruel, as the vision is cruel. And in that respect the final lines of the canto provide a telling conclusion.

Here for the last time we are asked to listen to the voice – which was raised first against Fucci and Pistoia – as the poet works to exhaust the evil he has seen:

> Così vid' io la settima zavorra
> mutare e trasmutare; e qui mi scusi
> la novità se fior la penna abborra.
>   E avvegna che li occhi miei confusi
> fossero alquanto e l'animo smagato,
> non poter quei fuggirsi tanto chiusi,

> ch'i' non scorgessi ben Puccio Sciancato;
> ed era quel che sol, di tre compagni
> che venner prima, non era mutato;
> l'altr' era quel che tu, Gaville, piagni.   (142–51)

(And so I beheld the ballast change and interchange in the seventh keel. The strangeness of it all will here excuse me if my pen has failed. And yet, although my eyes were reeling, my mind astray, these two could not make off so stealthily that I did not discern quite clearly Puccio Sciancato. Alone of the three who had come first in company, he was unchanged. The other is he, Gaville, who has made you weep.)

Of the sinners whom Dante has encountered in the seventh *bolgia*, only one remains unchanged. The apparent immunity, however, of this isolated figure wins him no credit. His name is spoken to single him out for especial odium. The name itself, indeed, carries with it an unrelenting contempt – Puccio Sciancato, Puccio the Cripple – as though in this entirely marginal, yet historical, figure Dante wished his reader to see how humanity, even apart from the effects of damnation, might be turned awry in body as in spirit. It would be hard to overestimate the viciousness of these lines, and it might perhaps be comforting to suggest that the voice was that of Dante-*personaggio*, still deeply involved with sin. Yet this cannot be. It is the voice of the author who has known from the opening lines of his poem that to remember evil is a labour 'so bitter that death is hardly more so'.

Notes

1 See E. Panofsky, *Studies in Iconology* (New York, 1962), p. 19.
2 Cf. A. Momigliano, '*Inferno*, Canto xxv' contained in *Letture dantesche: Inferno*, ed. G. Getto (Firenze, 1964), p. 470.
3 On the creative word in *Paradiso* xix, see K. Foster, 'The Son's Eagle: Paradiso xix' in *The Two Dantes* (London, 1977), pp. 137–55.
4 Cf. G. Almansi's essay on *Inferno*, Canto xxv in *L'estetica dell'osceno* (Torino, 1974).

Inferno XXVII

JUDITH DAVIES

In Canto XXVI Dante and Virgil reach the eighth *bolgia* of Lower Hell, and the Counsellors of Fraud. There Virgil has spoken to the shade of Ulysses, and Ulysses has given his magnificent account of how he and his fellow mariners, in their pursuit of experience, dared to sail beyond the limits of the known world, far down into the uncharted waters of the southern hemisphere, and how, coming at last to a great mountain (which we learn later in the *Comedy* was Purgatory) they perished there in a sudden, terrible storm. Ulysses has been the subject of almost an entire canto, and now Canto XXVII is to be devoted exclusively to another Counsellor of Fraud, Guido da Montefeltro, a Ghibelline general of the Romagna who died in 1298, just two years before the date at which Dante's imagined journey is set. So it is that we come from the classical world of the Greek heroes, celebrated in Virgil's verse, to an area of Dante's contemporary Italy that the exiled poet came to know well. We pass from the world of high, heroic legend that spoke of the destruction of Troy through the stratagem of the wooden horse, of Aeneas's flight and the foundation of Rome, to an altogether more domestic and painfully familiar story of ambition and sectarian strife. The two worlds that Dante has fused in the *Comedy* stand side by side. In the former, Virgil has been the interlocutor. In the canto of Guido da Montefeltro, Dante himself will be the speaker; while for the first and last time in Hell two major figures punished for the same crime are presented in parallel.

As a narrator building an immense poetic edifice, Dante is acutely aware of the value of structural and thematic variation and symmetry. These two cantos devoted to the Counsellors of Fraud, parallel yet contrasted, change the rhythm of the narrative that leads up to and away from them. Before he reaches Ulysses Dante has suffered extreme terror and extreme mental and physical exhaustion. He has been chased by, and narrowly escaped, a pack of quarrelsome and vengeful devils; in rapid, nightmarish succession he has seen sinners boiled in pitch, crucified and trampled, intolerably weighed down with leaden capes, or transformed into monsters by a repulsive process of metamorphosis. After he leaves Guido, there will be the same urgent rhythm in the narrative, the same horrific dwellings on physical deformity: bodies torn apart, or rotting and encrusted with scabs.

Thus the cantos of the Counsellors of Fraud mark a change in the pace of the narrative, and also, because Dante has invented a subtle punishment for their subtle crime, in the nature of its visual content. Here the sinners are completely enveloped in fire. Once so expert in the art of concealment, they are now concealed by flame. What Dante, however, stresses throughout the canto is not so much, or not alone, the pain of burning, but the effort required of the sinner in order to produce intelligible speech from amid the flame. Speech for Dante is an essential part of man's humanity. As he wrote in the second chapter of *De vulgari eloquentia*, angels who are possessed of immediate, intuitive knowledge, and animals who function by instinct alone, have no need of speech. But for man, whose distinctive quality is his reason, speech is the sensible means by which one rational mind, housed in flesh, may communicate with another. With Dante playing in the canto on what is fundamentally the familiar image of 'tongues of fire', that God-given spontaneity of speech disappears, the harmonious passage from thought to word is disrupted. This of course is entirely appropriate treatment for men who have misused their intellectual powers, have used their reason to excogitate schemes of treachery against their fellows. Remembering his visions of the wayward intelligences in this *bolgia*, the poet, even as he writes, curbs his own genius 'perché non corra che virtù nol guidi' ('so that it should not run where virtue does not guide it') (*Inf.* XXVI, 22). Guido's is intelligence unaccompanied by virtue, and speech, the instrument of reason, becomes a laborious process, which is emphasised throughout the canto.

When it opens, the flame of Ulysses has finished telling its story. Before the poets can resume their journey, their attention is attracted by another flame hurrying towards them:

Già era dritta in sù la fiamma e queta
per non dir più, e già da noi sen gia
con la licenza del dolce poeta,
　　quand' un'altra, che dietro a lei venìa,
ne fece volger li occhi a la sua cima
per un confuso suon che fuor n'uscia.　　　　　　(1–6)

(Already the flame was erect and still, having ceased to speak, and, with
the consent of the gentle poet, it was already moving away when another
flame coming on behind it made us turn our eyes to its tip because of a
confused sound issuing from it.)

With that 'confuso suon' Dante has already begun to characterise
his sinner. This is the perplexed spirit of Guido da Montefeltro,
who will tell the story of how he, a deceiver, was deceived and
who will take his leave at the end of the canto still lamenting and
bewildered.

Guido was the great Ghibelline general, one of the most
prominent and powerful figures in the Romagna of Dante's
youth, and his skill as a military tactician earned him the nickname
of the 'Fox'. In 1288 warfare in opposition to the Papacy also
earned him excommunication. But in 1296, after an adventurous
and successful military career, and by now an old man, Guido
joined the Franciscan Order. It was perhaps the dramatic nature of
the *volte-face* that surrounded the historical figure of Guido with an
aura of sanctity. At a point in his own *Convivio* where Dante
speaks of old age as the period in life when men should turn away
from worldly involvements in preparation for death, there comes
a reference to Guido. 'Like the good sailor, who nearing harbour
lowers his sails and glides gently into port', Dante writes, 'so we
too must lower the sails of our worldly concerns and turn to God
with all our understanding and heart, so that we reach that port
with all gentleness and in all peace.' As an example of pious and
contemplative old age he cites 'lo nobilissimo nostro latino Guido
montefeltrano' (*Con.* IV, xxviii, 8). The fourteenth-century commentator Benvenuto describes how the once proud general would
humbly beg for bread in the streets of Ancona, and he adds: 'I
have heard many things about him that would allow one to be of
good hope for his salvation.' It was also said, however, that in
1298 Pope Boniface VIII persuaded Guido to give him tactical
advice on subduing the fortress town of Palestrina not far from

Rome. Palestrina was the stronghold of the powerful Roman family of the Colonnas, who at that time were openly defying Pope Boniface, whose election to the Holy See, after the abdication of Celestine V, they regarded as fraudulent. The way in which Guido, having repented and become a friar, falls again from grace is to be the central episode of this canto. Since it is Boniface who persuades Guido to give the fraudulent counsel – the Pope, that is, who was indirectly responsible for Dante's own bitter exile, and whom he repeatedly condemns in the *Comedy* – a problem of interpretation arises: does Dante expect us to judge Guido less severely because of Boniface's role in his sin? Clearly by his very position in Hell Guido stands condemned, but some commentators have stressed that through Guido Dante's real target is the greater cunning and the greater evil of Pope Boniface. Momigliano, for instance, writes: 'We should not forget that it is Dante who pulls the strings here, and that the episode, which is of such vital interest to him as himself the victim of Boniface VIII, is thus permeated by a sense of bitterness . . . In reality infamy covers not Guido but Boniface VIII.' Guido's sin undoubtedly has the strongest of attenuating circumstances: he is a friar acting in obedience to the Church's highest representative, and he trusts in papal authority when Boniface proclaims his absolution. It is as though Dante for a moment invited the reader to question the justice of the condemnation. Of course there can be no real challenge; but from the momentary process of questioning the clarity of Dante's moral vision emerges the more triumphant. In this canto the moral issue is always clear: Guido is as guilty as he would have been had Boniface not been the occasion of his sin. For that sin to have occurred Guido's mind must have willed it. And in the canto this mind will be characterised very thoroughly: a sense of ambiguity and duality will run throughout it, unobtrusively but unmistakingly underlining the essence of Dante's poetic vision of Guido.

Before the 'confuso suon' can become intelligible to the travellers, Dante compares the predicament of the sinner enveloped in fire, and deprived of spontaneous speech, to that of the victims of the bull of Sicily:

Come 'l bue cicilian che mugghiò prima
col pianto di colui, e ciò fu dritto,
che l'avea temperato con sua lima,

> mugghiava con la voce de l'afflitto,
> sì che, con tutto che fosse di rame,
> pur el pareva dal dolor trafitto;
>   così, per non aver via né forame
> dal principio nel foco, in suo linguaggio
> si convertïan le parole grame.   (7–15)

(As the Sicilian bull – which bellowed first (and this was just) with the wailing of the man who had shaped it with his file – would bellow with the voice of the victim, so that although made of copper it seemed transfixed with pain; in the same way, because at first there was no passage or outlet for them in the fire, the doleful words were converted into the language of flame.)

Dante might have read in Ovid or Pliny the story of Perillus, who created a hollow brazen bull inside which the Sicilian tyrant Phalaris enclosed his enemies and burnt them alive. The cries of the tortured would issue from the metallic body of the animal, as though the bull itself were bellowing in agony. As the cries of the sufferer, deprived of their natural outlet, emerged as bellows, so in this *bolgia* the voice of the sinner, since it must pass through the intervening medium of fire, emerges first in the language of flames. But the parallels are soon to diverge:

> Ma poscia ch'ebber colto lor vïaggio
> su per la punta, dandole quel guizzo
> che dato avea la lingua in lor passaggio,
> udimmo dire: . . .   (16–19)

(But when they had travelled up to its tip and given it that same vibration which the tongue had given them in their passage, we heard say: . . .)

Certain critics, inheritors of the Crocean distinction between *poesia* and *struttura* in the *Comedy*, regard this meticulously detailed and almost technical passage as a piece of description of an essentially unpoetic kind, though characteristically ingenious. But it has a clear structural, thematic and poetic effect within the rest of the canto. Dramatic tension is increased by this delay in presenting the sinner, and the comparison with Perillus's bull, at first surprising, is in reality extraordinarily appropriate. In both terms of the comparison there is fire and there is the strange distortion of a human voice; both Perillus and Guido use their special intellectual gifts for evil purposes, and both devise a novel way of dealing with enemies. But the passage is perhaps most significant for what it suggests of Dante's attitude to Guido, and for its introduction of a central theme in the canto.

Dante has noted that it was Perillus himself whom the tyrant used to test the effectiveness of the invention; and adds in a parenthesis of severe simplicity 'e ciò fu dritto'. It is an unequivocal phrase that anticipates Dante's moral judgement on the man who advised deception and was himself deceived. As in the case of Perillus, Guido's abuses are justly punished by like abuse. Together with this moral judgement, itself an indication of how we should read this canto, Dante has introduced the important theme of the betrayer betrayed, the central situation of reciprocal evil, which Benvenuto's Latin expresses very neatly: 'Bonifacius astutissimus circumvenit me astutissimum.'

At last Guido's voice struggles out of the flame, and he addresses Virgil, whom he has heard dismissing the spirit of Ulysses:

> 'O tu a cu' io drizzo
> la voce e che parlavi mo lombardo,
> dicendo "Istra ten va, più non t'adizzo",
>   perch'io sia giunto forse alquanto tardo,
> non t'incresca restare a parlar meco;
> vedi che non incresce a me, e ardo!
>   Se tu pur mo in questo mondo cieco
> caduto se' di quella dolce terra
> latina ond'io mia colpa tutta reco,
>   dimmi se Romagnuoli han pace o guerra;
> ch'io fui d'i monti là intra Orbino
> e 'l giogo di che Tever si diserra.'   (19–30)

('O you to whom I aim my words, and who were just then speaking Lombard, saying: "Be on your way, I shall not urge you to speak any more", although I have perhaps arrived rather late, do not be unwilling to stop and talk with me; you see that *I* am not unwilling, and yet am burning! If you have just now fallen into this blind world, leaving behind that dear land of Italy from which I carry all the burden of my guilt, tell me whether the people of Romagna are at peace or at war; for I was from the mountains there between Urbino and the ridge from which the Tiber springs forth.')

It has puzzled many commentators that Virgil should have apparently spoken to Ulysses in Lombard dialect. Some like Grandgent and Zingarelli have found in *De vulgari eloquentia* sufficient evidence of Dante's belief that dialects existed in Italy contemporaneously with Latin. Virgil would therefore have been addressing Ulysses in a suitably ancient language. Benvenuto Terracini more recently has argued that the dialect phrase 'Istra ten va, più non t'adizzo' is not intended to reproduce Virgil's actual words. He points out that Guido alludes graphically to his own punishment in the word 'drizzo', which suggests the predicament of one who cannot see from within his flame, and must 'aim' his words in the general direction of Virgil. This concrete allusion to the nature of his punishment would then be continued in the verb 'adizzare', which spoken to a 'uomo-fiamma' carries almost the value of 'attizzare', to stir or poke a fire. Terracini argues that Guido reproduces the spirit of Virgil's words according to his own particular understanding, in his own rather concrete terms.[1] At all events, the dialect passage introduces a familiar note, which emphasises stylistically the antithetical nature of the two cantos on fraudulent counsel. In the previous canto the great Latin poet and the Greek hero have discoursed in a sustained high style. Now in the encounter between modern Italians the linguistic register is lowered. Guido's story will be told in a lively, direct manner, substantially free of stylistic decoration; and he will have his reply only when Virgil has unceremoniously nudged Dante and given him the colloquial prompting: 'Parla tu; questi è latino' ('You speak; this one is Italian': 33).

Guido's opening words, diplomatically cautious and even apologetic as they are, cannot finally contain his longing to hear news of the world he has left behind. And between lines 19 and 24 there is established a pattern of control and release that Dante will make characteristic of Guido. Virgil, whom Guido takes to be a sinner newly condemned, awakes in him a nostalgic memory of his fatherland; the poignant vision of lofty mountain ridges and springing water can, however, never be a source of pure consolation, for Guido's memories are clouded by his sense of guilt. Later in the canto, indeed, Guido will seem to deplore that part of his life that was connected with Romagna and her politics. Yet despite the heavy burden of his regrets, the word 'caduto' and the expression 'mondo cieco' suggest that for Guido condemnation to Hell has been an experience of sudden disruption, almost of surprise; and these will be the lines along which Dante develops the figure of Guido. He is a man theoretically aware of his sin, yet on some deeper level bewildered by his condemnation.

Like many of the sinners Dante has met in Hell, who can have no hope of future salvation, Guido's mind is anxiously fixed on the past. He has asked for news of Romagna, and the question whether Romagna is at peace or at war comes naturally from the former general. It will be Dante who eagerly replies to him:

> 'O anima che se' là giù nascosta,
>   Romagna tua non è, e non fu mai,
> sanza guerra ne' cuor de' suoi tiranni;
> ma 'n palese nessuna or vi lasciai.
>   Ravenna sta come stata è molt' anni:
> l'aguglia da Polenta la si cova,
> sì che Cervia ricuopre co' suoi vanni.
>   La terra che fé già la lunga prova
> e di Franceschi sanguinoso mucchio,
> sotto le branche verdi si ritrova.
>   E 'l mastin vecchio e 'l nuovo da Verrucchio,
> che fecer di Montagna il mal governo,
> là dove soglion fan d'i denti succhio.
>   Le città di Lamone e di Santerno
> conduce il lïoncel dal nido bianco,
> che muta parte da la state al verno.
>   E quella cu' il Savio bagna il fianco,
> così com' ella sie' tra 'l piano e 'l monte,
> tra tirannia si vive e stato franco.'   (36–54)

('O soul hidden down there, your Romagna is never, and nor has it ever been, free of warfare in the hearts of its tyrants; but when I left it now no war was in the open. Ravenna exists as she has existed for many years: the eagle from Polenta broods over her so that Cervia lies beneath its wings. The city [Forlì] that once withstood the siege and made a bloody mound of the French is again in the clutch of the green paw. And the old mastiff and the new one from Verrucchio, who once treated Montagna so wickedly, still sink their fangs where they always have [Rimini]. The cities on the Lamone and the Saterno [Faenza and Imola] are still ruled by the lion-cub of the white lair who changes sides from summer to winter. And the city [Cesena] whose flank is bathed by the Savio, sitting between plain and mountain, likewise survives between tyranny and freedom.')

Six terzinas summarise the recent history of Romagna, with Dante moving in an orderly manner from a general statement about the region to more detailed information on the political state of its main towns. After twenty-five years of constant warfare, in 1299 the cities of Romagna had agreed to a perpetual peace. The agreement apparently was still in force in 1300, the year in which Dante's journey is set, though, to judge from Dante's comments on the aggressive instincts of Romagna's rulers, the peace was a precarious one. The individual cities Dante names are the sites of battles where Guido won his reputation. The besieged town of line 43, for example, which inflicted such heavy losses on the French, is Forlì, and it was Guido himself who captained the resistance against the combined French and Italian forces of Pope Martin IV. Dante the traveller is still unaware of the spirit's identity (and Guido will never be explicitly named in the canto), but the choice of information given on the Romagna is clearly conditioned by the listening presence of Guido da Montefeltro. The rulers of the Romagna are presented in concrete visual terms, not named but evoked emblematically, usually by reference to their own heraldic devices. Guido da Polenta is seen as the eagle on his own escutcheon, brooding over Ravenna and Cervia; and the lion-cub of the white lair is Maghinardo Pagani, ruler of Faenza and Imola, whose arms were a lion azure on a field argent. As a political man Dante might have wished to distinguish between the merits of one ruler and another, but his poetic purpose is to suggest the hidden threat to Romagna's peace, with images of eagle, lion and mastiff creating a sense of latent rapaciousness behind a tranquil facade. This sense of ambiguity in the conditions prevailing in Romagna comes to a climax with the last-indicated town of Cesena, where two sets of balanced phrases underscore the precarious equilibrium of the area's political state. The impression of deviousness created by the presentation of the towns and their rulers links the passage to the rest of the canto; and the words 'Romagna tua', which open Dante's reply to Guido, come to seem not so much a sympathetic response to Guido's preceding mood of nostalgia, as a taunt associating him with the duplicity that Dante sees as characteristic of the political Romagna.

As happens so often in Hell, with Pier della Vigna, for example, in Canto XIII, or with Bocca and Ugolino in Canto XXXII, Dante offers as an inducement to speech the sinner's desire for vindication in the world of the living. Once again he must wait for the flame's speech to become intelligible, and the lines are a rhythmic accompaniment to the movement of the flame's tip, to the laboured emission of speech:

> Poscia che 'l foco alquanto ebbe rugghiato
> al modo suo, l'aguta punta mosse
> di qua, di là, e poi diè cotal fiato:
>   'S'i' credesse che mia risposta fosse
> a persona che mai tornasse al mondo,
> questa fiamma staria sanza più scosse;
>   ma però che già mai di questo fondo
> non tornò vivo alcun, s'i'odo il vero,
> sanza tema d'infamia ti rispondo.'   (58–66)

(When the fire had roared a while in its usual fashion, moving its pointed tip now to one side, now to the other, it then breathed out these words: 'If I thought that I was replying to someone who might ever return to the earth, this flame would never move again; but as no one ever returned alive from this abyss, if what I hear is true, I shall give you my reply without fearing that my reputation might suffer.')

Guido is no exception to the general rule that the sinners in Hell are anxious about their earthly reputations; but here Dante introduces a subtle variation, for Guido's concern is not to modify a bad reputation, but to preserve a good one. If Dante's return to earth might endanger it, we must assume that Guido's sin was not known, or not widely known, to contemporaries. They believed that his soul had been saved, and it is a fiction Guido wants preserved.

This brings us to the question of what Dante in the poem has made of the historical facts available to him on Guido. We saw that Benvenuto at one stage had been confident of Guido's salvation, though he clearly accepts as fact Dante's version of Guido's fate, including details of the encounter with Boniface not mentioned in the canto. But clearly even more noteworthy is that laudatory reference to Guido by Dante himself in the *Convivio*, which contrasts so markedly with the vision of Guido in Hell. Researches, however, have brought to light two contemporary witnesses of Guido's fateful meeting with Boniface, and both appear independent of the *Comedy*. We may assume therefore that after he had written the *Convivio* Dante came upon this information, and that it had limited currency – was unknown to his commentator Buti for instance. In the poem Dante ingeniously exploits this circumstance of Guido's personal history. It is on the mistaken assumption that Dante cannot return to earth and tarnish his reputation that the Guido of the canto consents to speak. Yet, just as he hopes to deceive his contemporaries about his true fate, so Guido is deceived by the traveller, Dante, who sees fit not to reveal that he is a mortal man, destined to return to earth. The seemingly unimportant fact that Guido's spiritual salvation was widely taken for granted becomes, in the poem, the means by which Dante reveals the essential personality of his sinner. Guido is a deceiver still as he was on earth, and, for all his prudent enunciation of the law that governs the inhabitants of Hell, he is as easily misled now as he was by Boniface. Meanwhile the motif of the deceiver deceived, introduced in the image of Perillus, and soon to be the subject of Guido's own story, now invests the narrative framework itself of the canto.

The facts of Guido's life, then, were puzzling. Contemporary chronicles not only praised Guido's military skills, but exalted his private character: Salimbene calls him 'a nobleman, intelligent, discreet, and gracious, generous, courtly and openhearted'. Yet Dante's own 'nobilissimo' Guido was in reality a sinner. The poet of course may make of documented facts what he likes; yet the intellectual and moral fascination of Guido for Dante may well have resided precisely in the contradictoriness of those facts. His task now as with other sinners in Hell is not simply to record the fact of sin, but to explore the spiritual terrain where sin took root and flourished; and in Guido's case there was the additional challenge that lay in fusing the baldly contradictory images of history so that they formed a unity. The poet presents us with a character who is a mixture of caution and forthrightness. There is in Guido the shrewdness of the tactician as well as the vigour and the energy of the fighter. And Dante will suggest that it is precisely this combination of the astute and the impulsive that accounts for Guido's sin. Into Dante's vision of a man who calculates finely and at the same time trusts too hastily in superficial reasoning is written the cause of his ultimate fate; and the characterisation begins with the first words of Guido's story:

'Io fui uom d'arme, e poi fui cordigliero,
  credendomi, sì cinto, fare ammenda;
e certo il creder mio venìa intero,

se non fosse il gran prete, a cui mal prenda!,
che mi rimise ne le prime colpe;
e come e *quare*, voglio che m'intenda.'   (67–72)

('I was a man of arms, and then I was a friar; girded like this with a cord,
I believed I was making amends; and my belief would certainly have
proved well founded, if it had not been for the High Priest – may the
devil take him! – who plunged me back into my former sinful ways; and
I want you to hear how and why.')

These first two terzinas are a concise summary of the whole
content of Guido's confession, with his entire existence neatly and
tellingly apportioned in line 67 between the flesh and the spirit.
The long years of military glory have become mere prelude to the
brief two years as a tertiary. And how certain Guido is that his
contrition will bring its reward! In line 70 the controlled and
balanced movement of the phrases breaks down. Guido erupts
with impotent rancour into the first of several imprecations
directed at Boniface, the man who showed how fragile was that
certainty of peace. In seeing Boniface linked irrevocably to him in
sin, the cause of his sin, Guido shows the enduring bluntness of
his moral sense. The more resolute his speech, the more Dante
shows him to be in error. At the end of these introductory
terzinas, the circumspect Guido is back in control. His torment in
Hell is the thought of the way he lost his salvation and it is the
'how' and the 'why' of that loss that he will recount to Dante:

'Mentre ch'io forma fui d'ossa e di polpe
che la madre mi diè, l'opere mie
non furon leonine, ma di volpe.
    Li accorgimenti e le coperte vie
io seppi tutte, e sì menai lor arte,
ch'al fine de la terra il suono uscie.
    Quando mi vidi giunto in quella parte
di mia etade ove ciascun dovrebbe
calar le vele e raccoglier le sarte,
    ciò che pria mi piacëa, allor m'increbbe,
e pentuto e confesso mi rendei;
ahi miser lasso! e giovato sarebbe.'   (73–84)

('While my soul was still in the form of the flesh and blood my mother
gave me, my actions were not those of the lion but those of the fox. I
knew every wile and subterfuge, and so expert was I in their use that my
fame reached to the ends of the earth. When I saw that I had reached that
part of my life in which everyone should lower the sails and gather in the

rigging, I came to hate what once I had delighted in. I repented and confessed, and became a friar. And – miserable dupe that I was! – this would have served me well.')

The Guido of history might have laid claim to valour as well as to cunning but the Guido of the poem is concerned primarily with his reputation as a tactician, since it was this that drew the disastrous attention of Boniface. His acrid tone, which transforms what might have been the boast of his fame into a bitter torment, is not entirely caused by pious regret over his worldly life, for what is welling up within him, and is soon to burst into the open, is once again the sense of dolorous outrage that such carefully laid plans for his salvation should have been disturbed. On the whole Guido is content to pass quickly and blandly over the most spiritually significant moments of his life, in the familiarly balanced phrases of line 82. There has been, it is true, a reflective pause as Guido recalls the temporary peace of his repentance: it is noticeable here that there recurs, in a light imaginative touch, the image of the sailing ship with its lowered sails that Dante had used in the *Convivio* (and in passing he may expect us to remember the fate of that other Counsellor of Fraud, Ulysses, who as an old man hoisted his sails for the 'folle volo' – the 'mad flight' – that was to end in death). But the respite is brief, lodged between a passage of controlled bitterness and the explosion of Guido's anger.

Yet for all the anguish that Guido will express and for all the soldierly directness of his speech, there is still an ordering and a precision in self-presentation suggestive of the calculating mind, and not entirely free of oratorical cadences. It is as though by freely acknowledging regrets over his worldly existence, Guido may better stress the purity of the later portion of his life, which only an invincible evil in the shape of Boniface could contaminate. And indeed the calculating mind is back in evidence in line 83 where the emphasis falls on Guido's scrupulous observation of correct theological procedure, his repentance duly preceding confession. All that a man must do for his salvation, Guido seems to say, had been carefully carried out. As before, it is the contemplation of redemption, so nearly grasped, that provokes the exclamation of grief and the indirect allusion to Boniface, 'e giovato sarebbe', so eloquent in its suggestion of repressed fury. The movement of Guido's thought is here identical to that of lines

61

69 and 70, and Boniface emerges as a torturing *idée fixe* at this point in the canto where he is about to become chief protagonist in Guido's account:

> 'Lo principe d'i novi Farisei,
> avendo guerra presso a Laterano,
> e non con Saracin né con Giudei,
>   ché ciascun suo nimico era Cristiano,
> e nessun era stato a vincer Acri
> né mercatante in terra di Soldano,
>   né sommo officio né ordini sacri
> guardò in sé, né in me quel capestro
> che solea fare i suoi cinti più macri.'   (85–93)

('The prince of the new Pharisees, being at war near the Lateran, and not against Saracens or Jews – for every enemy of his was Christian, and none of them had helped to reconquer Acre for the Moslems, nor traded for profit in the Sultan's land – showed regard neither for his own supreme office and holy orders, nor for my own wearing of that cord which used to make its wearers thinner.')

These terzinas and the ones that follow them are a passionate indictment of the Pope (even in some respects the Papacy), which seems to transcend Guido's personal animosity. It is in part the poet's own sense of moral, political and religious indignation that animates the fierce catalogue of papal sins. Between the subject of line 85, in itself an accusation of corrupt hypocrisy, and its related verb there comes a mounting sequence of subordinate clauses, a heaping-up of negatives: the aggravating circumstances of Boniface's war against the Colonna family. It is a crusade not against the infidel, but against Christians; not at Acre in the Holy Land, but near the Vatican City. When Palestrina resisted him, anger and pride induced Boniface to ignore all spiritual considerations. So ends the first part of the accusation with a final allusion to the present moral decay of the Franciscan order. Dante's vision of a corrupt and corrupting Papacy has ranged freely over the whole of Christendom and beyond, the disparate accusations being drawn together in one solemn act of indictment. Now the focus narrows; it is once again Guido's narrative:

> 'Ma come Costantin chiese Silvestro
> d'entro Siratti a guerir de la lebbre,
> così mi chiese questi per maestro

a guerir de la sua superba febbre;
domandommi consiglio, e io tacetti
perché le sue parole parver ebbre.
    E' poi ridisse: "Tuo cuor non sospetti;
finor t'assolvo, e tu m'insegna fare
sì come Penestrino in terra getti.
    Lo ciel poss' io serrare e diserrare,
come tu sai; però son due le chiavi
che 'l mio antecessor non ebbe care." '   (94–105)

('But as Constantine asked Sylvester to come from Soracte to cure him of leprosy, so this man asked me to be his doctor and cure him of the fever of his pride. He asked for my counsel, and I was mute, for his words seemed drunken. And then he spoke again: "Free your heart of all doubt; from this moment on you have my absolution; now show me how to cast down Palestrina to the ground. I have power to lock and unlock Heaven, as you know, because the keys for which my predecessor cared little are two." ')

Guido presents his interview with Boniface as a savage parody of the encounter between Constantine and Pope Sylvester, which according to legend led to the Emperor's conversion; and his controlled anger at the vastly different outcome of his meeting with a Pontiff emerges in this carefully articulated parallel, with its sarcastic rhyming of 'lebbre' and 'febbre'. The figure of Boniface begins to emerge, drunk with greed and pride, yet capable of a sinister and threatening logic. The heavy caesura in line 98 ('domandommi consiglio // e io tacetti') suggests Guido's foreboding hesitation; and in the following dialogue the dramatic tension of the confrontation between friar and Pope emerges out of the pauses, reticences and hesitations of the characters. As long as Guido stands silent, Boniface's words will mirror, and aim to offset, the secret, fearful workings of his conscience. It is Guido's dismayed silence that warns the Pope to moderate his language and adopt a more paternal and insinuating approach. Then follows the promise of immediate absolution in return for advice: the pact has a false blandness, and is expressed in two balanced phrases – the stylistic translation of duplicity that Dante has used repeatedly in the canto – 'finor t'assolvo, e tu m'insegna'. In a little while, when Guido resolves to speak, his words will follow a similar pattern, beginning with a circumspect reiteration of the bargain, 'da che tu mi lavi' (108). In both men there is an appearance of logic, an acknowledgement of a fair reciprocity in the arrangement. At the end of the canto it will be a subtly arguing devil, in the cruellest blow of all, who convinces Guido in the only terms he can understand that his sin derives from a logical contradiction. For the deeper source of his sin seems always to elude Guido, and so it is that he may continue to regard his condemnation with dismayed amazement, and Boniface's appearance on his tranquil horizon as a piece of ill luck not bargained for in the careful planning of his existence. Yet Dante's own presentation of Guido depends on the view that Boniface's role is not casual: he merely brings to light the spiritual superficiality that, in Dante's vision, has always been rooted in Guido's soul. Boniface is the occasion, not the cause, of Guido's sin.

Meanwhile the process of persuasion continues, hushed and menacing in the sibilants of line 103. As Peter's successor in the Holy See Boniface holds the keys with which to lock and unlock the gates of Heaven. Of the two keys, as Aquinas, and Dante himself in *Purgatorio* IX, tell us, one symbolises the knowledge required to determine whether the sinner's repentance is sincere, and the other symbolises the authority to give absolution. In this context Boniface's remark is grimly ambivalent: he reasserts his power to absolve Guido, but also reminds him that he is able to deny access to Heaven as well as to grant it. And the phrase 'come tu sai' seems to invite the friar to remember not only his theology but his vows of obedience. Finally Boniface can contain the fever of his pride no longer and he ends with a derisive sneer at Pope Celestine V, who 'from cowardice made the great refusal' (*Inf.* III, 60), the Pope who stepped down from the papal throne, persuaded, it was thought, by Boniface himself. This is the last we shall see of Boniface in the canto. Dante leaves us with the fearful vision of the supreme priest inebriated by his own vast power, and abusing the authority of his holy office for personal and temporal aims.

Boniface's jubilant insistence in this passage on the power of the papal keys must be seen in the context of Dante's misgivings about the contamination of the spiritual by the temporal power. The symbolic meaning of the two keys derives from Matthew 16.19, where Christ gives Peter the keys of the kingdom of Heaven and tells him: 'whatsoever thou shalt bind on earth shall be bound in heaven; and whatsoever thou shalt loose on earth shall be loosed in heaven.' Dante may well have been recollecting at this point how in his papal bull of 1302, *Unam Sanctam*, Boniface had cited precisely this source, among others, to assert that the Pope had authority over all things – temporal as well as spiritual. In the third book of his *Monarchia* Dante had refuted one by one the interpretation of those passages, including the one from Matthew, on which Boniface had based his claims to omnipotence. If this portion of the *Monarchia* cannot be seen as a specific refutation of *Unam Sanctam* (though it reads remarkably like one) it is at least evidence that Dante was alert to the argument for the Pope's temporal power based on the symbol of the keys. Clearly at this moment in the canto where Boniface is warlord not Pontiff, and where his frenzied ambition is about to erupt into a sneer at the naivety of his predecessor, the keys are to be seen not only as assertions of spiritual power but as symbols confirming the legitimacy of a political involvement, which to Dante was deeply repugnant in the head of Christ's Church.

Guido, however, is ready to capitulate:

> 'Allor mi pinser li argomenti gravi
> là 've 'l tacer mi fu avviso 'l peggio,
> e dissi: "Padre, da che tu mi lavi
>   di quel peccato ov' io mo cader deggio,
> lunga promessa con l'attender corto
> ti farà trïunfar ne l'alto seggio."'   (106–11)

('Then weighty arguments drove me to the point where silence seemed to me the worst course, and I said: "Father, since you wash me clean of that sin into which I now must fall, generous promises with scanty fulfilment will give you triumph on the High Throne."')

Again what is remarkable about this passage is the way that Dante suggests in this hard, crafty man a fatal combination of resolution and deviousness. Guido squarely faces the inevitability of his sin, and yet his expression otherwise remains oblique and shifty: the 'argomenti gravi' are never specified, and the impersonal construction 'mi fu avviso' seems to want to avoid any implications of personal responsibility; and finally the counsel that Guido gives is indirect, phrased in a proverbial form that seems to allow the speaker to dissociate himself from his own utterance.

The final section of Guido's confession opens abruptly and dramatically with his death. The intervening period is irrelevant, for Dante is concerned only with the essentials of a spiritual history:

> 'Francesco venne poi, com' io fu' morto,
> per me; ma un d'i neri cherubini
> li disse: "Non portar; non mi far torto.
> Venir se ne dee giù tra ' miei meschini
> perché diede 'l consiglio frodolente,
> dal quale in qua stato li sono a' crini;
>   ch'assolver non si può chi non si pente,
> né pentere e volere insieme puossi
> per la contradizion che nol consente."
> Oh me dolente! come mi riscossi
> quando mi prese dicendomi: "Forse
> tu non pensavi ch'io löico fossi!"
> A Minòs mi portò; e quelli attorse
> otto volte la coda al dosso duro;
> e poi che per gran rabbia la si morse,
>   disse: "Questi è d'i rei del foco furo";
> per ch'io là dove vedi son perduto,
> e sì vestito, andando, mi rancuro.' (112–29)

('Francis came to fetch me when I died; but one of the black cherubim said to him: "Don't carry him off; don't cheat me. He must come and join my slaves below, because he gave fraudulent counsel. Ever since then I've been lurking behind him, for without repentance there is no absolution; and it's impossible to repent of a thing and to will it at the same time, because the contradiction makes it inadmissible." Oh wretch that I am, how I started when he seized me, saying: "Perhaps you didn't realise I was a logician!" He carried me off to Minos, who coiled his tail eight times around his rough back, and when he had bitten it in great anger, said: "He belongs with the sinners in the thieving fire"; and so it is that I am damned in the circle where you see me now, and clothed in flame go my way, bitterly grieving.')

This short scene between the head of Guido's order, St Francis, and the devil is in effect the enactment of Guido's struggle with his own conscience after death, and it has a particular force in showing the element of surprise that attaches to Guido's condemnation. With the devil's final viciously jubilant taunt comes Dante's last play on the theme of the too-calculating intellect.

The scene of messengers from God and from Satan contending for the possession of a soul was familiar in medieval times. A biblical source is the Epistle of Jude, where Michael the archangel is seen struggling with the devil over the body of Moses. It is worth noticing that the image of a contest over a departing soul recurs once again in the *Comedy*, when Dante is climbing the Mountain of Purgatory; and it is clear that Dante intends his readers to relate Canto v of Purgatory to Canto xxvii of Hell, because the penitent in Purgatory is none other than Guido's own son, Buonconte.

Like his father, Buonconte was a Ghibelline leader. He was killed at the Battle of Campaldino in 1289, when he led the Aretine Ghibellines against the Florentine Guelphs, among whose number was Dante himself. It would have been at least humanly understandable if Dante had placed his political enemy in Hell: especially as there was the mysterious and sinister fact that after the Battle of Campaldino Buonconte's body was never found. We have therefore a seemingly contradictory situation: Guido who repented and whom Dante calls 'nobilissimo' is in Hell; Buonconte, who fought Dante's faction, and never had a Christian burial, is in Purgatory. It is clear that the parallels and divergences between the two cantos are intended not merely to provide links between the canticas of Hell and Purgatory, but are intended to make a forceful doctrinal point. The peculiar disappearance of Buonconte's body had perhaps captured the imagination of his contemporaries, for it is the subject of a question that immediately suggests itself to Dante, the pilgrim, who asks him: 'How is it that your burial place was never known?' (*Purg.* v, 93) As in the case of Guido, Dante once again is reversing the common expectation on the eternal destiny of the sinner. For he makes Buonconte go on to explain how 'wounded in the throat', he died on the banks of a tributary of the Arno river. On the night following the battle the river-waters rose, swollen by heavy rain, and sweeping up Buonconte's body carried it into the Arno, where it finally sank to the river-bed. But Buonconte dies with the name of the Blessed Virgin on his lips. After death there had been a struggle between the forces of Heaven and Hell, in which the devil's words in line 105: 'O tu del ciel, perché mi privi?' ('Oh you of Heaven, why do you deprive me?'), were an echo and a variation of the black angel's words in *Inferno* xxvii. But the outcome is different, for it is 'una lagrimetta', a tiny, belated tear of repentance, that deprives the devil of his prey. Up to the last moment, in Dante's concrete and dramatic vision, the destinies of Guido and Buonconte hang in the balance. Guido is condemned for a single act of false contrition, Buonconte is saved by a moment of true repentance. In the judgement of men the father, turned friar, seemed worthy of salvation, the son destined in all likelihood for perdition. With one canto reinforcing the implications of the other, Dante shows the mysterious workings of the Divinity: God's mercy is as great as his justice is inexorable and all-seeing.

We may note finally that it is in the portion of the *Monarchia* mentioned earlier that Dante makes an emphatic point about false contrition. Referring to that same passage from Matthew, he refutes the arguments of those who contend that the Pope's power is absolute in both temporal and spiritual matters. He concedes that their claim would be correct if the word 'whatsoever' in the phrase 'whatsoever thou shalt bind' were taken as absolute, but argues that the Pope would also be able, as Dante says, 'to grant me absolution even if I had not repented' (III, viii, 8). This is impossible – since not even God, Dante vigorously asserts (and therefore still less a Pope), can grant absolution where there is no remorse.

Guido's account, after all its vigour and drama, now falls again into the elegiac tones of his opening words. His parting line with its double caesura suggests the unending restlessness of the condemned soul, the suppressed rancour that is Guido's lot for all eternity. As one commentator has remarked, Guido is like a card-player who has lost a game and now obsessively goes over and over in his mind the misplaying of his hand. Unlike Ulysses, whose flame at the end of his speech was 'dritta' and 'queta', Guido leaves the poets grieving, and tossing the tip of his flame as he has done when he first approached them:

> Quand' elli ebbe 'l suo dir così compiuto,
> la fiamma dolorando si partio,
> torcendo e dibattendo 'l corno aguto.   (130–2)

(When he had finished speaking these words, the sorrowing flame moved away, twisting and tossing his pointed horn.)

In this canto perhaps more than in any other we have a sense of the eternity of punishment, of the tragic fixity of the sinner, whose only existence is the endless recapitulation of a fatal mistake. Guido's confession evokes no direct response in Dante the character. He has regarded the sinner with the detachment of a man anxious to understand how a mind, apparently so full of virtue, may nonetheless nurture the seeds of sin. Guido's confession has been a total act of self-revelation: the answer to Dante's question.

After the long pause with the Counsellors of Fraud, Dante and Virgil resume their journey soberly and without further comment, passing over the bridge that spans the ditches until they come to the place where the Sowers of Discord are punished.

Note

1 Benvenuto Terracini, '*Inferno* XXVII', in *Letture dantesche: Inferno*, ed. G. Getto (Firenze, 1964), pp. 521–4. I take this opportunity to express my particular indebtedness for their discussion of this canto to Terracini and to Edoardo Sanguineti, in *Interpretazione di Malebolge* (Firenze, 1961), pp. 257–82.

Inferno XXXIII

PIERO BOITANI

The last three cantos of *Inferno* – from XXXII to XXXIV – make up a deliberate unity of matter and form. In the tenth *bolgia* of the eighth circle Dante and Virgil meet the giants. One of them, Antaeus, carries the poets down to the frozen lake of Cocytus, which constitutes the ninth circle of Hell. Here the traitors, the worst of all sinners, are punished, divided into four groups that occupy four adjacent areas of the lake (*Caina*, those who betrayed their relatives; *Antenora*, political traitors; *Tolomea*, traitors of their guests; *Giudecca*, traitors to their benefactors). Cantos XXXII–XXXIV describe this last circle of Hell, the sinners who inhabit it, and Dante's encounter with some of them. Halfway through Canto XXXIII we pass from *Antenora* (Ugolino and Ruggieri) to *Tolomea* (Frate Alberigo and Branca Doria). Halfway through Canto XXXIV Dante and Virgil climb past Lucifer and, through a narrow passage, emerge – at the end of the canto – on the other side of the world, on the shore of the Mountain of Purgatory, and finally see the stars again.

Dante himself clearly points to the unity of the last cantos of *Inferno* by prefacing Canto XXXII with a grand formal *exordium* where he announces that his subject will now be the 'dismal hole on which all the other rocks converge and weigh' – the 'bottom of the whole universe'. He then declares that he does not command the 'harsh and grating rhymes' that would befit this circle, and finally he invokes the Muses. I shall go back to this passage later. But it is perhaps worth remarking at the outset that this is not the only sign of the unity of form among the three cantos of which XXXIII occupies the centre.

In the first place, Cocytus dominates Dante's imagination and our reading throughout: the frozen lake that looks like glass, the eternal icy darkness, the 'gelate croste', form the immobile background against which Dante and Virgil move (XXXII, 24–5, 71–5). The sinners' tears are frozen, too: the glazed tears of Alessandro and Napoleone degli Alberti are the same that Frate Alberigo will later ask Dante to remove from his eyes (XXXII, 46–8; XXXIII, 127–8). All these sinners are tormented by the cold and the ice: some lie on the surface, some are half immersed, some are completely covered and shine through like straw in glass (XXXIV, 12).

All the sinners of the ninth circle are – as befits their 'matta bestialità' – animal-like. Dante himself comments that it would have been better for them to be sheep or goats (XXXII, 15) rather than human beings; but they look like frogs, sound like storks and butt each other like rams; later, Ugolino is like a dog and Lucifer himself, the 'vermo reo', is like a horrible bird, or rather, a bat (XXXII, 31–6, 50; XXXIII, 78; XXXIV, 47–9).

The traitors to whom Dante pays particular attention are presented in couples – as if they were sculpted, dynamic pairs: the brothers Alessandro and Napoleone degli Alberti are so pressed against each other, that their hair is tangled together; Ugolino and Ruggieri, as we shall see, lie frozen in one hole, one on top of the other, Ugolino's head looking like a 'hood' over Ruggieri's skull; in his three mouths Lucifer champs Judas, Brutus and Cassius (XXXII, 41–2, 125–6; XXXIV, 55–67).

Finally, all we are given to see of these sinners – the focus of Dante's attention in the ninth circle – is their heads (XXXII, 21, 77, 126; XXXIII, 3; XXXIV, 38), their hair (XXXII, 42, 97–105), the frozen faces, the eyes filled with glazed tears, and, above all, their mouths and teeth, with which they torment each other and with which they speak – teeth that clatter making the sound produced by storks' beaks, sharp fangs, dogs' teeth, the teeth like those of a fulling mill in the mouth of Lucifer, the mouth of Evil (XXXII, 36; XXXIII, 35, 78; XXXIV, 55–6).

It is with 'la bocca' that our canto begins – the mouth of darkness, as it has been called.[1] It is the mouth, not the head, that rises and opens and will remain the focus of the first seventy-eight lines of the canto, which are given over to Count Ugolino. The mouth that is wiped on the hair of his victim's head is the mouth that speaks and recounts the story of hunger, telling of the five mouths that were denied all food, of the sharp fangs that ripped the flanks of the victims, and of the teeth that bit the hands for grief. This is the mouth to which the children offer their own flesh, the teeth that seize the wretched skull, crunching the bone like a dog's; the mouth of the traitor betrayed, of the man who sold his city. In the next canto, it will become the mouth of Hell, the bottom of the universe: the three mouths of Satan, the angel who betrayed God and mankind, chewing those who betrayed Caesar, the founder of an empire preordained by God, chewing the disciple who sold the Son of God.

Our first sight of Ugolino is of his mouth: thus, abruptly, the canto opens with the 'bestial segno', the 'beastly mark', of hatred. Dante had closed Canto XXXII with a description of Ugolino and Ruggieri that concentrated on head, teeth, brain, nape, skull. Ugolino was like Statius's Tydeus, 'befouled with Menalippus' shattered brains', 'his jaws polluted with living blood' (XXXII, 124–32). And it was there, at the end of Canto XXXII, that the image of hunger was for the first time associated with that of the mouth, for Ugolino's teeth gnawed the marrow 'as bread is devoured for hunger' (127). The savage meal, the tower of hunger, the children crying in their sleep and asking for bread, the hour of food that never came, the boys' flesh offered in the supreme sacrifice, the ambiguous fasting that did more than grief had done – these are the images of hunger, bread and food that will dominate Canto XXXIII.

Ugolino, the traitor, was betrayed by the archbishop, Ruggieri, and condemned to die of hunger. An ancient chronicle says that Ugolino 'made the people of Pisa die of hunger' for he sold wheat at an exorbitant price; 'then at last', it adds, 'he died of hunger with all his family', a kind of rough justice that prefigures the more terrible poetic justice of the *contrappasso* Dante will devise.[2] Here, the law of Dante's Hell gives the traitor his betrayer's skull to gnaw: Ruggieri will forever satisfy his former victim's hunger with his own brain. And yet Ugolino, too, is condemned to eternal hunger, for he will never satiate himself with the archbishop's head. Natural love and human trust are put out of mind by traitors (*Inf.* XI, 61–6), who are therefore 'eternally consumed' in the deepest and smallest of Hell's circles, the abyss of human degradation, as 'foul and terrible' as Dante suggested it would have to be in his letter to Cangrande (*Epist.* XIII, 29, 31).

The beginning of the new canto isolates Ugolino's mouth, 'la bocca'. Its position in the first line is not orthodox: grammatically, it is an object; the emphasis placed on it by Dante with the inversion almost makes it a subject. The portrait of Ugolino, beginning with his mouth, is sketched in the first terzina. Yet there is no stasis, each line contains a verb, indicates an action:

> La bocca *sollevò* dal fiero pasto
> quel peccator, *forbendola* a' capelli
> del capo ch'elli *avea* di retro *guasto*.　　　(1–3)

(That sinner lifted his mouth from his grisly meal, wiping it on the hair of the head whose rear he had destroyed.)

Ugolino's punishment does not allow him much movement, for he is imprisoned in the ice, yet Dante makes him move as much as logic permits. Ugolino makes two gestures: he raises his mouth and he wipes it on his victim's hair. Halfway between beast and man, he cleans his mouth before he speaks – a highly civilised gesture indeed! But no mention is made of what he tries to wipe from his mouth; the reader must fill the gap with the most horrible sights he can imagine. The picture drawn in the first terzina is indirect and yet completely self-sufficient.

At the end of his story Ugolino goes back to his 'fiero pasto':

> Quand' ebbe detto ciò, con li occhi torti
> riprese 'l teschio misero co' denti,
> che furo a l'osso, come d'un can, forti.　　　(76–8)

(When he had said this, with eyes askew he seized the wretched skull with his teeth, which grated brutally on the bone like those of a dog.)

The portrait is, again, the description of an action: three verbs bring the sinner back to his eternal repast. But we notice also the rhetorical devices: there is a terzina at the beginning of the episode, a terzina at the end; three verbs there, three here; the verb in the compound past comes at the end there, and here at the beginning; the teeth of line 77 come right at the end of the clause, the mouth of line 1 comes at the beginning. The simile, 'come d'un can', makes explicit the identification of Ugolino with an animal, which, in the first terzina, existed only in the reader's imagination. The 'occhi torti' (another borrowing from Statius) are the only new element: 'bent', 'crooked', 'twisted', they mark Ugolino's new metamorphosis. The unknown sinner of line 1 becomes a dog. The victim, meanwhile, has not moved: by the supreme nemesis of the divine *contrappasso*, Ruggieri is no more than a skull, a pure object in both terzinas.

There is no pause between Ugolino's first movement and his first words. A sense of slowness and heaviness seems to dominate his movements and his first sentence. Dante remains, and will remain, silent: 'all fell silent, turning their gaze in complete attention', as Virgil had said at the beginning of Book II of his poem. And Dante's next line is an echo of Aeneas's words to Dido (which follow immediately on the line just quoted): 'You want me, queen, to renew an unspeakable grief.' But Ugolino's grief is greater than Aeneas's. It is not just 'inexpressible' or 'terrible', but desperate,[3] and it wrings his heart. The very sound itself of his outburst with its five 'r's, seems to express Ugolino's raging despair.

> Poi cominciò: 'Tu vuo' ch'io rinovelli
> disperato dolor che 'l cor mi preme
> già pur pensando, pria ch'io ne favelli.
> Ma se le mie parole esser dien seme
> che frutti infamia al traditor ch'i' rodo,
> parlare e lagrimar vedrai insieme.
> Io non so chi tu se' né per che modo
> venuto se' qua giù; ma fiorentino
> mi sembri veramente quand' io t'odo.'   (4–12)

(Then he began: 'You ask me to renew a grief so desperate that it crushes my heart even to think of it, before expressing it in speech. But if my words are to be a seed that will yield a fruit of infamy to the traitor whom I gnaw, you shall see me speak and weep at the same time. I don't know who you are nor by what means you came down here; but, in truth, when I hear you, you seem a Florentine to me.')

The beast of the first terzina has become a human being: by simply speaking and recalling his tragedy, Ugolino leaves the infernal dimension and returns to earth. Dante is, after all, the poet of our world, the natural and historical world.[4] Ugolino's answer incorporates a metaphor sustained from one term (*seme*) to another (*fruttare*), and it expresses precisely the reaction that Dante

74

had expected when he first addressed the sinner at the end of Canto XXXII (133–9). Dante appealed to Ugolino's hatred, and Ugolino now responds. The words 'al traditor ch'i' rodo' (three 'r's in so short a space) are uttered with such force of hatred and contempt that Ugolino could well sink back into animality. The verb, 'gnaw', particularly stressed as it closes a line and an entire clause, belongs to a non-human dimension. But Ugolino halts soon enough on this dangerous slope. He will speak; and speaking and weeping are linked (as in Francesca's case) as marks of Ugolino's humanity.

Six lines are enough for Dante to sketch Ugolino's psychology: despair, prompt reaction to a stimulus from without, hate and grief. Ugolino is not, as some have said, a one-dimensional man, but a man *tout court*. He ignores Dante as a person. As usual, the poet's 'loquela', his way of speaking, reveals that he is a Florentine (10–12), and this is enough for Ugolino, who does not wish to converse with Dante but only to speak to him. The sinner's words become almost matter-of-fact: he gives us his name, and the name of the head he is gnawing, both hitherto unknown as befits dramatic technique. We are about to enter our world of change and time.

It is the powerful – and tragically ironical – contrast between the 'fui' (I was Count Ugolino) and the 'è' (this is Archbishop Ruggieri) that marks the beginning of the *recherche du temps perdu*. The lost time in question has two dimensions: one that of the episode in history, known to all; the other beyond history, unknown to all, 'interred with men's bones'. It is precisely this second dimension that Dante explores and that interests Ugolino himself. For, as he says, everyone knows his story, how, as a result of Ruggieri's ill devising, he was taken and put to death. But no one knows how 'cruel' his death was, no one can understand the wrong Ruggieri had done him.[5]

> 'Tu dei saper ch'i' fui conte Ugolino,
> e questi è l'arcivescovo Ruggieri:
> or ti dirò perché i son tal vicino.
>   Che per l'effetto de' suo' mai pensieri,
> fidandomi di lui, io fossi preso
> e poscia morto, dir non è mestieri;
>   però quel che non puoi avere inteso,
> cioè come la morte mia fu cruda,
> udirai, e saprai s'e' m'ha offeso.'   (13–21)

('You must know that I was Count Ugolino, and this is Archbishop

75

Ruggieri. Now I will tell you why I am his neighbour. There is no need to relate how I put my trust in him and was captured and later killed as a result of his evil plans. But what you cannot have learnt – the cruelty of my death – you shall now hear. Then you will know if he has done me wrong.')

I shall return to this second dimension shortly. But we have first to deal with the historical dimension of Ugolino's story. Ugolino, Count of Donoratico, was born in the first half of the thirteenth century. The Gherardeschi, Ugolino's family, were Ghibellines: Pisa itself, his native town, was Ghibelline at first. When he saw that the Guelphs, after the death of Manfred at Benevento in 1266, were taking over the whole of Tuscany, Ugolino thought it better to become a Guelph. Together with his son-in-law, Giovanni Visconti, he therefore tried, in the years 1274–5, to establish a Guelph government in Pisa; but he failed, was imprisoned and was finally exiled with other Guelphs. In 1276, however, he was allowed to return, accompanied by his grandson Nino Visconti, Giovanni's son. This time, Ugolino was successful in gaining the favour of the Pisans and became very powerful. When, in 1284, Pisa fought against Genoa, Ugolino himself led the Pisan fleet, which was defeated. Nevertheless, back in Pisa, and supported by the Guelphs of Florence, Ugolino became *podestà* and *capitano* of the city. A little later, Pisa found itself dangerously alone against an alliance of Genoa, Lucca and Florence. Ugolino decided to break the alliance by buying off Genoa's associates: he allowed a few minor Pisan castles to be ceded to Lucca and Florence. This move provoked harsh reactions in Pisa, and Ugolino found himself at variance with Nino Visconti. The party split. Weakened by polemics and struggles, Ugolino drew closer to the surviving Ghibellines, headed by the Archbishop Ruggieri with the support of the Lanfranchi, Gualandi and Sismondi families. Ruggieri and his allies made Ugolino pay for their friendship: they demanded exile for Nino Visconti, and Ugolino accepted. Nino left Pisa before they could harm him, while Ugolino, 'to cover his treason', as Villani says,[6] retired to his castle of Settimo for a short time. He then returned to Pisa and took over again: Villani maintains that he had one of his opponents, Anselmo di Capraia (his sister's son) poisoned. After this episode, events are not clear. It seems that Ruggieri, to show that he was not Ugolino's accomplice, accused him of having sold the castles to Lucca and Florence. The mob attacked Ugolino's palace. One of his sons and one of his nephews were killed, and Ugolino was captured along with two of his sons and two (according to Dante) or three (according to Villani) of his grandsons (but they all appear as 'figli', children, in Ugolino's narrative). Ugolino's family and his allies were driven out of Pisa; he himself and the children were imprisoned in a tower, where they died the following year, February 1289. Thus, Ugolino betrayed first the Ghibellines, then the Guelphs, including his grandson Nino Visconti, and finally Anselmo di Capraia. Ruggieri did not betray his party, for he remained a Ghibelline; but he betrayed Ugolino and made innocent people die in prison.[7] This, then, is history: Ugolino's tragedy, like everything in Dante, must be seen within the general frame of the political life of thirteenth-century Italy. It is history that condemns Ugolino to the frozen lake of Cocytus, and history that echoes in the *contrappasso*.

We enter, now, a new dimension, that of the 'secrete cose', the 'secret things'. Here, beyond history, the poet chooses his own subject and the way in which to deal with it. The death of Ugolino and his children is an historical fact, but how it took place is Dante's invention. We have already seen how a series of images centred on the mouth dominate Dante's portrait of Ugolino as a character both animal and human, whether in the reality of his damnation or in his remembrance of life. Now the story of Ugolino's death begins with another strong image, that of the 'breve pertugio', the narrow hole of the Mew where Ugolino was imprisoned. The image becomes even stronger three lines later, when the word 'forame' closes the line, at the centre of three very significant rhymes: 'fame', 'forame', 'velame' ('hunger', 'opening', 'veil'):

> 'Breve pertugio dentro da la Muda,
> la qual per me ha 'l titol de la fame,
> e che conviene ancor ch'altrui si chiuda,
>   m'avea mostrato per lo suo forame
> più lune già, quand' io feci 'l mal sonno
> che del futuro mi squarciò 'l velame.' (22–7)

('In the garret where they penned the hawks, which through my death has acquired the title of Hunger, and which will be closed on yet another victim, there is a narrow slit. It had already shown me several moons through its opening when I had the nightmare that tore aside the veil of the future.')

It seems to me that there is a sort of evocative affinity between the mouth with which the canto begins and this narrow hole with which Ugolino's tragedy starts. It is as if the image that Dante found there became wider in its significance here, one cavity larger than the other. There, at the beginning, the mouth was the 'beastly mark' of Hell and the instrument and symbol of human speech; it was the focus of Ugolino's portrait against the background of the timeless, frozen lake of eternal life. Here the narrow hole is the victims' only indicator of space, time and light. Through the hole Ugolino catches a glimpse of the several moons that have risen and set (26); the hole scans the passing of the eight days within which the final act of the tragedy is consummated; the hole lets a little ray make its way into the prison (55). Light and dark are determined for the prisoners by this hole, which separates them from, and links them to, the world outside. Both time and space are governed by this 'pertugio', which is not simply little, but, significantly, 'breve', 'short'. Space and time seem to close in with the two 'u's of 'pertugio' and 'Muda' which make us think of 'buio' and 'oscuro' in this context rather than 'luce' or 'lume'. The spatial dimension is deepened further by the use of the word 'Mew', a dark and enclosed place where falcons were kept fasting before the hunt, their strength failing little by little, their fury tamed by lack of air and light.

The third most important word of the terzina is 'fame', 'hunger'. If we were reading Canto XXXIII of *Inferno* for the first time in our lives, we would read this word here without knowing anything except that Ugolino was imprisoned in the Mew and that his death, as he himself has declared, was 'cruel'. Now we find ourselves suddenly reading this 'title' of Hunger (23). Once again Dante avoids direct statement, building up suspense and enunciating a narrative theme that will, in due course, become the dominant one.

The dream now interrupts our train of thought and adds expectation to expectation, doom to doom. Suspended between the past and the future, the first two terzinas describe the situation that had brought Ugolino to the Mew: Ruggieri leading the

Ghibelline families and the mob against the Count and his children. Ruggieri, now simply 'questi', 'this man', 'this skull', appears in the dream as he was in reality, 'maestro e donno', 'master and lord'. It is he who chases the wolf and the whelps (Ugolino and his children), he who gathers the nobles, he who incites the mob. The hunt has an obsessive rhythm: the animals flee towards the mountain that separates Pisa from Lucca (Ugolino had perhaps thought of taking refuge in that city, which was Pisa's enemy). But the 'bitches' (as in Canto XIII, the female of the species is more deadly than the male) are lean and eager, the running becomes more and more difficult for the wolf and the whelps, who turn into human beings again – 'father and sons' (35), an expression that gives us the clue for the understanding of the prophetic dream and reveals, at the same time, Ugolino's feelings. Then comes the inevitable tragedy: the sharp fangs of the bitches tear the victims' flanks open. Preceded by the tearing ('squarciò') of the veil (line 27 – violence explodes in the psyche even before being evoked by memory), Ugolino's nightmare is an extraordinary example of indirectness as a narrative technique. Ugolino, now in Hell, is telling Dante his story. He is evoking the past and he begins with the Mew. But in the Mew he has a dream that alludes to what had actually happened before he was imprisoned and at the same time announces what in the end will take place, his and his children's death.

> 'Questi pareva a me maestro e donno,
> cacciando il lupo e ' lupicini al monte
> per che i Pisan veder Lucca non ponno.
>   Con cagne magre, studïose e conte
> Gualandi con Sismondi e con Lanfranchi
> s'avea messi dinanzi da la fronte.
>   In picciol corso mi parieno stanchi
> lo padre e ' figli, e con l'agute scane
> mi parea lor veder fender li fianchi.'   (28–36)

('This man appeared in my dream as master and lord, hunting the wolf and its whelps on the mountain that prevents the Pisans from seeing Lucca. He rode at the head, followed by bitches that were well-trained, lean and eager, and by the Gualandi, Sismondi and Lanfranchi. After a brief chase the father and his sons seemed exhausted, and I seemed to see their flanks torn open by the sharp fangs.')

This technique is used again in the following lines. The anguish that the dream has left in the prisoner's heart is confirmed by reality. When Ugolino awakes before morning, he hears his children cry and ask for *bread* in their sleep. It is the primeval cry, the 'Give us this day our daily bread' of the *Pater Noster*, the desperate clinging of men to life, and it comes after the 'title' of *hunger* of line 23. Ugolino's heart sees with foreboding that which Dante and we with him already suspect (line 41 – again, we are not told what). Furthermore, when the children awake, at the very time when their *food* is normally brought to them (43–4), they are all anxious and afraid 'because of their dream' (45). This is a total surprise for us, for Ugolino has never said that everyone had a dream. He is – once more, indirectly – projecting his own dream onto the children.

> 'Quando fui desto innanzi la dimane,
> pianger senti' fra 'l sonno i miei figliuoli
> ch'eran con meco, e dimandar del pane.
>   Ben se' crudel, se tu già non ti duoli
> pensando ciò che 'l mio cor s'annunziava;
> e se non piangi, di che pianger suoli?
>   Già eran desti, e l'ora s'appressava
> che 'l cibo ne solëa essere addotto,
> e per suo sogno ciascun dubitava . . .'   (37–45)

('When I awoke just before dawn I could hear my children who were with me crying in their sleep and asking for bread. You must be cruel indeed if you feel no pain in thinking of what my heart foretold. And if you do not weep, what could ever move you to tears? They were awake now and the hour was approaching at which our food was usually brought, and each was fearful because of his dream . . .')

Then space is definitively closed.

> 'e io senti' chiavar l'uscio di sotto
> a l'orribile torre; ond' io guardai
> nel viso a' mie' figliuoi sanza far motto.'   (46–8)

('And I heard the door nailed up below in the tower of horror; at which I looked into my sons' faces without uttering a word.')

No specific person nails up the door. Ugolino simply hears the hammering, and utters no word. He will keep silent till the end: silence is the measure of his impotence as the frozen lake is the measure of his damnation. Only his eyes can move. He cannot even weep, for, as we are told in the very next line, he turns to stone within himself. The expression, 'sì dentro impetrai' opens up a new horizon. 'Impetrai' is, again, an active verb; it is, again, allusively indirect. 'Dentro' adds to it, specifying where this reaction is taking place. 'Dentro' makes manifest to the reader something that goes on in the entire episode, the echo that all external events have inside the human being. The space of the tower is not purely external, it is an interior dimension as well. We see everything through the character's feelings: the Mew has its title of hunger through him, through Ugolino ('per me'); he has the 'mal sonno'; he hears the children's cries and the nailing-up of the door; he looks; he falls silent. His silence is, in fact, that of a stone, inside which reactions take place that cannot be described. Ugolino is a petrified man: impotent, silent, totally alone. He cannot disclose his inner agony except by looking and, later, biting his hands. He cannot communicate with his children: it is only after they die that he breaks his silence.

Ugolino cannot even weep, but the children, whose eyes he is searching, do weep: the contrast is underlined by the mirror-like opposition, 'io non piangea . . . piangevan elli' (49–50). When Anselmuccio breaks the silence and catches his father's gaze, his words try to penetrate inside the stone: 'che hai?' ('what's the matter?'). He picks up Ugolino's mute glance with his simple words 'you've got such a look' ('tu guardi sì': 51). 'Tu guardi *sì*' sounds like '*sì* dentro impetrai' reversed and ripped open by 'che hai?' While Anselmuccio's question remains suspended in Ugolino's silence, the inexorable passing of time is witnessed through the hole ('that day and the night after': 53). And as space was closed by the 'chiavar', so now time is closed in the extremely powerful line at the climax of the next two terzinas.

> 'Io non piangëa, sì dentro impetrai:
> piangevan elli; e Anselmuccio mio
> disse: "Tu guardi sì, padre! che hai?"
>   Perciò non lagrimai né rispuos' io
> tutto quel giorno né la notte appresso,
> infin che l'altro sol nel mondo uscìo.'   (49–54)

('I was so completely turned to stone within that I did not lament. They did. And my little Anselmo said: "Father, you look so strange, what's the matter?" So I did not weep, neither did I make any reply all through that day and the following night until another sun rose on the world.')

81

Here we have doom, hope definitively crushed, the beginning of a Passion. The sun, shining brightly on the world of the living, becomes a little ray in the woeful prison of the dying (55). And yet that single thread of light is enough for the impotent father to recognise his own aspect in the four mute faces (56–7).

When Ugolino bites both his hands for grief (58) – as he will later bite Ruggieri's skull for hatred – his gesture prompts the reaction of the 'choir of the four immortal children', as De Sanctis called them.[8] They rise and offer themselves for the sacrifice, their primeval cry for bread transformed into a Christ-like readiness to give their own flesh. A law stronger than life prompts them: like Job, they tell their Lord – this father who seems to present himself more and more like the Father – to take away what he gave; like Christ, they are ready to let their bodies be eaten.

> 'Come un poco di raggio si fu messo
> nel doloroso carcere, e io scorsi
> per quattro visi il mio aspetto stesso,
>   ambo le man per lo dolor mi morsi;
> ed ei, pensando ch'io 'l fessi per voglia
> di manicar, di sùbito levorsi
>   e disser: "Padre, assai ci fia men doglia
> se tu mangi di noi: tu ne vestisti
> queste misere carni, e tu le spoglia." '   (55–63)

('When a feeble ray of sunlight had struck into the dreadful prison, I caught sight of my own expression in four faces, and I bit both my hands for grief. They thought I had done so because I wanted to eat, so they got to their feet on the instant and said: "Father, you would cause us far less pain if you took us as your food. You clothed us in this miserable flesh, and you must *un*clothe." ')

But again, Ugolino does not answer. Two more days pass in total silence till the fourth day comes and Gaddo dies. Between the fifth and the sixth day the other three fall before their father's eyes. The undoing of Ugolino's children looks like the six days of the Creation in reverse, but, more significantly, it resembles Christ's passion. Gaddo's dying cry recalls 'Eli, Eli, lama sabachthani?' ('My God, my God, why hast thou forsaken me?': Matthew 27.46). Later, in his invective against Pisa, Dante himself will exclaim: 'non dovei tu i figliuoi porre a tal *croce*' ('you ought not to have put his children to such a cross').

'Queta'mi allor per non farli più tristi;
lo dì e l'altro stemmo tutti muti;
ahi dura terra, perché non t'apristi?
    Poscia che fummo al quarto dì venuti,
Gaddo mi si gittò disteso a' piedi,
dicendo: "Padre mio, ché non m'aiuti?"
    Quivi morì; e come tu mi vedi,
vid' io cascar li tre ad uno ad uno
tra 'l quinto dì e 'l sesto . . .'   (64–72)

('I calmed myself then so as not to make them suffer more. That day and
the next we all remained dumb. Ah! too solid earth, why didn't you
open? When he had come to the fourth day, Gaddo threw himself down
full length at my feet, saying: "Father, why don't you help me?" There
he died. And just as you see me now, so I saw the other three die one by
one from the fifth day to the sixth . . .')

Then the light disappears: Ugolino is blind and, groping over
the corpses, he calls his children for two more days. Everything is
ready for his own death: sight is gone, silence is broken, space and
time and light and living beings have come to an end.

                'ond' io mi diedi,
    già cieco, a brancolar sovra ciascuno
    e due dì li chiamai, poi che fur morti.
    Poscia, più che 'l dolor, poté 'l digiuno.'   (72–5)

('And so, blind as I had become, I let myself go and groped over each
body in turn; and for two days I called their names after they were dead.
Then fasting proved stronger than grief.')

'Dolor' and 'digiuno' include all the images that build up the
episode: the desperate grief, the woeful prison, the hands bitten
for grief; the savage repast, the gnawing, the bread, the wretched
flesh. 'Dolor' and 'digiuno' are the sounds of Ugolino's story:
repetition and the alchemy of poetry have made the 'r' and 'u'
themselves seem harsh, dim and dark.
    Fasting killed Ugolino: did it also kill his humanity to the point
of making him eat his dead children's flesh? Did the mad groping
become a tearing to shreds? Did the desire to eat lead to a savage
repast before Ugolino found Ruggieri's skull to gnaw? Did the
father consummate a last, devilish Eucharist? What is certain is the
following. First, the Chronicle mentioned earlier on, which was
compiled towards the end of the thirteenth century (seemingly

before Canto XXXIII of *Inferno* was written) says, 'and here it was found that they ate each other's flesh'.[9] Secondly, the commentary on the *Inferno* by Jacopo della Lana may well have been written when Dante was still alive, and in any case apparently before 1328. Several, but not all, of the Lana manuscripts say: 'here the author shows that, after they [the children] died, fasting overcáme grief, for he [Ugolino] ate of some of them'.[10] In other words, rumours of what has been called not just 'cannibalism' but 'tecnophagy' – the eating of children by the father – were circulating already in the thirteenth century; and at least one commentator, as early as the fourteenth century, accepted this version.[11] Dante must have been aware of these rumours, and although he does not accept their truth explicitly, there is enough in his text to hint very strongly that Ugolino did eat his sons' flesh. He is like Tydeus (XXXII, 130–2), who did eat Menalippus's head; throughout the canto he insists on the images of mouth, hunger, biting, eating; finally, as Contini suggested,[12] 'tecnophagy' would agree with the conception of tragedy that Dante sketched in the Letter to Cangrande, which is certainly not isolated in the general context of thirteenth-century culture. Yet Dante left the matter uncertain. He left the interpretation to his readers, as he left it to them to imagine what Ugolino wipes away from his mouth or what Ugolino's heart forebodes after the dream. Dante, then, is again relying on the technique of indirectness that is so typical of this canto. The tension of the text increases almost unbearably in the ambiguity of a sentence that cuts Ugolino's voice forever. There is no peace, no catharsis, just 'the last syllable of recorded time'.

Then the sinner sinks back into his animality, his teeth crunching the bone like a dog's, and Dante himself bursts into a violent and rhetorically elaborate invective against Pisa (79–90) in order to express his own moral and, perhaps, political judgement. Parallel as it is to another outburst, later in the canto (151–7), directed against Genoa, it might indicate Dante's condemnation of two cities that had fought against each other while neglecting their common duty of war against the infidel.

Thus in the first ninety lines of Canto XXXIII of *Inferno* we can follow a process that is typical of the entire *Comedy*. The reality of the other world suddenly finds a focus of attention in a character, who is presented as an *exemplum* of a moral dilemma. He is described through his actions; he speaks and hints at an historical situation, then recounts his own story. The poet expresses his personal reaction. He uses classical authors,[13] scriptural echoes, medieval rhetoric. Above all, he consistently uses a narrative technique that is active, dramatic and indirect, and is constructed throughout the episode by a hammering of certain images.[14]

Alliteration ('disperato dolor'; 'poscia', 'più', 'poté'; 'dolor', 'digiuno'; 'e che conviene ancor ch'altrui si chiuda'), and the prevalence of certain sounds ('r' and 'u') combine to give Dante's poetry in *Inferno* XXXIII its peculiar quality, that of the 'rime aspre e chiocce', the harsh and grating rhymes with which Canto XXXII had opened. It is to that passage that we can turn to find in Dante's own words his conception of the last three cantos of the *Inferno*:

> S'ïo avessi le rime aspre e chiocce
> come si converrebbe al tristo buco
> sovra 'l qual pontan tutte l'altre rocce,
> io premerei di mio concetto il suco
> più pienamente; ma perch'io non l'abbo,
> non sanza tema a dicer mi conduco;
> ché non è impresa da pigliare a gabbo
> discriver fondo a tutto l'universo,
> né da lingua che chiami mamma o babbo.
> Ma quelle donne aiutino il mio verso
> ch'aiutaro Anfïone a chiuder Tebe,
> sì che dal fatto il dir non sia diverso.
>
> (*Inf.* XXXII, 1–12)

(If only I had the harsh and grating rhymes that would match the pit of misery on which all the rocks of the earth bear down, I would squeeze out more fully the juice of my conception; and since I do not have them, it is not without fear that I bring myself to speak. For it is no trifling matter to describe the bottom of the whole universe, and not possible in the language in which children call for their mummy and daddy. But may those ladies come to the aid of my verse who helped Amphion to build the walls of Thebes, so that there may be no discrepancy between the fact and the word.)

The tongue that cries 'Mummy' and 'Daddy', the child's first and natural language, is not enough for the bottom of the universe. What the poet needs is harsh and grating rhymes; what, above all, he asks for is the help of the Muses to find words that, as Chaucer put it, 'moote be cosyn to the dede': 'sì che dal fatto il dir non sia diverso'. Language reshapes reality, but it also offers an imitation of that reality – a mimesis.

For all readers Canto XXXIII of the *Inferno* is – and rightly so – Ugolino's canto. Dante himself, however, added another sixty-six lines to the ninety that he used for Ugolino and for his own invective against Pisa. As he and Virgil leave *Antenora*, they enter *Tolomea*, where the souls of those who betrayed their guests lie on the ice, not bent downwards, but with their faces upturned (93). Their agony is increased by the fact that they cannot even weep, because their tears freeze on their eyes (94–9). Dante is stopped by a sinner who begs him to lift from his face the 'hard veils' so that, before the weeping freezes again, he may give vent to his misery (109–14). Dante consents to do so, on condition that the sinner shall reveal his name (115–17). The man is Fra' Alberigo, condemned to *Tolomea* for betraying his relatives Manfredo and Alberghetto. Pretending to come to an agreement with them on a matter of discord, Alberigo had invited them to dine with him. When the fruit was served, Alberigo's servants entered the room and killed the guests. Hence the proverb, apparently common in the fourteenth century, 'he got the fruit of Fra' Alberigo', and hence Dante's pun: 'I am he of the fruits of the evil garden, and here I receive date for fig' (119–20).

This phrase, which Alberigo himself pronounces, can be considered the anticlimax of the Canto. The tone of the two lines is 'low' as opposed to Ugolino's 'high' tragic style. The irony behind Alberigo's pun is, however, quite different, for the fig means treason, and the date means the deepest part of Hell. 'Fig' and 'date' are the two terms of the *contrappasso*, which is tragic here as everywhere else in the *Inferno*. Thus the two lines suggest a sense of absurdity that is confirmed by Alberigo's speech. Dante thinks that Alberigo is still alive. But the sinner explains: 'How my body fares in the world above I have no knowledge. This *Tolomea* has the particular advantage that often the soul falls down here before the body dies. As soon as the soul commits treason its body is taken from it by a devil who thereafter rules it until its time comes to die' (122–6).

Some maintain that Dante invented this absolutely monstrous doctrine by interpreting literally that passage in John's Gospel where Satan is said to have entered into Judas 'after the sop' (John 13.27). But this interpretation is theologically unjustifiable because, as Dante knew perfectly well (cf. Buonconte da Montefeltro in *Purg.* v, 85–129), it excludes the possibility of a last-minute repentance. Dante knows that Alberigo and Branca Doria, who is indirectly introduced immediately afterwards as 'the shade that is wintering here behind', are still alive. He takes some liberty with theology because he wants to place them in Hell. But there is something more, namely, the element of absurdity. It will be seen that Alberigo calls all this an 'advantage'; and in his invective against the Genoese at the end of the canto, Dante refers to the Genoese Branca Doria as follows: 'With the worst spirit of Romagna [Alberigo] I found a Genoese who is bathed in Cocytus, whilst his body still appears alive on earth!' Dante seems to suggest that here, at the bottom of Hell, all normal assumptions have lost their validity and that there is no place for the logic of theology.

Dante the character's reaction to this situation is comprehensible. When Alberigo tells him that the soul behind him is that of Branca Doria, he replies that Branca is still alive, 'e mangia e bee e dorme e veste panni' (141). But this sentence, which seems to express an objection, is in perfect agreement with Alberigo's words. Eating, drinking, sleeping and putting on clothes are things pertaining to the body, not to the soul. Once again the revealing ambiguity stresses the element of absurdity.

The pun reappears in Dante's final gesture. When Alberigo had asked him to remove the glazed tears from his eyes, the protagonist played on the sinner's misunderstanding (Alberigo had believed that Dante and Virgil were souls condemned to the 'last station', the last area of the ninth circle), and promised to do so. Otherwise, 'may he be sent to the bottom of the ice!' (117). But it was precisely to the bottom of the ice that Dante was being led by Virgil, though for his salvation rather than damnation. So after Alberigo has entertained him for a while, Dante gives him . . . date for fig: 'and to be brutal to him was an act of courtesy' (150).[15] The two expressions, 'dattero per figo' and 'e cortesia fu lui esser villano' close the circle of irony and bring the anticlimax of Canto XXXIII to completion.

This element of absurdity and irony together with the ambiguously light tone are contrasted, however, with a series of images to which our attention is constantly drawn even in the second half of Canto XXXIII. I am referring to the 'fredda crosta', the cold crust of line 109; to the 'invetriate lagrime', the glazed tears of line 128; to the two splendid terzinas from line 94 to line 99, where all the images of the ninth circle and of Ugolino's episode are echoed:

> Lo pianto stesso lì pianger non lascia,
> e 'l duol che truova in su li occhi rintoppo,
> si volge in entro a far crescer l'ambascia;
> ché le lagrime prime fanno groppo,
> e sì come visiere di cristallo,
> rïempion sotto 'l ciglio tutto il coppo. (94–9)

(It is crying itself that prevents crying there, and the pain that finds a blockage at the eyes turns back to increase the anguish within; the first tears form a frozen barrier and like crystal visors they fill the whole socket underneath the brow.)

Once more these are 'rime aspre e chiocce', once more we have a description that omits no detail but uses no adjective. The first, almost baroque, line unfolds in the two following, which maintain the quality of abstraction ('pianto', 'pianger', 'duol', 'ambascia'). The second terzina transfers all this onto a concrete level ('lagrime', 'groppo', 'ciglio', 'coppo') and introduces the simile ('e sì come visiere di cristallo') that closes the eyes of the damned forever.

We are back to blindness, ice, silence. When the pain and the grief of man cannot be expressed, it turns inwards, becomes anguish, despair, and multiplies forever. This is the bottom of the universe.

Notes

1 A. Pézard, 'Le chant XXXIII de l'Enfer', in *Letture dell'Inferno* of the *Lectura Dantis internazionale* (Milano, 1963), pp. 343–96.

2 P. Villari (edn.), *Cronica Fiorentina compilata nel sec. XIII*, in *I primi due secoli della storia di Firenze*, vol. I (Firenze, 1898), p. 250.

3 A distinction is to be made between *tristitia* and *dolor*, following Aquinas's and Dante's own thought; see V. Russo, 'Il "dolore" del Conte Ugolino', in *Sussidi di esegesi dantesca* (Napoli, 1967), pp. 147–81.

4 E. Auerbach, 'Dante, poeta del mondo terreno', in *Studi su Dante*, Italian trans., 3rd edn. (Milano, 1971), pp. 3–161.

5 This would be the point of departure of Ugolino's 'oration'. See G.

Barberi-Squarotti, 'L'orazione del Conte Ugolino', now in *Letture classensi*, vol. IV (Ravenna, 1973), pp. 147–82.

6 G. Villani, *Cronica* (Firenze, 1845), vol. I, p. 450.

7 Ugolino, according to Barberi-Squarotti, never mentions *his* treasons.

8 F. De Sanctis, 'Il Canto XXXIII dell'Inferno', now in *Letture dantesche*, ed. G. Getto (Firenze, 1964), pp. 629–49.

9 Villari (ed.), *Cronica*, p. 251.

10 L. Scarabelli (ed.), *Commedia di Dante degli Allagherii col commento di Jacopo della Lana* (Bologna, 1866), p. 501.

11 F. D'Ovidio, *Nuovi studi danteschi* (Napoli, 1932), vol. I, pp. 51–96.

12 G. Contini, 'Filologia ed esegesi dantesca' now in *Un'idea di Dante* (Torino, 1976), pp. 125–8.

13 The following is a table of the sources and correspondences for the passages I have examined:

Inf. XXXII,	130–2:	Statius, *Thebaid* VIII, 749ff.
XXXIII,	4–5:	Virgil, *Aeneid* II, 3 and 11.
XXXIII,	62–3:	Job 1.21.
XXXIII,	66:	Virgil, *Aeneid* X, 675–6 and XII, 883–4.
XXXIII,	69:	Matthew 27.46.
XXXIII,	73:	Ovid, *Metamorphoses* VI, 274.
XXXIII,	76:	Statius, *Thebaid* VIII, 757.
XXXIII,	79–90:	Lucan, *Pharsalia* VIII, 827–30.

For further reading on the Ugolino episode, see 'Ugolino', in *Enciclopedia dantesca*, vol. V (Roma, 1976), pp. 797–9.

14 I have more fully examined the narrative technique used by Dante in Ugolino's story in 'Ugolino e la narrativa', to be published shortly in *Studi danteschi*.

15 On 'cortesia' in this passage see R. Kirkpatrick, 'The Principle of Courtesy in the *Convivio* and the *Comedy*', *Italian Studies* XXXV (1980), 25–30.

Purgatorio III

PHILIP McNAIR

There are many things we do not know about the author of the *Comedy*, and some we shall never know; but one thing is morally certain, and that is the trichotomous structure of his mind. Like Julius Caesar's Gaul, all Dante may be divided into three parts; for he was a tripartite man who lived in a three-storeyed universe and worshipped a three-personed God; and when he composed his sacred poem he projected it in three canticas and wrote it in threefold rhyme. It is not altogether surprising, therefore, how naturally and obligingly so many of his cantos fall into three parts at the critic's touch: and the third canto of *Purgatorio* is no exception.

Lines 1–45 form the canto's first part, and poignantly belong to Virgil; lines 46–102 form the second part, which is pervaded by the peaceful movement of 'una gente d'anime' and is crowned by a simile of sheep; lines 103–44 form the third part, which is dominated by the figure of Manfred. Aesthetically the canto is a poetic sandwich, with the idyllic Part Two compressed between the elegiac Parts One and Three.

Traditionally this has been called the Canto of Manfred, and of course it *is* Manfred's Canto just as surely as *Inferno* x is Farinata's or *Paradiso* xv Cacciaguida's; but the tragic figure of the vanquished king is only revealed on its last page after more than a hundred lines of moving verse. The true subject of the canto is the inscrutable interpenetration of the justice and the love of God, the unsearchable interaction of His right hand and His left.

As the canto begins, the two characters Dante and Virgil are on the sloping coastal plain between the sea-shore (described in Canto I) and the foot of Mount Purgatory, the region that Forese Donati in Canto XXIII will call 'la costa ove s'aspetta' ('the slope

90

where one awaits'). It is outside Purgatory proper, and hence it answers to the Vestibule of the Uncommitted in *Inferno*; and just as that Vestibule is known as *Antinferno*, so this region is called *Antipurgatorio*, or Ante-Purgatory. Here await their entry through the Gate of Purgatory the spirits of the Late Repentant, who turned to God *in extremis* but did not avail themselves of the means of penitence provided by the Church.

Dante's analytic and scholastic mind divides them into four classes. First come those who died in contumacy of the Church: they wait in Ante-Purgatory thirty times the period of their contumacy, unless this period should be shortened by the prayers of the faithful on their behalf in this life. They form the subject of this third canto, and the example Dante brings before us is the excommunicated King Manfred of Sicily. The second class comprises those who put off their repentance through indolence or indifference until the point of death: they must wait in Ante-Purgatory for as long as they lived upon earth, unless this period should be shortened by prayer on their behalf. They form the subject of Canto iv, and the example Dante gives of them is a Florentine friend of his called Belacqua. Those who died a violent death but repented *in articulo mortis*, yet without absolution, form the third class, and they are described in Cantos v and vi with no less than ten examples. The fourth and final class contains kings and princes who deferred their repentance under the crushing pressure of temporal business. These negligent rulers wait in a valley decked with flowers and are described in Cantos vii and viii with eleven examples.

Dante and Virgil do not reach the Gate of Purgatory until the seventy-sixth line of Canto ix, and do not cross the threshold of Purgatory until the first line of Canto x. The first nine cantos of *Purgatorio*, therefore, are spent outside Purgatory proper, just as the last six and a half are also spent beyond Purgatory proper: and taken together they account for nearly half the cantica.

Canto i has introduced us to the beauty of the natural setting of Dante's Purgatory; Canto ii has begun with the sea-dawn and has ended in shamefaced flight – for at sunrise of their first day out of Hell the two poets find Casella the musician among the souls who have just arrived at the shores of Ante-Purgatory from Tiber's mouth. This old friend has begun to sing one of Dante's own songs at his request, and a crowd has gathered to listen, when they are all brusquely interrupted by Cato, the old man venerable who is Warden of the Realm. He sends them about their business with the words: 'What is this, dawdling spirits? What negligence, what loitering is this? Run to the Mountain to despoil yourselves of the husk that hinders God from being manifest to you!' And so the crowd of shades has dispersed in shame and confusion, like frightened doves disturbed when feeding, and the two poets have fled with them.

The third canto opens with their headlong flight, the spirits of the Late Repentant fanning out across the plain as they scurry to the foot of Mount Purgatory:

> Avvegna che la subitana fuga
> dispergesse color per la campagna,
> rivolti al monte ove ragion ne fruga,
>   i' mi ristrinsi a la fida compagna:
> e come sare' io sanza lui corso?
> chi m'avria tratto su per la montagna?   (1–6)

(Although the sudden flight scattered *them* over the plain, turned back to the mountain where justice probes us, I drew close to my trusty companion: and how should I have run without him? Who would have drawn me up the mountain?)

This second realm of the dead is sited on the Mountain 'ove ragion ne fruga' (3) – an arresting phrase, and the most telling of all Dante's descriptions of Purgatory. 'Ragion' of course means reason, but it is here the Divine Reason which is the justice of God. In many Italian towns the seat of justice is still called *il palazzo della ragione* – and this is the sense in which the word is used here. 'Ne' in this context is the archaic form for *ci*, meaning 'us'. *Frugare* is a verb most non-Italians first come across in descriptions of women rummaging in their handbag: *frugare nella borsa* – just as *frugare una casa* means to ransack a house. If we add these meanings together, we find that on Mount Purgatory it is the justice of God that probes us through and through, that rummages to the bottom of that ragbag of our conscience, that ransacks our inmost self.

One of the many lovely things about the *Comedy* is the affection and respect that poets are shown to feel for one another. Here the sudden flight that scatters the other souls serves only to bring

Dante closer to his faithful comrade. Virgil is a poet's poet, and nothing is more engaging in our study of *Inferno* and *Purgatorio* than to trace the developing and many-faceted companionship of these two devotees of Apollo, the vernacular Muse keeping step with the classical epic, the ancient and the modern world advancing hand in hand. Their relationship is no doubt intended to symbolise for us the subtle interplay of reason and faith in the Christian life: for the Schoolmen, reason was the handmaid of faith, just as for St Paul the Law is our schoolmaster to bring us to Christ. But through all the symbolism of the poem Virgil remains Virgil – 'la fida compagna' of line 4, 'il mio conforto' of line 22 – a very human shade of a very human person; and nowhere in the whole of the *Comedy* do we find such a searching and convincing portrait of him as in the first third of this canto.

For Dante imagines Virgil to be touched to the quick by Cato's rebuke:

> El mi parea da sé stesso rimorso:
> o dignitosa coscienza e netta,
> come t'è picciol fallo amaro morso! (7–9)

(He seemed to me gnawed by self-reproach. O noble and stainless conscience, how bitter a bite is a little fault to you!)

Virgil's essential tragedy is all summed up in that 'dignitosa coscienza e netta'. Dante's characters are whole men and women, even though damned; they are never simply personified attributes. Ugolino, for instance, is a damned traitor, but he is still a tender father. Hell is no annihilation: as now, so then. Death has bereft Virgil of his shadow-casting body, but it has not diminished the sensitivity of his soul. In his disembodied state he is still a sentient moral being: he is pre-eminently a 'coscienza', and it is both 'dignitosa' and 'netta'. To retain a conscience in Hell, and a pure conscience at that, is the ultimate tragedy. Though he has abandoned all hope in passing through Hell-Gate, the poet of the Roman Empire has not abandoned all virtue, all morality: line 7 portrays him as a self-correcting creature, as all moral beings must be.

In the best sense, the Virgil of history and the Virgil of Dante is a good Victorian. The criterion of decency in literature adopted by our great-grandfathers was whether a fellow could leave the book lying about in the drawing-room where his daughter (or one of the servants) might see it. Virgil and his *Aeneid* measured up to this requirement as did no other poet and poem of Antiquity: his 'coscienza' is 'dignitosa e netta'. Ausonius might invest his lines with obscene meaning by crafty manipulation, but in themselves they are as blameless as they are beautiful.

Because in these opening lines Virgil is troubled and uneasy in his conscience, his 'onestade' (11) is impaired by the unaccustomed haste of his flight. We are far from his eternal habitat in Limbo, where 'li spiriti magni' of Antiquity move with immense dignity and deliberation. Here all is urgent hurry, for time is of the essence of Purgatory.

As the two poets slow down, Dante's mind is free to take in their strange and exciting environment. The risen sun is flaming red behind them as they walk side by side from the sea-shore to the mountain foot, when all at once in a dramatic moment of truth and incipient panic he realises that only he is casting a shadow before him:

> Lo sol, che dietro fiammeggiava roggio,
> rotto m'era dinanzi a la figura,
> ch'avëa in me de' suoi raggi l'appoggio.
>   Io mi volsi dallato con paura
> d'essere abbandonato, quand' io vidi
> solo dinanzi a me la terra oscura.   (16–21)

(The sun, which was flaming red behind, was broken in front of me by my figure, for it had in me an obstacle for its rays. I turned sideways in fear of being deserted when I saw the ground dark before me only.)

In Hell there had been no sun, and hence no occasion for observing that – curiously enough – shades cast no shadow. Here in *Purgatorio* Dante employs this effective device more than once to emphasise his otherness, to impress upon the spirits of the dead and upon his readers that he is alive, a living man in the realms of the departed. It is akin to his discovery in the eighth canto of *Inferno* that only when *he* clambered aboard the boat that was to ferry the two poets across the Stygian marsh did it appear to be laden.

Delightful and complete though it is in itself, this incident of Dante's shadow seems to have been introduced as a visual aid to enable Virgil to propound an argument that stems from Cato's rebuke at the end of Canto II. Many of the cantos of the *Comedy* are self-contained, but this third canto of *Purgatorio* is not: it is the apple-tree that lavishes its fruits upon our lawn but yet is rooted in our neighbour's garden. To catch the drift of this next long speech of Virgil's we must peep back over the garden wall and discover what provoked that rebuke.

We find Casella singing to an admiring audience one of Dante's major love-poems, which begins 'Amor che ne la mente mi ragiona' ('Love that speaks to me in my mind'). Now the poet had commented at length on this *canzone* in the third tractate of his *Convivio*, where he explained that the Lady whom it praises is none other than Philosophy. In view of this equation, seen in the total context of Dante's conversion from the dark wood of sin to the beatific vision, it seems that Cato is castigating not only the frivolous negligence of souls content to listen to sweet love-songs on the beach rather than dash into action on the Mountain (for this much is obvious), but also the particular brand of metaphysics that had held Dante in thrall – and, by implication, the human confidence in its own capacity to reason out ultimate issues that is personified by Virgil. So, in effect, Cato's is a triple reproof: of the crowd, of Dante and of Virgil. Anyhow the crowd and Virgil take it that way, as the opening of this third canto has shown.

What Cato's rebuke has brought home to Virgil is that the human intellect has its limits: it can establish by the exercise of ratiocination *that* God is, but not *what* God is, which is the subject of divine revelation. And yet within those appointed limits Virgil is Dante's guide, for reason is worthy of trust as far as it goes:

> . . . e 'l mio conforto: 'Perché pur diffidi?',
> a dir mi cominciò tutto rivolto;
> 'non credi tu me teco e ch'io ti guidi?'   (22–4)

(. . . and my comforter, having fully turned round, began to say to me: 'Why do you still distrust? Do you not believe that I am with you and that I am guiding you?')

Reason is indeed worthy of trust as far as it goes, but it does not go far enough. It cannot lead Dante home to Heaven, nor can it bridge the abyss between Man and God. Profiting from Cato's rebuke, Virgil in pensive mood traces the limits of human ratiocination for the next six and a half terzinas. He moves from

Dante's fear in line 19, and his incomprehension of the fact that Virgil's shade casts no shadow, to an apostrophe of the whole human race – and in particular 'li spiriti magni' of Antiquity - for failing to realise the inadequacy of the human intellect; and this leads him logically (for he is the embodiment of reason) to rue his own inadequacy, his ultimate failure and his eternal grief; and this, in turn, induces in him the depression that overcomes him in lines 44–5.

Virgil's closely reasoned and admirably articulated discourse begins on a note of purest elegy:

> 'Vespero è già colà dov' è sepolto
> lo corpo dentro al quale io facea ombra;
> Napoli l'ha, e da Brandizio è tolto.'   (25–7)

('It is already late afternoon over there where the body within which *I* used to cast a shadow is buried; Naples has it, and it was taken from Brindisi.')

The tone of wistful nostalgia seeps through his words and pervades his argument. The Roman poet had planned to spend three years in Greece revising his *Aeneid*, but before he could begin he sickened in Megara while travelling with Augustus, and lived only a few days after landing at Brindisi (Brundisium) on the heel of Italy: there he died on 21 September of the year 19 B.C, but was buried between Naples and Pozzuoli at the Emperor's command (as he tells us at the beginning of *Purgatorio* VII, when he returns to this haunting theme). What shadows would be cast that very evening around his tomb!

Virgil develops his argument in the following two terzinas:

> 'Ora, se innanzi a me nulla s'aombra,
> non ti maravigliar più che d'i cieli
> che l'uno a l'altro raggio non ingombra.
>   A sofferir tormenti, caldi e geli
> simili corpi la Virtù dispone
> che, come fa, non vuol ch'a noi si sveli.'   (28–33)

('Now if before me no shadow is cast, do not marvel at this more than you wonder at the heavens, that one heaven does not obstruct another's ray. The Supreme Power ordains such bodies as mine to bear torments, heat and frost, but He does not will that it should be revealed to us how He does it.')

Although Virgil has quit his shadow-casting body, the creative power of God ('la Virtù' of line 32) has furnished him with another vehicle of being, which is not flesh and blood but diaphanous to the sun's rays as are the nine concentric spheres of Heaven to one another's beams, and yet made subject to the elements that it might suffer extremes of heat and cold – as indeed we have already seen similar bodies suffering in Hell. How this can be is a divine mystery that God is unwilling to make manifest to us (but the 'a noi' of line 33 may refer to the virtuous heathen of Antiquity who had not faith, rather than to the Christian who enjoys the revelation of God in Christ).

This discussion of the material–immaterial quality of man's *post mortem* body harks back to the risen body of Jesus as described in the Gospels (Luke 24.36–43; John 20.19–29), and finds its *locus classicus* in the New Testament in St Paul's explanation to his Corinthian converts:

But some one will ask, 'How are the dead raised? With what kind of body do they come?' You foolish man! What you sow does not come to life unless it dies. And what you sow is not the body which is to be, but a bare kernel, perhaps of wheat or of some other grain. But God gives it a body as He has chosen, and to each kind of seed its own body. For not all flesh is alike, but there is one kind for men, another for animals, another for birds and another for fish. There are celestial bodies, and there are terrestrial bodies; but the glory of the celestial is one, and the glory of the terrestrial is another. There is one glory of the sun, and another glory of the moon, and another glory of the stars; for star differs from star in glory. So it is with the resurrection of the dead. What is sown is perishable, what is raised is imperishable. It is sown in dishonour; it is raised in glory. It is sown in weakness; it is raised in power. It is sown a physical body, it is raised a spiritual body.

(1 Corinthians 15.35–44)

'God gives it a body as He has chosen' – therefore Dante's panic at the thought of being abandoned arose from his ignorance of that *Virtù* which can and does create more than one quality of body, and from his foolish arrogance in supposing that his unaided intellect was capable of understanding all the mysteries of God's universe. And so the next link in the argument treats of the inadequacy of human reason:

'Matto è chi spera che nostra ragione
possa trascorrer la infinita via
che tiene una sustanza in tre persone.'   (34–6)

97

('Foolish is he who hopes that our reason can traverse the infinite way that one Substance in three Persons follows.')

If our finite minds cannot comprehend the elementary fact that in sunlight a body of one order casts a shadow, whilst a body of another order casts none, then it is sheer madness to hope that our natural reason may be capable of apprehending the mystery of the Trinity – '*una* sustanza in *tre* persone'. The proposition is reciprocal: the mystery of the Trinity should warn us that the operations of its *Virtù* are no less mysterious.

But it is not only the mystery of the Trinity that Virgil is evoking here, but also the mystery of the Incarnation; for that 'infinita via' followed by the triune God was the way of the Cross, which entailed the Virgin's womb. Therefore:

> 'State contenti, umana gente, al *quia*;
> ché, se potuto aveste veder tutto,
> mestier non era parturir Maria;
> e disïar vedeste sanza frutto
> tai che sarebbe lor disio quetato,
> ch'etternalmente è dato lor per lutto:
> io dico d'Aristotile e di Plato
> e di molt' altri'; e qui chinò la fronte,
> e più non disse, e rimase turbato. (37–45)

('Rest content, human race, with the *quia*; for if you had been able to see everything, there was no need for Mary to give birth; and you have seen the fruitless longing of men [whose understanding was] such that [if this knowledge had been possible] their desire would have been satisfied – the desire that is given them eternally for grief: I speak of Aristotle and Plato and many others'; and here he bowed his head and said no more, and remained troubled.)

Line 37 alludes to an Aristotelian distinction that was fundamental to the teaching of the Schoolmen and is best defined by St Thomas Aquinas: 'Demonstration is of two sorts: the one proves by means of the cause, and is called *propter quid*; the other by means of the effect, and is called the demonstration *quia*.' In other words, we distinguish the knowledge *why* a thing is what it is from the knowledge *that* a thing is what it is. The first is knowledge derived by arguing from cause to effect (or *a priori*), and we call this argument *propter quid*. The second is knowledge derived by arguing from effect to cause (or *a posteriori*), and we call

98

this argument *quia*. A homely illustration may make this distinction clear. If I plant a rose-bush, I expect it to bear roses, because I
know that in its essential quiddity it is a rose-bush: this is the
argument *propter quid*. If on the other hand I find roses on a bush, I
conclude that it must be a rose-bush because it is bearing roses:
and this is the argument *quia*.

Here Dante (through Virgil) is calling on the human race to rest
content with the *effects* of God's sovereignty without attempting
to pry into its essential quiddity: to be satisfied with the *quia* and
not to probe into the *propter quid*. He is, of course, in harmony
with much biblical teaching; the Lord (through Isaiah) says: 'My
thoughts are not your thoughts, neither are your ways my ways
. . . For as the heavens are higher than the earth, so are my ways
higher than your ways, and my thoughts higher than your
thoughts' (Isaiah 55.8–9); and St Paul exclaims: 'O the depth of the
riches and wisdom and knowledge of God! How unsearchable are
His judgements and how inscrutable His ways!' (Romans 11.33).

But the rest of this terzina is patient of a double interpretation,
according to whether we consider Mary's child as the Word of
God or as the Saviour of mankind – in other words, whether the
context here is revelation or Redemption. Both interpretations are
valid, for both were surely in the mind of Dante. First, if Man had
been able to know everything there would have been no need for
God to reveal it to him in Christ. Secondly, had God judged Man
capable of all knowledge He would not have forbidden him to eat
of the tree of the knowledge of good and evil in the Garden of
Eden; and if Man had not disobeyed God he would not have
fallen; and if he had not fallen there would have been no need for
Christ to save him. But God forbade, Adam ate, Man fell, and
Christ saves – and with St Augustine we can bless the *felix culpa*
that caused the Blessed Virgin to conceive and bear.

And so line 39 sounds a warm and human note from the poet of
the Fourth Eclogue. The womb of Mary becomes the vehicle of
all the divine counsel and everlasting purpose of Heaven, since it
contains God manifest in flesh, the wonder of His universe and the
end of all knowledge, for in Christ 'dwells all the fulness of the
Godhead bodily' (Colossians 2.9). But the tone of pathos invades
this fleeting reference to the Incarnation, for Virgil survived
almost long enough to enjoy the golden age of the Messiah; when

he sickened and died on his return from Greece at the modest age of fifty he had less than twenty years to go (within his God-allotted span) before that day of days when 'mestier . . . era parturir Maria'. Why, the poet of the *Aeneid* was younger than Anna the prophetess, younger than Simeon, who held the baby Jesus in his arms! No wonder he broods on the timing of his death in distant Brindisi, and the site of his sepulchre near Naples.

In its obvious sense, the 'sanza frutto' of line 40 means 'fruitless' or 'in vain', but – given the complexity of Dante's mind – it may also convey a subtle comment on the Fall. For natural, unregenerate Man has tasted the forbidden fruit of the tree of the knowledge of good and evil; he is no longer innocent, but a morally responsible creature with longings after good yet vitiated by evil. But he has not tasted the fruit of the tree of life, which stood with the forbidden tree in the midst of the Garden, and which in the Apocalypse is revealed to be none other than Christ Himself (Revelation 22.2). He is thus without that vital, sustaining and satisfying fruit which is the eternal life of the spirit. He is indeed 'sanza frutto' in himself, and not having tasted Christ he is in consequence also 'sanza frutto' toward God – the barren fig-tree cursed by Jesus.

That wistful tone of elegy creeps back into Virgil's voice as his despondent speech peters out halfway through line 44. Still apostrophising the human race, he conjures up that world of poignant desire, that eternity of heartfelt longing – for ever stimulated and never assuaged – which is the life of the virtuous pagan in Limbo. For if there is no physical torment in that first circle of Hell, there *is* an inner endless grief, which issues in sighs that keep the air for ever trembling, the piercing grief of lovers deprived of their love. Even the shades of 'li spiriti magni', honoured though they may be, have passed through Hell-Gate and abandoned all hope. They are lost, and know that they are lost, condemned in Virgil's telling words to live without hope in desire (*Inf.* IV, 42). What they desire is the vision of God, 'il ben de l'intelletto', the Good that they have known too late and irrevocably missed.

The premise of lines 40–42 is still, of course, line 38. 'If, O human race' – Virgil declares – 'you had been able to see the whole counsel of God by natural reason, then not only would there have been no need for the Incarnation, but also you would have seen satisfied the desire of those great minds of Antiquity in whom reason rose to its highest power; but since this is not the case, that very desire is given them for everlasting grief.' And then his sad voice tails away as he says: 'I speak of Aristotle and Plato and many others . . .' – and he finishes mid-line, too modest to mention himself, too chastened to add another word. It is a memorable poetic effect, gained with a stringent economy of means, eked out by the haunting repetition of the copulative *e*.

The inadequacy of reason is the inadequacy of Virgil: we await the coming of Beatrice and the glorious revelation of the mind of God.

The second part of the canto begins with line 46, in which the two poets at last reach the foot of the Mountain, and there find the rocky ascent so steep that the nimblest legs would have tackled it in vain. Little by little we are forming our picture of this place where the souls of repentant sinners are purged; it is, as we have been told in those impressive words from lines 14 and 15, 'il poggio / che 'nverso 'l ciel più alto si dislaga' ('the hill that towards heaven distances itself furthest from the sea'); it is, we shall find, a mountain of such stupendous eminence that it soars thousands of miles beyond the atmosphere of this earth.

On the summit of this mountain Dante places the Earthly Paradise, the Garden of Eden, from which Man fell by disobedience. I often puzzled over this lofty mountain-setting for the scene of the Fall until I found the visual clue in the prophecy of Ezekiel (a book after Dante's own heart), where the Lord reminds the King of Tyre (a figure of Satan): 'You were in Eden, the Garden of God . . . you were on the holy mountain of God . . . you were blameless in your ways from the day you were created, till iniquity was found in you . . . so I cast you as a profane thing from the mountain of God . . . I cast you to the ground' (Ezekiel 28.13–17).

And here, characteristically, the poet gives us a point of reference in the familiar world we know in order that we may see the unfamiliar world of his imagining:

> Tra Lerice e Turbìa la più diserta,
> la più rotta ruina è una scala,
> verso di quella, agevole e aperta.   (49–51)

101

(Compared with that, the wildest and most broken rockfall between Lerice and Turbia is an easy and open stairway.)

All those exasperating steeps and precipices between one end of the Italian Riviera and the other, which generations of pilgrims have toiled over, are as nothing compared with the ascent of Mount Purgatory. In this unwonted realm, human reason is at a loss, for little less than wings seems to avail here; Virgil the trusted guide and mentor, still depressed and 'turbato' from line 45, confesses himself stumped, bows his head, and seeks to excogitate the way by introspection. His pupil, more practical and curious, looks out and around him, and from the left there appear to him a crowd of souls moving their steps in the direction of the two poets, and yet not seeming to approach, so slowly are they coming.

> 'Leva', diss' io, 'maestro, li occhi tuoi:
> ecco di qua chi ne darà consiglio,
> se tu da te medesmo aver nol puoi.'   (61–3)

('Raise your eyes, Master', I said; 'see on this side people who will give us counsel, if you cannot obtain it from yourself.')

'Maestro' is by now a courtesy title for Virgil, who knows no more about Purgatory than his apprentice, and line 63 seems to be flavoured with a pinch of irony: 'Stop looking inside yourself' – Dante is saying – 'you won't find the answer in there: try these people over here.' The inadequacy of the human intellect is beginning to show. The perplexed guide brightens up with obvious relief, and suggests they go to meet them; and then, with a touch of the old paternal admonition, he adds: 'e tu ferma la spene, dolce figlio' ('and you, sweet son, be steadfast in hope': 66). But Virgil's dear son is growing up fast.

This 'gente d'anime' approaching like snails are, of course, the company of the Late Repentant who have died in contumacy of Holy Church, and who are condemned to wander on this slope like sheep without a shepherd until they have expiated thirty times the period of their contumacy: such is their *contrappasso*. When they see Dante and Virgil coming towards them, although they are still a stone's throw away, they all huddle together under the rocky mass of the Mountain 'com' a guardar, chi va dubbiando, stassi' ('as the traveller uncertain of his way stands still to reconnoitre':

72). Virgil addresses them with elaborate courtesy, but his congratulatory 'O ben finiti' seems calculated to suggest that they were 'mal andati', for it was only their end that was good about them:

> 'O ben finiti, o già spiriti eletti',
> Virgilio incominciò, 'per quella pace
> ch'i' credo che per voi tutti s'aspetti,
>   ditene dove la montagna giace,
> sì che possibil sia l'andare in suso;
> ché perder tempo a chi più sa più spiace.'   (73–8)

('O you who have finished well, O spirits already elect', began Virgil, 'by that peace which I believe awaits you all, tell us at what point the Mountain slopes, so that it may be possible to make the ascent; for waste of time most irks the expert.')

In Hell time stands still, in Purgatory it is of the utmost moment, as Virgil early realises – not for himself but for his charge, 'a chi più sa'. It is a realisation that will increase in urgency the higher they climb the Mountain. But the haste of purgation is here contrasted with the peace of Heaven, and the mention of 'quella pace' so intensifies his own *disio* destined never to be *quetato* that it brings back that wistful note into Virgil's voice.

The next three terzinas are filled with one of Dante's most idyllic and pastoral similes, Franciscan in its natural simplicity:

> Come le pecorelle escon del chiuso
> a una, a due, a tre, e l'altre stanno
> timidette atterrando l'occhio e 'l muso;
>   e ciò che fa la prima, e l'altre fanno,
> addossandosi a lei, s'ella s'arresta,
> semplici e quete, e lo 'mperché non sanno;
>   sì vid' io muovere a venir la testa
> di quella mandra fortunata allotta,
> pudica in faccia e ne l'andare onesta.   (79–87)

(As sheep come out of the fold by one, by two, by three, and the others stand timid, keeping eye and muzzle to the ground, and what the first one does the others do also, huddling up behind her if she halts, simple and quiet, and not knowing the reason why; so I saw the head of that favoured flock move then to come forward, modest in expression and seemly in bearing.)

Having refused the Church's leading, the souls of the contumacious are likened to a shepherdless flock. Twice (84 and 93) we are

103

told that they do not know *il perché*, in marked contrast to the foolish people of lines 34–6 who would pry into *il perché* that is denied them. For it is not so much the stupidity of sheep that Dante is stressing in this analogy as their timid modesty and helplessness, their simple-minded dependence on each other. Here, as always, the poet is a patient and most accurate observer of nature, for this is not the first time that he has remarked on the psychology of the flock. In the opening tractate of his *Convivio* he has told us:

If one sheep were to throw herself from a cliff a thousand yards high, all the others would go after her; and if one sheep for any reason in crossing a road makes a leap, all the others leap, even though they see nothing to leap over. And before now I have seen many of them jump into a well because of one who jumped into it, perhaps believing that they were jumping over a wall, despite the fact that the shepherd set himself with arms and breast before them, weeping and shouting (I, xi, 9–10).

There is an evident note of censure in this prose passage, which is quite missing from the simile in Canto III, where we are shown the hesitant but intuitive movements of a 'mandra fortunata'; indeed, in these terzinas Dante is holding up the sheeplike qualities of *semplicità* and *mansuetudine* for our admiration and emulation. These are the moral attributes that the proud and contumacious – the Manfreds of this world – must learn to cultivate in Purgatory.

The Late Repentant boggle at Dante's shadow, just as Dante earlier had turned in fear at Virgil's lack of shadow, until the master explains to them that he is still alive and is on a Heaven-powered mission to scale this mountain wall ('di soverchiar questa parete': 99). At that the worthy people ('gente degna') – and seemingly the description is not ironic – afford Virgil the direction he has craved, 'coi dossi de le man faccendo insegna' ('signalling with the back of their hands': 102).

This second part of the canto is played with muted strings in a minor key between two arresting bravura passages in the major.

With line 103 begins the third and final part, and it is dominated by one of Dante's heroes. We are not left long in suspense: the shade who accosts the poet with the imperious command to turn his face and recognise him soon identifies himself for us with majestic simplicity in the three words 'I am Manfred':

E un di loro incominciò: 'Chiunque
tu se', così andando, volgi 'l viso:
pon mente se di là mi vedesti unque.'
   Io mi volsi ver' lui e guardail fiso:
biondo era e bello e di gentile aspetto,
ma l'un de' cigli un colpo avea diviso.
   Quand' io mi fui umilmente disdetto
d'averlo visto mai, el disse: 'Or vedi';
e mostrommi una piaga a sommo 'l petto.
   Poi sorridendo disse: 'Io son Manfredi,
nepote di Costanza imperadrice;
ond' io ti priego che, quando tu riedi,
   vadi a mia bella figlia, genitrice
de l'onor di Cicilia e d'Aragona,
e dichi 'l vero a lei, s'altro si dice.'   (103–17)

(And one of them began: 'Whoever you are, turn your face as you are going: consider whether you ever saw me over there [in the other world].' I turned towards him and looked at him intently: he was fair-haired and handsome and of noble appearance, but a blow had cleft one of his eyebrows. When I had humbly disclaimed ever having seen him, he said: 'Now look!' and showed me a wound in the upper part of his breast. Then he said smiling: 'I am Manfred, grandson of the Empress Constance; therefore, when you return, I beg you to go to my beautiful daughter, mother of the vaunted rulers of Sicily and Aragon, and tell her the truth, if another story is told.')

Manfred was the bastard son of the Emperor Frederick II of Hohenstaufen by Bianca, daughter of Count Bonifazio Lancia: that makes him the grandson of the Emperor Henry VI and Constance of Sicily. He was born about 1232, and at his father's death in 1250 he assumed the government of Southern Italy. Unlike Frederick, he was never Emperor of the Holy Roman Empire; but in 1258, at the urgent insistence of his barons, he was crowned King of Sicily at Palermo. Like his father, whose politics he continued, he came into head-on collision with the Papacy, and was excommunicated twice by successive Popes. It was Urban IV who invited Charles of Anjou into Italy to dispossess him, and it was Clement IV who confirmed the invitation and engineered Manfred's destruction; for in February 1266 the invading French defeated the armies of Sicily at the battle of Benevento, and Manfred was killed in the encounter without having made his peace with Rome.

For the poet of the *Comedy*, Manfred is much more than a king who was unmade the year after Dante was made: he is a symbol of an age, a world, a glory that was past. We tend to pay more attention to his stupendous father, and find in him one of the most fascinating figures of medieval times; but Dante gives scant attention to Frederick in his *Comedy* – Farinata in a single line points out his tomb in the Circle of Heretics in Hell (*Inf.* x, 119) – in order to focus our gaze on his tragic son. For although he was not Emperor himself, Manfred was the victim of the imperial–papal conflict that, in Dante's eyes, curdled all Christian charity between temporal and spiritual rulers in thirteenth-century Italy.

Manfred's apparently absurd question to Dante if he had ever seen him before in this life is sometimes explained by the fact that at the time of his death he was about thirty-five, which was Dante's age when they met; and that Manfred, forgetting that he had been wandering beneath the Mountain for thirty-four years, mistakes the poet for a contemporary. My own view is rather different, and I offer it to you here for your consideration.

Lines 109–11 suggest to me that Manfred's question is related to his wounds, and that in this outcast figure we see a reflection of Dante himself. When we come to think of it, there was a remarkable parallel between the political situation in Italy of 1300 and that of 1266; in both cases the Papacy had invited a French Charles into the country to sort out the tangle of the South. Like Manfred, Dante would be the victim of a confederacy between a vindictive Pope and the French invader – that Charles of Valois who 'with the lance of Judas burst the paunch of Florence' (*Purg.* xx, 73–5). Like Manfred, Dante was to suffer sharp reverse at the hands of his enemies and bear for ever the wounds in his heart and head. In effect what Manfred asks is: 'Do you recognise me, Dante? No? Then look at this!' – and holds before his eyes a looking-glass in which the poet sees himself reflected.

There is more in the encounter with the King of Sicily than this, of course, and here I must tread with reverence and caution. Not only is there a Dante-reflection in Manfred but also there is a Christ-echo, however faint. Who was it that was hounded to death by an iniquitous confederacy of the spiritual and temporal rulers of His day? Who bears for ever the marks of His suffering in His glorified body? This world last saw Jesus of Nazareth hanging on a villain's gibbet in seeming weakness and defeat, but Dante is telling us here that we cannot always judge by appearances: the last word rests with God.

Though wounded and slain, a wandering shade who casts no shadow, Manfred still preserves his natural charm and personal beauty: 'biondo era e bello e di gentile aspetto'. Dante's portrait of him is no doubt modelled on the biblical description of King David, who 'was ruddy, and withal of a beautiful countenance, and goodly to look to' (i Samuel 16.12); but it also wakes cultural and social echoes from the Magna Curia. Fair hair carried with it an imperial and poetical cachet in thirteenth-century Sicily, where its actual incidence made it a statistical rarity; yet every woman loved by every poet of the *scuola poetica siciliana* (and indeed for centuries later in Italy) was blonde. I used to think that this could be explained by analogy with the angels, who are always depicted as fair; but I now believe that the explanation is literary. Every age has its archetypal lovers – soon after the publication of *Gone with the Wind* a popular song declared: 'Those famous lovers we'll make them forget / From Adam and Eve to Scarlett and Rhett' – and in the early generations of vernacular love poetry they were Tristan and Isolda. Since she was of Nordic stock, Isolda was a natural blonde; therefore in praising his madonna after the manner of *l'amour courtois* every would-be Tristan approximated her to Isolda, to *Isotta la bionda*, even though she were a native Sicilian and her tresses as black as night.

The one family for whom we have particular evidence was the reigning Hohenstaufen, who, despite the mixture of blood within their veins, were basically Nordic and, like Isolda, fair. Contemporaries remarked on the Emperor Frederick's auburn hair, and Re Enzo's legendary attempt to escape captivity in a barrel was foiled when a tell-tale lock of his golden hair gleamed from an unlucky chink. Manfred bore this mark of distinction also: in that otherwise panmelantrichophorous Kingdom of Sicily he stood out as *biondo*.

The fact that Manfred sprang from such an illustrious father makes line 113 all the more surprising. We should have expected him to say: 'I am Manfred, son' (and he might have added: 'favourite son') 'of the Emperor Frederick the Second'. Instead we hear: 'Io son Manfredi, / nepote di Costanza imperadrice.' It is as though Sir Winston Churchill's late son should announce his presence in the other world with the words: 'I am Randolph, grandson of Jeanette Jerome, the American heiress.' But Dante himself provides a clue to this bypassing of Manfred's father in his *Convivio*, where, treating of the four ages of Man and arguing that shame as 'una paura di disonoranza per fallo commesso' ('a fear of being dishonoured through sin committed') is proper to adolescence, he gives the following example from Statius:

Therefore the same poet says . . . that when Polynices was asked by King Adrastus who he was, he hesitated at first to say, through shame for the sin he had committed against his father, and also because of the sins of Œdipus his father, which seemed to leave their trace in the son's shame; and he did not name his father, but his ancestors and his native city [Thebes] and his mother [Jocasta] (IV, xxv, 10).

Shame attended Manfred's birth, for he was born out of wedlock, and already his father Frederick is in Hell; whereas his grandmother, the Empress Constance, is in Heaven, where Dante will shortly see her in the Moon (*Par.* III, 109–20).

Manfred continues his self-declaration with an account of his repentance *in articulo mortis*:

> 'Poscia ch'io ebbi rotta la persona
> di due punte mortali, io mi rendei,
> piangendo, a quei che volontier perdona.
>   Orribil furon li peccati miei;
> ma la bontà infinita ha sì gran braccia,
> che prende ciò che si rivolge a lei.'   (118–23)

('After I had my body rent by two mortal thrusts, weeping I gave myself up to Him who willingly forgives. My sins were horrible, but the infinite Goodness has arms so wide that He receives whatever turns back to Him.')

Repentance – confession – absolution – pardon – acceptance. Here the 'bontà' that embraces is contrasted with the 'Virtù' that conceals of line 32, just as the 'sorridendo' of line 112 contrasts with the 'piangendo' of this passage: at the point of death, tears of contrition; at the foot of Mount Purgatory, smiles of acceptance.

The fourteenth-century chronicler Giovanni Villani (who began his *Cronica* in 1300, the year of Dante's imagined journey through Hell, Purgatory and Heaven) gives us a detailed description of the circumstances of Manfred's death in battle near Benevento on

Friday, 26 February 1266; but he knows nothing of a last-minute conversion – indeed, how could he or anyone else know of such a thing? Yet Dante, sovereign of the poetic realm he creates, saves Manfred in the teeth of ecclesiastical censure and excommunication. It cannot fail to strike the reader of the *Comedy* how prone its author is to play 'the divinity that shapes our ends, / Rough-hew them how we will'. For Dante's imagination testifies to what no human witness has seen, and to former generations his testimony enhanced his mystique as a poet. He has the key to Francesca's bedroom and to the hunger-tower at Pisa; he follows Ulysses to his overwhelming at the Antipodes, and overhears the wrangle for the soul of Guido da Montefeltro. But of all the tragic deaths re-enacted in the *Comedy* this battle-agony of Manfred is the most dramatic and the most daring. Here is drama within drama: the outward passion of the broken body enshrines the inward passion of the broken spirit.

The *possibility* of Manfred's repentance *in articulo mortis* is not, of course, in dispute. St Augustine speaks somewhere of the suicide finding the 'misericordia Dei inter pontem et fontem', and I have no doubt that many a soul may have experienced the same thing in those vertiginous seconds between Clifton Suspension Bridge and eternity. From the third Gospel we have the example of the penitent thief crucified beside Christ, and William Camden's 'Epitaph for a Man Killed by Falling from his Horse' warns:

> My friend, judge not me,
> Thou seest I judge not thee.
> Betwixt the stirrup and the ground
> Mercy I asked, mercy I found.

But Manfred's battle-field repentance is poetic fiction and not fact, although Novati tells us that there was a legend to this effect which went the rounds in Dante's day. The legend was probably based on an incident that occurred just before Manfred charged into the heat of battle. 'Whilst he was putting on his helmet' – records Villani – 'a silver eagle, which he wore as crest, fell down before him on his saddlebow; and he, seeing this, was much dismayed, and said to the barons who were beside him, in Latin: "*Hoc est signum Dei*, for I fastened this crest with my own hand after such a fashion that it should not have been possible for it to fall" ' (*Cronica* VII, 9).

It is not impossible that this recognition of the hand of God upon him at such a crisis could have led to Manfred's conversion *in extremis*, but Dante seizes upon the possibility from theologico-political motives which, I suspect, were not unmixed. For commentators have seen in *Purgatorio* III the obverse of *Inferno* XXVII: the Pope was powerless to condemn Manfred when God forgave, just as he was powerless to pardon Guido da Montefeltro when God and conscience condemned.

Manfred's repentance and pardon underline the theme of the inscrutability to Man of the sovereignty of God which Dante has stressed in the first part of this canto. Many reformed theologians distinguish between the covenanted and the uncovenanted mercies of God; the covenanted mercies flow through the channels of the Church in terms of absolution, reconciliation and communion; the uncovenanted mercies operate without reference to the Church and solely in accordance with His sovereign will. The Lord says to Moses: 'I will have mercy on whom I will have mercy, and I will have compassion on whom I will have compassion' (Romans 9.15; cf. Exodus 33.19). Dante's Manfred avails himself at the point of violent death of the uncovenanted mercy of 'quei che volontier perdona' – the God who willingly forgives, who freely pardons: and no Pope on earth has power to prevent him.

I have called Manfred one of Dante's heroes, but he by no means glosses over his faults. It is true that in his *De vulgari eloquentia* he writes:

The two illustrious heroes, the Emperor Frederick and his high-born son Manfred, exhibited the nobility and rectitude of their character, while fortune remained faithful to them, in attaching themselves to the higher pursuits of mankind, disdaining what was brutal. Therefore all noble-hearted and gifted men strove to attach themselves to the majesty of such great princes, and thus all that was most excellent in Italian letters made its first appearance at their court (I, xii, 4).

But here Dante makes Manfred confess: 'Orribil furon li peccati miei' – and indeed the King of Sicily had much to repent, if Villani is to be believed, or Manfred's Guelph contemporary, Brunetto Latini.

But whatever his sins, and however horrible, when Manfred turns in repentance he finds the arms of God's infinite goodness wide open to embrace him. Perhaps never in all Dante's *Comedy* does the Christian evangel shine out so clearly and so attractively. 'Him that cometh to Me' – promises Jesus – 'I will in no wise cast out' (John 6.37), and stretched out His arms on the Cross to prove it.

But Manfred's mortal remains were cast out by the Bishop of Cosenza, as his shade tells Dante:

> 'Se 'l pastor di Cosenza, che a la caccia
> di me fu messo per Clemente allora,
> avesse in Dio ben letta questa faccia,
>   l'ossa del corpo mio sarieno ancora
> in co del ponte presso a Benevento,
> sotto la guardia de la grave mora.
>   Or le bagna la pioggia e move il vento
> di fuor dal regno, quasi lungo 'l Verde,
> dov' e' le trasmutò a lume spento.
>   Per lor maladizion sì non si perde,
> che non possa tornar, l'etterno amore,
> mentre che la speranza ha fior del verde.'   (124–35)

('If the shepherd of Cosenza, who was then sent to hunt me by Clement, had read aright this face in God, the bones of my body would still be at the bridge-head near Benevento beneath the guardianship of the heavy cairn. Now the rain soaks them and the wind blows them about outside the kingdom, near the banks of the Verde, where he removed them with lights extinguished. Through their curse souls are not so utterly lost that the eternal love cannot return while hope has left a scrap of green.')

'Illius hominis pestilentis cadaver putridum': Pope Clement IV's words describing all that was left of a dead enemy speak for themselves, and form part of the sorry story of man's inhumanity to man. By contrast Manfred mentions both Pope and bishop – now seen *sub specie aeternitatis* – with noble restraint and Christian charity, and the call for vengeance is eloquently absent from his speech.

Villani's account of what happened to Manfred's corpse is informative but non-committal, and may derive in part from this canto, for it uses the same word, *mora*, for the cairn of stones:

But forasmuch as he was excommunicated, King Charles [of Anjou] would not have him laid in a holy place; but he was buried at the foot of the bridge of Benevento, and upon his grave each soldier of the [French] army threw a stone, so that there arose a great cairn of stones. But by some it was said that afterwards, by command of the Pope, the Bishop of Cosenza had him taken from that sepulchre and sent forth from the kingdom, which was Church land, and he was buried beside the river Verde [Garigliano], on the borders of the kingdom and Campagna; this, however, we do not affirm (*Cronica* VII, 9).

Both Virgil and Manfred have their corpses removed from their place of death – the one in honour, the other in dishonour – the one at the command of the Emperor, the other at the command of the Pope – and both speak poignantly of the removal to an understanding Dante. Virgil is haunted by the memory of that shadow-casting body in which he wrote the immortal work and which was 'tolto' from Brindisi like a chattel. Manfred is no less wistful about his broken body and derelict bones, but it is a wistfulness tinged with hope.

Line 126 is patient of more than one meaning and has been much discussed. Many commentators take 'faccia' to mean the page of a book, and refer it to that text of God's word in which Jesus issues the all-embracing invitation to sinners to come unto Him. I prefer to see in it a reference to the two faces of God – His justice and His love, His vengeance and His mercy. The Pope and bishop who banned that putrefying corpse had read only the one face of God – His inexorable justice towards the excommunicated sinner who dies in contumacy of Holy Church; but Manfred saw the face of everlasting love. His dead body was cast out of the kingdom of Naples, but his undying soul was received into the kingdom of Heaven.

In that inscrutable relationship and interaction between the two faces of God we place our finger on the crux of this canto, and in a Christian context such as this, crux is the operative word – the *Crux Christi* in which the justice and love of God meet and find their consummation. Despite his 'dignitosa coscienza e netta', Virgil the virtuous pagan without faith is shown only the face of God's justice, and is banned from His presence for ever. Manfred the dissolute excommunicate, who lived like a Saracen Sultan but died like a pitiful penitent, sees at the last the face of God's compassion and love, and is received into His presence with joy.

Vividly we see – through Manfred's eyes – Bishop Pignatelli removing his carcase from its burial-place beneath the 'grave mora', dragging it darkly at dead of night beyond the confines of the kingdom, and abandoning it to the elements beside the river Verde. Dante's poetic symbolism is obvious here, for the green waters of the Garigliano speak of hope – and no papal curse can so damn a soul that the eternal love (that other face of God) may not return while hope has left a scrap of green (133–5).

And so it is a message of faith, hope and charity that the shade of Manfred entrusts to Dante. 'When you return to the world of the living' – he commands him in lines 114–17 – 'go to my beautiful daughter [mother of Frederick, King of Sicily, and James, King of Aragon] and tell her the truth [about my repentance, forgiveness, acceptance and hope of glory] if another tale is told.' And of course Dante knew perfectly well that another story of Manfred's end was current when he wrote, which crystallised in the pitiless words of his contemporary Villani: 'Without doubt there came upon Manfred and his heirs the malediction of God, and right clearly was shown the judgment of God upon him because he was excommunicated, and the enemy and persecutor of Holy Church' (*Cronica* VII, 9). For the chronicler also could see only one of the two faces of God.

Christ receives Manfred because He has borne the penalty of his sins, so many and so horrible; but the laws of the kingdom still bind the forgiven sinner as justice excludes him from Purgatory until thirty times the period of his presumption is fulfilled (136–41).

Manfred concludes his speech by naming the daughter to whom he has already alluded (line 115), and the canto ends on a note of mutual care within the family, tuned to that tenderest of ties between a father and his daughter, but not entirely without self-interest, as the last line reveals:

> 'Vedi oggimai se tu mi puoi far lieto,
> revelando a la mia buona Costanza
> come m'hai visto, e anco esto divieto;
> ché qui per quei di là molto s'avanza.' (142–5)

('See now if you can make me glad by disclosing to my good Constance how you have seen me, and also this ban [on my entering Purgatory]; for much headway is made here through [the prayers of] those who are over there [on earth].')

Purgatorio XXIX

*The Procession**

PETER DRONKE

The canto of the procession is not generally much loved. The sensitive commentator Attilio Momigliano, writing in 1946, called it 'one of the poorest in poetry in Dante's entire work';[1] an interpreter in 1967, E. N. Girardi, alluding to Croce's formulation of the dilemma: allegory, or poetry? – writes, 'If Dante's *non-poetry* is not to be found here . . . where ever could one look for it?'[2] The most recent *lectura* of the canto which I have read, that of Paolo Brezzi, tries to mitigate this harsh judgement by suggesting that the canto would have given pleasure to its own age, if not to ours: even if Dante's technique here 'may appear cold and confused to us . . . such poetic procedures [as are seen in Canto XXIX] suited the intellectualistic taste of the Middle Ages, and helped to integrate its most profound religious convictions'.[3]

On the other hand, this canto has for a long time been one of those that have drawn me and fascinated me most in the whole of the *Comedy*. I do not think we need be patronising towards medieval taste; we need not suppose that intellectual or religious uplift would have made a cold and confused piece of poetry seem poetically finer to a medieval sensibility. (One wonders how,

* This essay is an extensive reworking of a *lectura* given in Cambridge on 3 March 1975. It has already appeared under the title 'The Procession in Dante's *Purgatorio*' in *Deutsches Dante-Jahrbuch*, vol. 53/54 (1978–9), pp. 18–45, and is reprinted by kind permission of the Deutsche Dante-Gesellschaft. The text of the article is uncut and unchanged except for minor typographical details in the interests of uniformity, but the editors have been compelled through shortage of space to sacrifice almost two thirds of Mr Dronke's original and most valuable notes. The author has also asked us to point out that his translations, here set as continuous prose, were conceived to match Dante's text line by line.

114

among Dante's friends, for instance, Guido Cavalcanti would have reacted to such a suggestion?)

The problem, rather, has been the general assumption that Dante in this canto uses certain poetic procedures that are 'typically medieval'. One looks for such procedures in the canto (and naturally finds what one is looking for), and then uses the 'typically medieval' as a stick to beat Dante the poet with. Whereas I am convinced that the most important imaginative procedures in this canto were untypical – or better, were taking a known aspect of medieval poetic beyond its previous frontiers. To evoke these procedures swiftly, before beginning a more detailed study, the most illuminating first comparison may be from the sphere of drama. Two plays in particular – one ancient, one modern – seem to me to use an imaginative technique similar to that of Dante in this canto: the *Prometheus Bound* of Aeschylus, and Strindberg's *Dream-Play*. These are dramas in which a succession of encounters with beings in various degrees natural and supernatural, or surreal, can be seen as the manifold projection of a single central conception, that underlies and controls them. In the same way *Purgatorio* XXIX has a single conception underlying and controlling all that passes; and this conception, in my view, is not the procession of the Church or the pageant of Revelation, as is commonly held. It is Dante's reawakening to Beatrice.

If we view the dominant elements in the canto as a pageant or *trionfo*, they will almost inevitably seem artificial and external. I believe we should see them primarily – to put the matter now in medieval terms – as an exceptionally sustained use of 'hidden comparison' (*collatio occulta*): a foreshadowing of, and symbolic equivalent to, the process by which Dante regains full cognizance of his beloved, and of all the personal and visionary understanding she reveals to him. The poetic principle of *collatio occulta* was defined by the finest of the thirteenth-century theorists, Geoffrey of Vinsauf, as 'a new, wondrously ingrafted transplantation, where something assumes its place so surely in the design as if it were born of the theme itself – yet it is taken from elsewhere, though it seems to be from there . . .' (*Poetria Nova*, 247–53). And it is clear that much of Dante's imagery in this canto is 'taken from elsewhere' (from Ezekiel and from St John's Apocalypse, for instance, as Dante himself notes in lines 100–5). But what we must observe is the nature of Dante's 'new, wondrously ingrafted transplantation' – a possibility of which not only Aeschylus and Strindberg were aware, but which constituted, critically and creatively, one of the most sensitive insights of Dante's age.

Canto XXIX begins with the music of the earthly paradise: Matelda is still nearby, though on the farther shore of the stream Lethe, her beauty, as sensual as it is innocent, subsuming and crowning the beauty of the place. The two ancient poets, Virgil and Statius, are still present close behind Dante, though Dante is so engrossed in Matelda and her realm that for the most part he is scarcely aware of them: only once does he briefly turn back to Virgil, in the hope of having a marvel explained to him – a hope that is left unfulfilled, as Virgil too stands amazed.

Matelda had closed the previous canto with her beautiful, profound explanation of how the earthly paradise is an inherent human longing, that may feature in the dreams of poets who knew nothing of the Judaeo-Christian account of the Fall;[4] now she sings a verse, 'Blessed are they whose sins pardon has covered' (*Beati . . . quorum tecta sunt peccata* – words drawn from the opening of Psalm 32), evoking not uncorrupted innocence but rather, paradise regained. Her song prefigures the pardon that in their different ways both Dante and Statius will receive before *Purgatorio* closes: Statius as a soul purified and redeemed, Dante as destined to have his visionary foretaste of paradise in Beatrice's company. Both poets' sins will be 'covered' in another sense, too – submerged in the waters of the stream of forgetfulness.

While Matelda gives this hint of what is to come, she herself remains the incarnation of an Arcadia that knows nothing of sin and has no need of pardon. The words 'Cantando come . . . innamorata' in the opening line, and 'givan sole' in the fourth, deliberately echo phrases in a *pastourelle* of Dante's 'primo amico', Guido Cavalcanti, a lyric which had conjured up a fantasy of graceful, uncomplicated sensual bliss; already in the previous canto Dante had linked the language of this song with Matelda.

But when Dante and Matelda, walking delicately in unison, though still held apart by the stream, come to face eastwards, we sense that the Arcadian landscape is about to be transfigured. Matelda's urgent admonition to Dante (15), 'Frate mio, guarda e ascolta', with its forceful use of caesura, marks the change of

consciousness. Facing the East ('levante': 12) has symbolic connotations – it is the region of heaven in which the divine first reveals
itself ('Look at the rising sun, there God doth live!'); it also holds
the apocalyptic associations of an imminent judgement: 'For as
lightning comes forth from the East, and appears as far as the
West, thus will be the coming of the Son of Man' (Matthew
24.27). And lightning is indeed the first impression that passes
through Dante's mind at the beginning of the revelation he now
experiences. Yet it is no isolated flash, but an intensifying
radiance, conjoined with a gentle melody: the synaesthesia here
prefigures that of *Paradiso* XIV, where the luminous cross in the
heaven of Mars shows Christ lightening in that dawn ('in
quell'albor balenar Cristo'), and at the same time 'from the lights
that there appeared to me / a melody . . . was forming, / that made
me rapt' ('da' lumi che lì m'apparinno / s'accogliea . . . una melode
/ che mi rapiva . . ': 108 and 121–3).

Here too the beauty of light and sound is joyful and captivating.
The sudden excess of light causes Dante no fear, as we might have
supposed. Yet the sense of hesitancy revealed in his wondering
thought – is it lightning? – is also important for what follows:
from the spell of idyllic certitude in the earthly paradise he is
moving into uncertainties again. He will experience illusion and
hallucination and varying degrees of clarity of vision – all these
are aspects of the dreamlike foreshadowing of the momentous
event, the confrontation with Beatrice. Throughout this foreshadowing, we can observe Dante's intense striving for descriptive
accuracy: he wishes to show all the nuances of perception in his
visual and visionary experience, and will use not only natural
imagery but philosophical terms, theological references and mythical allusions to achieve this end.

This use of varied techniques to achieve a perceptual complexity
is one of the distinctive aspects of Dante's art in this canto.
Umberto Bosco, in a *lectura* of it that contains many sensitive
insights,[5] compared the vision Dante here conjures up with the
mosaics of Sant'Apollinare Nuovo at Ravenna, which Dante
could indeed have contemplated. Yet how far these mosaics are
from Dante's evocative diversity. At Sant'Apollinare all is hieratic
and still, the figures set against an unvarying background of gold;
there is no sense of illusions, of indistinct forms that gradually

become clearer, of a dark forest sky filled with flame-tinted streaks and an intense moonlike radiance, nor of contrasting motions, the slow majesty of Dante's chariot and procession set against the dancing nymphs that circle it; least of all can Sant' Apollinare's limpid solemnity suggest the phantasmagoria of Dante's vision. Visually, we might say, the effects of light and the hallucinating quality of the whole are closest to El Greco; the surreal forms in Dante look forward in painting to Hieronymus Bosch; the incandescent spirits, to Grünewald. It seems to me unlikely that any painting Dante could have seen would have suggested quite this conjunction of qualities to him.

The resplendence and harmony stir in Dante an impulse of resentment at the shameless disobedience of Eve: but for Eve's self-will and refusal to be loyal ('divota': 28), would not he, Dante, like the rest of mankind, have had lifelong possession of these wondrous delights from the moment of birth? While it is possible to adduce not only misogynistic poets but authoritative theologians, such as Augustine and Aquinas, who argued that Eve's blame in the Fall was greater than Adam's – that is, this could be a perfectly serious and tenable view in Dante's time – I cannot help feeling that, in its dramatic context in the *Purgatorio*, Dante's 'zelo' concerning Eve comes a little strangely at this moment, and that it may be 'good' ('buon') in the sense of 'abundant' rather than of 'morally admirable'. Does not Dante's zealous reproach of Eve come to appear in a somewhat different light in the next canto, when Beatrice reproaches Dante: Dante who has failed to be 'divoto' to her, straying from the heavenly ideal that she, a woman, embodies – Dante who has come to the brink of losing heaven for himself? Was it really a good moment for indulging in righteousness – however genuinely felt – at a woman's expense?

With the first of the synaesthetic changes – the lightning turn-ing into fire-suffused air, the melody into songs (though the words are still not distinguishable) – Dante pauses to invoke the Muses (37ff.). It is one of a number of such prayers for renewed poetic inspiration in the course of the *Comedy*, and perhaps these demand a special kind of empathy today. When we know so much poetry where such an invocation is little more than a topos or an ornamental flourish, it needs a particular attentiveness to recall here the sheer wretchedness of existence that Dante endured for so long for the sake of his inspiration, for the sake of completing his *Comedy*, and to sense that at moments like these he is most intensely conscious of the difficulty, urgency, or grandeur of what he must next try to express.

What, then, does this exhilarating light and music become? It turns into the surreal procession of a heavenly host, culminating in the appearance of Beatrice. Yet in an important sense the entire procession constitutes the epiphany of Beatrice, she whose coming is identified with that of the heavenly Bride in the Song of Songs, 'beautiful as the moon, peerless as the sun, and terrible as a host with its panoply of banners'. Scholars often call it a pageant of Revelation, and in a sense this is not inept; but only if it is remembered that Revelation came to Dante in a unique way – in the form of the beloved woman who was his *revelatrix*, his hope of love, of inspiration, and of heaven, but also the summation of his religious and political ideals: the finest aspect of his earthly consciousness, and the terrible self-judgement of falling short of his ideals that this entailed.

Now to turn to the procession in some detail. Its general symbolism, wrote Bosco, is extremely simple: 'la simbologia generale . . . è semplicissima' (p. 1259). Starting from the fact that certain elements can be traced back to St John and to Ezekiel – seven candelabras, twenty-four elders, four living creatures – Dante's commentators have, with remarkable unanimity, attributed precise emblematic significance to the other aspects of the procession also. The chariot, we are told, is the Church; its two wheels are the Old Testament and the New Testament; the gryphon that draws it along is Christ; the three girls dancing at its right wheel are Faith, who is white, Hope, who is green, and Charity, flame-coloured.

Yet if we look more closely, we see there are considerable difficulties in the assumption that Dante was here simply making his verse a vehicle for traditional theological emblematics. Admittedly it was one of the chief concerns of the early commentators on Dante to give his work didactic respectability, to show by means of allegorical exegesis that it contained a wealth of profoundly edifying doctrine – but did they truly by this method reach the centre of Dante's poetic intent? Is this unanimity about emblematic meanings not a little artificial, and often achieved by ignoring those aspects of the poetry that do not fit? That Dante means the four living creatures of Ezekiel and John, it would be foolish to deny; but where in the tradition are these creatures ever crowned with fronds of green ('coronate ciascun di verde fronda': 93), and where before Dante are their eyes compared with those of the pagan mythical Argus (95–6)? If the chariot were the Church, would it have quite so many pagan associations? – Dante compares it with the chariots for Scipio's triumph and that of Caesar Augustus, and, more pessimistically, with the doomed chariot driven by Phaethon, which was destroyed and burnt. In Canto XXXII Dante's chariot is broken up by a dragon and is itself transformed into a monster, in Canto XXXIII Beatrice says: 'it was, and is no more' ('fu e non è': 35). On the traditional interpretation, this could only mean that for Dante the Church, which Christ had promised to protect even to the consummation of the world, had ceased to exist – could he really, at this moment in his poem, have come so close to saying: 'God is dead'?

As for the chariot's two wheels – while most scholars have seen them as signifying the two Testaments, others, as Sapegno notes in his commentary, have plumped for the active and the contemplative life, others again for wisdom and charity, still others, for love of God and love of one's neighbour. If Dante had intended any one of these emblematic significances, would he not have made his meaning clear? If this was what mattered to him poetically about the chariot-wheels, were his powers of expression so inadequate that he would have left us in confusion?

When one turns to the gryphon, the scholars are so unanimous about its being an emblem of Christ that for many years I assumed this must be a traditional Christian usage – like the eagle for St John, or the dove for the Holy Ghost – but one which I had strangely failed to observe. After long and strenuous gryphon-hunting, however, I must fully confirm the negative conclusion of Dr Colin Hardie:[6] there is no single instance in Christian tradition of a gryphon associated with Christ before Dante – or rather, before Dante's commentators. Various well-known modern Dante commentaries, and an impressive new encyclopaedia of Christian iconography, claim that the gryphon as Christ can be found in Isidore of Seville; even a spurious chapter reference is often given for this erroneous assertion. It is an heirloom that several generations of scholars have handed down one to another – a tissue of a fabrication as priceless as the Emperor's clothes.[7]

Even such an apparently innocuous identification as of three maidens with Faith, Hope and Charity raises problems if it is scrutinised. Why, in Canto XXXI (line 106), should these maidens be both nymphs and stars in the sky? Why (XXIX, 127–8) should the green nymph, if she is Hope, never be allowed to lead the dance, as her two companions do? Some scholars answer, because Hope belongs to the future – that is, she isn't really there at all. And yet, if any of the three virtues could be seen as leading into the future – as leading the dance, in Dante's image – would it not have to be Hope? And why, if Dante simply wanted an image for a virtue, should he give this nymph a magical-macabre aspect – 'as if her flesh and bones / had all been made of emerald'?

Once more, I do not wish to deny that Dante was aware of the connotations of theological virtues which the colours of his three nymphs could have. But I believe these connotations were not central to his purpose in using this imagery, and also, that Dante had the poetic tact to avoid emblematic meanings here, because he would indeed have sensed to what absurdities a total explicit *allegorêsis* could lead. In the imagery of the procession, in short, nothing is simple, because the images take on a life of their own in the contexture of Dante's vision. Their primary purpose is imaginative: it lies in their significant interrelations with all the other aspects of the vision that unfolds from here to the end of *Purgatorio*, and they exist in the poem for their contributions to that entire vision, that sustained *collatio occulta* by which Dante evokes not only his private emotions and aspirations but also his public ones. Clearly Dante in his *collatio occulta* is relying on and playing on a vast range of inherited associations, biblical, classical, Christian–allegorical. At the same time, he himself in this canto stresses that these are secondary to his individual imaginative structure: having succinctly mentioned the characteristics of the four living creatures, he adds:

> A descriver lor forme più non spargo
> rime, lettor; ch'altra spesa mi strigne,
> tanto ch'a questa non posso esser largo;

> ma leggi Ezechïel, che li dipigne
> come li vide da la fredda parte
> venir con vento e con nube e con igne;
> e quali i troverai ne le sue carte,
> tali eran quivi, salvo ch'a le penne
> Giovanni è meco e da lui si diparte.   (97–105)

(Reader, I shall not squander further rhymes to describe their shapes, for other expense compels me so much that I cannot be spendthrift in this; but read Ezekiel, who depicts those creatures as he saw them coming from the region of cold, coming with tempest and with cloud and fire; as you will find them in his writings, such were they here, except that for the wings John is of my view and diverges from him.)

That Dante should take up three terzinas in this way is not lengthy pedantry, as some commentators have complained; one might almost say, it is Dante's ironic look at the kind of pedantry that his future commentators would perpetrate – an irony pointed by Dante's light triple wordplay on the poet's way of spending. If iconology is uppermost in your concern, he is saying, then why not go to the appropriate sources for it? He is not competing with these – he is assuming them, insofar as he needs them. And he needs them here not for their own sake, but for his 'new, wondrously ingrafted transplantation'.

The reason that many of the things Dante now evokes are 'obdurate to thought' ('forti cose a pensar': 42) is partly their perceptual complexity, as shapes and sounds continually transform themselves in dreamlike alterations, partly the width of their spectrum of meaning, ranging from universally accepted significations – seen in a perspective that gives them individual nuances in Dante's vision – to evocative symbols that retain something indefinable and enigmatic to the end.

The first of Dante's images – the seven trees of gold (43) – is visually and psychologically complex, but also exploits inherited mystical complexities from St John's Apocalypse, whence it derives. The trees of gold are a sensory illusion – Dante explains this in precise Aristotelian terms, to which he had already alluded in his *Convivio*: illusion of this kind is possible in such matters as 'shape, size, number, motion, and rest – which are called common sense-objects, that we comprehend with more than one sense' (III, ix, 6). So here, as the distance diminishes, the faculty of perception is able to synthesise the sense-impressions in such a way as to give reason a basis for correct judgement: the gold trees are then recognised to be candelabras, the indistinct singing that had from the start been linked with the luminous vision is understood as *Hosanna*, the Hebrew call which the medieval West knew to mean *salva, quaesumus* ('save, we beseech!'), the call with which the crowds in Jerusalem had greeted Christ at his entry.

This image of light and sound, which had begun to impinge on Dante's consciousness in line 16 of the canto, would seem to have at last been clarified; yet this is by no means the last of its modulations. After marvelling at the serenity of its flaming, like a full moon in the nocturnal sky (54), and seeing that Virgil shares his own stupefaction and has no explanation to offer, Dante seems to perceive it in a gentle, for a moment almost humorous, way. That the vast candelabras are moving towards him of their own accord is magical and astounding, yet strangely not frightening: their motion is so slow that what comes to Dante's mind is human brides, perhaps dawdling, bemused and absorbed, as they emerge from church in a wedding-procession. A little later (73) he notes the effect of their advance: they have left the sky behind them painted in woven bands, the colours of the rainbow or of the lunar halo, as if the vertical stem of each of the walking candlesticks had been the stem of a paintbrush, held upright by an invisible artist, the bristles sweeping across the sky in their wake as they moved:

> e vidi le fiammelle andar davante,
> lasciando dietro a sé l'aere dipinto,
> e di tratti pennelli avean sembiante;
> sì che lì sopra rimanea distinto
> di sette liste, tutte in quei colori
> onde fa l'arco il Sole e Delia il cinto. (73–8)

(and I saw little flames moving forward, leaving the air flame-tinted in their wake – they seemed painter's brushes drawn across so that the air above remained emblazoned with seven bands, all in the colours of which Sun makes his bow and Delia her girdle.)

There is an intriguing minor problem in lines 77–8. Did each of these seven 'liste' show one colour, or several? We who are familiar with Newton's division of the rainbow into seven bands of colour might naturally assume that each of Dante's bands displayed one colour of the rainbow; but while there are many diverse accounts of the rainbow's colours in the Middle Ages, no one before Newton specifies as many colours as seven – though, interestingly enough, a twelfth-century manual for artists (Theophilus, *De diversis artibus* I, xvi) says that to imitate a rainbow in painting you need seven colour-*combinations*. This, however, is a unique and isolated testimony, if one can judge by what survives. (Perhaps artists looked more closely than philosophers or scientists, but seldom wrote about what they saw.) At all events, if we assume that Dante meant each of the seven bands to have one rainbow-colour – and certainly at least one of his fourteenth-century commentators thought this was what he had meant – it implies that his intuitive vision here anticipates Newton's scientific analysis.

The final visual modulation of the image follows with line 79: now that the candelabras have left their flame-painting in the sky, they are like shafts of standards ('ostendali'), and the flames are the gonfalons flying from those shafts; they have become the insignia of a host from heaven, a heaven so beautiful that Dante, with a self-conscious aside (82), admits he is half-enamoured of his own description.

Yet a little earlier Matelda had reproached Dante for his too-exclusive engrossment in the beauty of those candelabras:

> 'Perché pur ardi
> sì ne l'aspetto de le vive luci,
> e ciò che vien di retro a lor non guardi?'   (61–3)

('Why so ardent to see the spectacle of living lights – and yet you don't see what comes after them?')[8]

The function of those lights was to be heralds: to herald the blessed company, and above all to herald Beatrice, the integration and summit of all that is glimpsed partially in them. The cry *Hosanna*, that now follows, likewise heralds Beatrice: it is the very cry that the angels had used in Dante's vision of the death of Beatrice in the *Vita Nuova* (XXIII, 7). Here we must reckon with the total seriousness of Dante's sense that Beatrice was the bearer of divine revelation to him – that is why to Dante there is nothing playful, let alone sacrilegious, in such a transference of the invocation from Christ to his own beloved, any more than there was in the *Vita Nuova* in associating Beatrice's death with portents that echo the death of Christ: the darkening of sun, and immense earthquakes (*VN* XXIII, 5). That the *Hosanna* here as in the *Vita Nuova* is destined for Beatrice is, I believe, made certain in that, in the same chapter of the earlier work, Dante's faltering attempt to say the words 'Oh Beatrice, blessed be you' ('O Beatrice, benedetta sie tu') is deliberately echoed and fulfilled in line 85 of this canto, when the entire blessed host greets Beatrice, '*Benedicta* tue . . .' That it is she who is being acclaimed, however, is deliberately not spelt out at these moments in Canto XXIX, which retain their sense of mystery. At first we may well wonder, is it Mary for whom all this is meant? The Song of Songs had expressed just such a state of wonderment: 'Who is she who is descending, in her radiant whiteness?' (a line Cavalcanti had echoed at the opening of his love-sonnet 'Chi è questa che vèn'). Only in Canto XXX does Dante show the acclamations converging in Beatrice.

A glance at Dante's prophetic, apocalyptic inheritance will indicate something of what he relies on and presupposes in this part of his vision. John, in his trance on the island of Patmos, was commanded to write what he beheld and to send it to seven churches; he looked to see what voice was commanding him, and turning saw seven golden candelabras ('septem candelabra aurea'), and in the midst of them one like to the Son of Man; his hair was like snow ('tamquam nix'), his eyes like the flame of fire ('velut flamma ignis'); in his right hand he held seven stars; from his mouth came a sword sharp ('acutus') on both sides; his face was like the sun shining in all its strength (Revelation 1.12–16). John gazed on him with mortal fear, but the figure calmed him and continued his message: he told that the seven stars are the angels of seven churches, and the seven gold candelabras, the churches themselves, or (according to some interpreters) the tutelary spirits of these. Each church is then rebuked for its corruption, and its future is envisaged with threats and with promises of celestial help and grace. In the fourth chapter, John's vision continues: he now sees one seated on a throne in heaven, with a rainbow encompassing the throne, like a vision of emerald ('similis visioni smaragdinae'). On twenty-four other thrones are seated the twenty-four elders, robed in white, but with crowns of gold – not lilygarlands – on their heads. From the central throne come lightnings, and voices, and thunder; and seven lamps burn before the throne, which are the seven spirits of God. Also around the throne are the four living creatures ('animalia'), each with six wings, and these wings full of eyes. Both the creatures and the elders ceaselessly adore and blazon the glory of the divine figure on the central throne.

Clearly Dante relied also on some details of Ezekiel's vision, on which John's had been modelled; yet imaginatively John was more vital to him here, as Dante himself notes ('Giovanni è meco': 105). What is poetically important is that his sources, John and Ezekiel, showed Dante that this vein of macabre and resplendent imagery could be worked in two ways which were not exclusive: it could relate to both the spiritual experiences of the visionary and the spiritual future he dreamed for the world around him; the biblical imagery had been used to illuminate microcosm and macrocosm together. In portraying the individual fears and hopes of the prophet, it evoked his general fears and hopes for mankind; for if his particular vision was true and God-given, then it was universally valid too.

Thus the seven gold candelabras can convey a meaning that relates to the inner experience of Dante the individual – they are the first heralds of Beatrice for him – and, radiating from that meaning, they can evoke his wider aspirations for Church and world, thereby recalling John's seven spirits of God and seven churches; thereby linking also with the seven stars of John's vision: the seven angelic stars, which Dante sees as seven nymphs in his procession – he makes this remarkable identity of stars and nymphs explicit in Canto XXXI, where at the same time he calls them the seven handmaidens of Beatrice (106–8). But these heptads of divine spirits, manifest in the candelabras and the star-nymphs, must also, I believe, relate in Dante's imagination to another heptad near the close of the *Purgatorio*, a nightmarish, demonic counterpart: for it is seven monstrous heads – divided, like the nymphs, into a group of three and a group of four – which Dante's chariot sprouts after it has been attacked (XXXII, 142–7).

The way in which the blessed company that follows the candelabras both proclaims and prefigures the epiphany of Beatrice can be seen especially in its ductile colour-symbolism, that captivates perception. The twenty-four elders advance 'garlanded with lilies' ('coronati venien di fiordaliso': 84) – unlike their gold-crowned prototypes in the Apocalypse. So, too, the four living creatures in Dante are 'each one garlanded with fronds of green', (93) – again an unbiblical trait. The final company, which incidentally is yet a third heptad of blessed spirits, is described as follows:

> E questi sette col primaio stuolo
> erano abitüati, ma di gigli
> dintorno al capo non facëan brolo,
>   anzi di rose e d'altri fior vermigli;
> giurato avria poco lontano aspetto
> che tutti ardesser di sopra da' cigli.   (145–50)

(These seven were robed in the same way as the first company, yet not with lilies had they fashioned the garland for their heads – rather, with roses and other crimson flowers. Looking from a brief distance, one would have sworn that, above their eyebrows, they were all aflame.)

Lilies, fronds of green, flowers crimson with a flamelike intensity: this triad of colours appears a second time in this canto in the bodies of three of the nymphs:

> . . .l'una tanto rossa
> ch'a pena fora dentro al foco nota;
>   l'altr' era come se le carni e l'ossa
> fossero state di smeraldo fatte;
> la terza parea neve testé mossa.   (122–6)

(. . .one, of so fierce a red, she would scarcely have been noticed in the flame; another was as if her flesh and bones had all been made of emerald; the third appeared to be new-fallen snow.)

And it is precisely this colour-triad that appears for the third time, consummated in the moment Beatrice herself is seen in the next canto:

> sovra candido vel cinta d'uliva
> donna m'apparve, sotto verde manto
> vestita di color di fiamma viva.   (xxx, 31–3)

(a lady appeared to me, garlanded with olive over her radiant-white veil, clothed beneath her green mantle with the colour of living flame.)

In other words, what Dante glimpses partially and in a frag-mented sequence in the course of Canto XXIX, he perceives unified in the presence of his beloved. The final triad, I would suggest, also makes of the colour symbolism a triple triad, a three times three, which – already in the *Vita Nuova* – constituted Beatrice's mystic number:

This number [nine] was she herself; I say it by way of a likeness, and intend it thus. The number three is the root of nine . . . as we manifestly see that three times three makes nine. So if the three is of its own accord maker of the nine, and the maker of miracles is of his own accord three – Father, and Son, and Holy Spirit . . . then she was a nine – that is, a miracle – whose root is uniquely the wondrous Trinity (*VN* xxix, 3).

What are the associations of the three colours? The traditional link that the commentators make with faith, hope and charity is clearly present, for one aspect of these dancing *donne* is the embodying of virtues: we notice this especially, for instance, at line 132, when one of the second group of *donne* is swiftly identified emblematically: she who has three eyes in her head can be no other than Prudence, the virtue that sees past, present and future. Here for a moment the meaning fully coincides with the emblem, though Dante is also aware of, and relies on, the poetic congruence of this three-eyed woman with the range of phantas-magoric beings engendered by Ezekiel and John. The almost perfunctory swiftness with which Dante alludes to the three-eyed emblem, however, should indicate that the more pervasive and subtle colour symbolism I have sketched is likely to be of a different imaginative order, that it will not be reducible to a simple emblematic aspect but will be rich in associations.

I should like to suggest at least two ranges of association that may be relevant here. One is in the colour symbolism for angels set down by pseudo-Dionysius: 'One must think, if they are white, that they are images of light, if red, images of fire' (light and fire were for Dionysius the most 'deiform' of all symbols); 'if green, then they are images of youth and of the flower of the soul'.[9] But must we not also, in Dante's use of these colours, recall the apocalyptic context in John, where they evoke key qualities in his vision: the one who is like the Son of Man is also like snow, and like the flame of fire; around the throne, it is like a vision of emerald. Is it not this 'visio smaragdina' that in Canto xxxi finds its echo in the 'smeraldi' (116), the emeralds, of Beatrice's eyes?

To return briefly to the twenty-four elders (xxix, 83): it has often been pointed out that they embody revelation in a particular way in this canto: that is, Dante conceives of them here as living books; each of the twenty-four is one of the books of the Old Testament. So, too, each of the four living creatures is the embodiment of a Gospel, rather than of an evangelist; and the final group of seven would show forth the remaining books of the New Testament: the Acts ascribed to Luke, who, known as a doctor, becomes Dante's old follower of Hippocrates (136–7); the Epistles of Paul embodied in the fierce figure who here – as in the iconographic tradition – carries the sword of the spirit; the four of lowly aspect, the minor Epistles of Peter, John, James and Jude; and at last the 'old man alone, coming, asleep, with piercing aspect', a particularly vivid incarnation of the Apocalypse. Numerous other candidates were proposed for these last seven figures, especially by the fourteenth- and fifteenth-century commentators on Dante; but the identification with 'living books' seems the most satisfying, as far as it goes. Yet I would stress 'as far as it goes': the very fact that in the century after Dante's death there could be disagreements about the precise significations should once more warn us that finding these is not equivalent to comprehending Dante's poetic intentions. (If it were, we should have to say Dante was at fault, for not having made himself clearer.) The exact identification of each member of this blessed host is a minor enigma, to delight such minds as are attracted by it; Dante's central poetic purpose is the orientation of the entire host towards Beatrice. Every element of revelation, first seen here part by part and successively, foreshadows and declares Beatrice: she who manifests revelation for Dante integrates and fulfils all the elements first beheld in this canto 'per speculum in enigmate'. Thus at line 85, the first poetic climax in the canto, the role of the elders is to be Beatrice's paladins, singing '*Benedicta* tue. . .': 'Blessed are you among Adam's daughters, and blessed be your beauty, unto eternity!'

It is Dante's individual transformation, for his beloved, of the angel's greeting to Mary: 'Blessed are you among women' ('Benedicta tu in mulieribus': Luke 1. 28) – the use of Latin amid the Italian, here as in the *Vita Nuova*, lending a hieratic, oracular quality to the words. In the next canto, one of these elders is indeed called a heavenly herald ('messo dal ciel'): he addresses

Beatrice as the heroine of the Song of Songs, again in Latin: 'Veni, sponsa de Libano!', 'Come, bride of Lebanon!' And it is with Latin words that all the rest take up his call: 'Benedictus qui venis', 'Blessed are you who come!' Here Dante by his choice of Latin text is able to achieve a unique poetic effect: by retaining the masculine forms of his original – the greeting to Christ as he triumphantly entered Jerusalem – he can superimpose the new moment on the old, make us momentarily see Beatrice's triumph as re-enacting that of Christ.

Again, there is nothing sacrilegious in these symbolic associations of Mary, of the heavenly Bride, or of Christ. Such connotations, which Dante affirms of his own beloved, can be valid for any one of the blessed souls in heaven. This is beautifully expressed – to give one instance among many – by the fourteenth-century English poet who composed *Pearl*, whose account and dramatic unfolding of this paradox were I believe inspired partly by Dante:

> The court of the kyndom of God alyue
> Hatz a property in hytself beyng:
> Alle that may therinne aryue
> Of all the reme is quen other kyng.   (445–8)

> The court of the kingdom of God alive
> has a property of its own being:
> each one who may therein arrive
> of all the realm is queen or king.

The human figure, the lost daughter whom the *Pearl* poet loves, becomes a celestial *revelatrix* for him, as Beatrice does for Dante. For both works, however, I would stress that poetically this transformation is achieved by investing the heroine with symbolic splendours, not by a use of equivalences such as allegory or emblem would demand. Thus Dante sees Beatrice as blessed among women, and as the beloved heavenly *Sponsa*; he also sees her as judging him and redeeming him; yet this is not the same as saying that Beatrice *stands for* the Church, or Theology, or for Christ. The danger of such formulations is that they may obscure the far more individual and imaginatively fecund situation that here prevails: it is as a woman, as Dante's beautiful beloved, whose womanly presence leaves Dante deathly-pale with awe and fear, that Beatrice reveals the meaning of judgement and redemption to her lover.

After the elders, and in the midst of the living creatures, Dante beholds:

> . . .un carro, in su due rote, trïunfale,
> ch'al collo d'un grifon tirato venne. (107–8)

(. . .borne upon two wheels, a triumphal chariot, which came drawn at the neck of a gryphon.)

Here more than ever I am convinced understanding depends on sensitiveness to poetic suggestion, and not on adopting a simple emblematic identification. If we recall what happens to the gryphon and the chariot in the following cantos, then on the traditional scholarly view that the gryphon is Christ and the chariot is the Church, the narrative movement would have to be described along these lines. In Canto XXIX Christ descends from heaven to the earthly paradise, in order to pull his chariot, his Church, which (Canto XXX) is crowned by the presence of Beatrice. Then (Canto XXXI) Christ, after performing some optical illusions for Dante and Beatrice, and after being commended for not tearing at the tree of Adam (Canto XXXII), ascends again, leaving his Church behind to be guarded by Beatrice. Beatrice guards it so unsuccessfully that it is annihilated by wild creatures and monsters – so that she at last has to say of the Church (XXXIII, 35): 'it was, and is no more'. This is how the account would have to proceed if one took the traditional allegorical meaning seriously and consistently through Dante's vision. Yet is this not to reduce the haunting poetic enigmas to a farrago of absurdities?

I have no doubt that, when Dante speaks of the gryphon as 'the wild animal that is one person only in two natures' (XXXI, 80–1), he is aware of the Christological overtones of his phrase, and is deliberately exploiting them. But that is a very different matter from saying, the gryphon is Christ. So, too, in a letter Dante attacks the cardinals of Italy as 'false Phaethons, who have failed to steer the chariot of the Bride along the clear orbit of Christ crucified' (*Epist.* XI, 6); clearly his 'carro' in the *Purgatorio* can have connotations of the Church as well. But the combined image – a monster, half-eagle, half-lion, drawing a chariot that is tied to its

131

neck – does *not* at once conjure up Christ guiding his Church, and certainly had never done so for anyone up to Dante's time. This strongly suggests that the principal connotations must lie elsewhere.

Dante, like most medieval poets and intellectuals, was familiar with a range of celestial journeys. That of Alexander the Great, whose ascent into heaven was precisely in a chariot drawn by gryphons, must be among the most relevant imaginatively; the interpretation of his ascent, however, was ambiguous: it was seen by some as unholy hubris, by others as an effort at holy contemplation. In the biblical account of Elijah, the awesome holiness of the prophet's ascent is left in no doubt: 'Suddenly there was a blazing chariot, drawn by a pair of blazing horses; and Elijah ascended through the whirlwind into heaven; but Elisha watched and shouted: "My father, my father: Israel's chariot, and her charioteer!" ' (II Kings 2.11–12).

Besides images of ascent, such as Alexander's and Elijah's, Dante would have recalled certain images of return: the chariot which, in a famous Platonic image of Boethius, is the vehicle by which a soul is brought down from the world of the stars to a mortal body (*Consolatio philosophiae* III, m. 9, 18–20); and above all the journey in the twelfth-century Latin epic *Anticlaudianus*, undertaken by Prudentia, the highest power of the human mind, in a chariot drawn by five horses (the senses), to win from heaven the idea of a new and perfect human being, an idea she will bring back to the earthly paradise, and realise in such a way as to renew the face of the earth. In the *Anticlaudianus* as in Dante, we have the sense of a symbolic event that is at the same microcosmic and macrocosmic.

In *Purgatorio* XXIX, both the chariot and the monster drawing it are of great splendour. The gryphon's wings pierce the heavens, but gently, leaving the rainbow streamers, the manifestations of the blessed candelabras, intact. The colours of the gryphon's body have connotations of the Lover of the Bride in the Song of Songs – 'my beloved, red and white, peerless among thousands, his head the choicest gold' (5.10–11). The chariot, too, is magnificent – it suggests the glory of ancient Rome, a glory for which Dante had deep feeling, though there is also a hint of the doom that will befall it in the allusions to the chariot of the Sun.

To try to comprehend the chariot and gryphon more fully, I would start from my earlier assumption that, as in the visions of Ezekiel and John, inner and outer meanings complement each other, that an outer range of meaning radiates from the inner: here one might say, that the political and theological reverberations of meaning, especially in Cantos XXXII and XXXIII, are rendered possible by a substrate of personal meaning, especially in the three preceding ones. Gryphon and chariot relate fundamentally to the concerns of the protagonists, Dante and Beatrice, and *thereby* to the concerns of mankind.

Thus I would see the symbolically rich meanings of the chariot beginning from a microcosm: the chariot, as in Boethius, the vehicle for a soul – in the first place for Dante's soul, which is crowned by Beatrice. By means of this chariot his soul can travel heavenward and back to earth again. And yet in the nightmarish vision of Canto XXXII Dante sees that wondrous vehicle being degraded and ruined – until Beatrice, who had tried in vain to guard it, and had lamented its ravagings, has to declare it utterly destroyed. Is this not an objective correlative for terrifying inner experiences of Dante's, and must it not relate essentially to the harsh judgement that Beatrice pronounces over him? And when he has been renewed in the stream Eunoe, and is ready to mount to the stars, in the last lines of the *Purgatorio*, does the wording not suggest he has acquired a new vehicle of flight for his heavenward ascent – namely, the presence of his beloved?

What is it that draws the chariot of the soul? If we were envisaging myth-making of the Platonic kind, the answer might well be: a *daimôn*. This could be a deliberately ambiguous answer, for a *daimôn* can have both 'demonic' attributes and divine ones. It is a hybrid, like the gryphon. How shall we imagine this particular *daimôn*, then? Proud, and superb, and wrathful as a lion, perhaps; keen and soaring as an eagle. Yet Dante's language also consciously evokes the divine aspect – one person in two natures, the red and white and gold of the Lover in the Song of Songs – just as Socrates had evoked it, when he characterised the *daimôn* as 'the god himself, who speaks within us', or Plotinus, who described it as 'the soul at its divinest'. What I would suggest, in a word, is that the gryphon here is the *daimôn* of Dante Alighieri.

It is only along such lines, I believe, that we can begin to

133

account for the enigmatic range of language used of the gryphon: for the use of divine and Song of Songs language – it is by virtue of what is divinest in him that Dante is lover of the celestial Bride, Beatrice[10] – together with expressions and incidents that cannot possibly apply to Christ himself. Thus for instance when the gryphon is praised for not tearing at the tree of Adam (XXXII, 43–4): this would be senseless if applied to Christ, who is divine; it can only be meaningfully said of a being who has the power and impulse to do wrong, yet does not do so – here, a *daimôn* that does not yield to its 'demonic' nature.

Crucial is the passage in Canto XXXI where Beatrice contemplates the gryphon, and Dante, looking into Beatrice's eyes, sees how 'like the sun in a mirror . . . the double animal shone in her eyes, now with certain ways of behaving, now with others ('or con altri, or con altri reggimenti'). Reader, imagine how I marvelled when I saw the thing in itself ('la cosa in sé') remain changeless, and yet changing in the image in her eyes' (121–7). Those who identify the gryphon with Christ must here suppose that in Beatrice's eyes Dante sees the human and divine natures of Christ alternately. This is not only an idea to my knowledge unparalleled in the Middle Ages, and somewhat far-fetched in itself, but it also depends on attributing a very peculiar meaning to the word 'reggimenti'. I rendered it 'ways of behaving'; it can also mean something like 'gestures' or 'attitudes' or 'actions' – I know no parallel for its meaning 'nature'. But what is worse is that, if we postulated such a meaning, we would have to admit that the changeless reality of Christ's two natures in one ('la cosa in sé') can be seen by Dante alone, but that with Beatrice's help he can only see it fitfully – now this way, now that. Beatrice's eyes, that is, would actually be hindering Dante from seeing 'the thing in itself'. All that we know of Dante's thought makes such an interpretation absurd. If we do not force the gryphon to be Christ, and do not force 'reggimenti' to mean 'nature', we can pose the problem in a far simpler way, almost like a children's riddle: 'What is it that remains the same, but looks different at different times in the eyes of one's lady-love?' Does not a far simpler kind of answer – a psychological answer – lie to hand?

Finally, when the gryphon flies aloft again, and leaves the chariot to its destruction, we need not think it is Christ abandoning his Church. Is it not, within Dante's own consciousness, a moment comparable to that in which 'the god . . . whom Anthony lov'd / Now leaves him'?

Gryphon and chariot are perhaps the most elusive of the prefiguring symbols of Canto XXIX. I have tried to suggest the principal orientation of these symbols, and, for some at least, have tried to indicate their place in the marvellously subtle poetic fabric. To conclude, I would pause at one other, both arresting and profound: it is the contrast Dante makes between two figures:

> L'un si mostrava alcun de' famigliari
> di quel sommo Ipocràte che natura
> a li animali fé ch'ell' ha più cari;
>   mostrava l'altro la contraria cura
> con una spada lucida e aguta,
> tal che di qua dal rio mi fé paura.   (136–41)

(One showed himself to be of the company of that supreme Hippocrates, whom Nature made for the living beings she holds most dear; the other showed the contrary concern, with a sword so radiant and keen that even on the far shore he caused me fear.)

The double image, the healer and the fearsome figure with bright threatening sword, has numerous echoes in the later cantos. It suggests to me a symbolic premonition of Beatrice's double role: she whose frightening words judging Dante are a sword ('spada': XXX, 57), a fierce cutting edge ('taglio . . . acro': XXXI, 3), and who thereby is also Dante's miraculous healer, reviving his faculties, which were as if dead, and restoring him.

As for the last figure in the procession, the old man, asleep yet with piercing aspect – overtly he is the living form of the Apocalypse. Indeed the ancient figure of the opening of St John's vision combines the keen sword of Dante's previous image with the keen eyes, blazing like a flame of fire. And yet, if we remember Dante's own face from portraits – the sharp features and the piercing eyes – was his not also 'una faccia arguta'? Does not this last, lonely figure in the procession – the visionary, walking asleep, perhaps like Webster's 'madman, with his eyes open' – carry a hint of the other visionary, Dante himself?

The thunderclap at which the grave assembly halt, as if forbidden to go on, once more evokes the atmosphere of St John's vision: the thunder heralds the unearthly presences. Now the vision will be consummated.

Yet the whole of the twenty-ninth canto has already revealed Beatrice *per speculum in enigmate*. It uses biblical and pagan and 'monstrous' imagery, both perceptually varied and hieratic; it uses an astonishing (though never merely virtuoso) diversity of poetic techniques, of types of imaginative evocation – from Cavalcantian idyll to Johannine apocalypse. Out of all this is built the revelation of Beatrice; and it is this that leads into Dante's confession in Beatrice's presence, into his individual apocalypse and sibylline oracle, and at the very close of the *cantica*, as if in release, to a moment of serene light-heartedness.

Notes

1 *La Divina Commedia*, commento di Attilio Momigliano (3 vols., Firenze, 1945–7), II, 490, 486.
2 *Lectura Dantis Scaligera: Purgatorio* (Firenze, 1967), p. 1076, n. 2.
3 *Nuove letture dantesche, V* (Casa di Dante in Roma, Firenze, 1972), p. 154. In the same year appeared Daniela Bertocchi's 'Segni e simboli in *Purgatorio* XXIX', in *Psicoanalisi e strutturalismo di fronte a Dante*, II (Firenze, 1972). This contains many stimulating observations, especially on the nature and function of the feminine figures in the final cantos of the *Purgatorio*. Notwithstanding the title, however, this essay does not include any detailed discussion of Canto XXIX itself – indeed Canto XXX is far more important to the author's arguments.
4 Cf. my discussion, 'Dante's Earthly Paradise: Towards an Interpretation of *Purgatorio* XXVIII', *Romanische Forschungen* LXXXII (1970), 467–87.
5 *Letture dantesche*, ed. G. Getto (Firenze, 1962), pp. 1251–68 (esp. pp. 1264ff.).
6 'The Symbol of the Gryphon in *Purgatorio* XXIX, 108 and following Cantos', in *Centenary Essays on Dante* (Oxford, 1965), pp. 103–31.
7 This assertion may cause surprise to many scholars, and so should perhaps be substantiated in detail. Among modern commentators, for instance, Sapegno writes: 'Il *grifone* . . . è certo il Cristo, in cui si congiungono la natura umana e la divina (cfr. Isidoro di Siviglia, *Orig.* XII, 2)'. Let us, then, compare the Isidore passage *in full*:

> Grypes vocatur quod sit animal pinnatum et quadrupes. Hoc genus ferarum in Hyperboreis nascitur montibus. Omni parte corporis leones sunt; alis et facie aquilis similes; equis vehementer infesti. Nam et homines visos discerpunt.

In the whole of Isidore's work, there is only one other sentence referring to gryphons (XX, 11, 3):

> Spingae sunt in quibus sunt spingatae effigies, quos nos gryphos dicimus.

Nonetheless, another passage in Isidore is often alluded to by Dante scholars (e.g. by Singleton, *Commentary*, p. 718), though without attention to context:

> Nam et Christus Agnus pro innocentia; et Ovis propter patientiam; et Aries propter principatum; et Haedus propter similitudinem carnis peccati; et Vitulus pro eo quod pro nobis est immolatus; et Leo pro regno et fortitudine; et Serpens· pro morte et sapientia; idem et vermis, quia resurrexit; Aquila, propter quod post resurrectionem ad astra remeavit (VII, 2, 42–3).

While this series of animal images that are used of Christ includes a lion and – somewhat later – an eagle, it should be clear from the surrounding lines that each of these images is self-contained, and that one cannot conceivably infer from this passage that Christ was likened to a gryphon by Isidore or anyone else. The assertion in the *Lexikon der christlichen Ikonographie* (Freiburg i. Br., 1968ff.), s.v. *Greif* (II, 202ff.), that it is 'Sinnbild Christi (Isid Sev) wegen seiner Beziehung zur Unsterblichkeit, Vollkommenheit und seiner Doppelnatur', is preposterous.

In a recent article, 'Traces of Servius in Dante', *Dante Studies* XCII (1974), 117–28, Erich von Richthofen, while he rightly sees that Isidore cannot support his claim, believes that one can use Servius to show 'that we have here (in the gryphon) an allegory of Christ' (p. 120). This too is mistaken. Servius (*in Ecl.* v, 66) explains that Apollo has three emblems (*insignia*), indicating his triple power (*triplex potestas*) in heaven, earth and hell – a lyre, image of heavenly harmony, a gryphon, showing him as an earth-god, and arrows, showing him as an infernal and noxious god – '*Lyram*, quae nobis caelestis harmoniae imaginem monstrat: *Gryphon*, quae eum (*cum*, Richthofen, p. 121) etiam terrenum numen ostendit; *Sagittas*, quibus infernalis deus et noxius iudicatur'. That Dante used Servius's commentary (or glosses based on it) is altogether possible; but Richthofen's conclusions from this passage (p. 121), that it shows 'the figure of a griffin allegorizing the actions of a divine being on earth', and that 'this simile, in Dante's *Commedia, continues to stand* for the Son of God who is Christ' (italics mine), are wholly unsupported by this or any other passage in Servius.

No scholar, on the other hand, seems to have noticed the text about the gryphon in Scotus Eriugena (cited below, n. 10), which does not identify it with Christ, but which could be genuinely relevant to Dante.

8 Petrocchi reads 'affetto', not 'aspetto' in line 62. This would give the meaning, 'Why so ardent to feel the affect of the living lights. . . .?'

9 *Hier Cel.* xv, 2 and 7 (ed. Roques-Heil-de Gandillac, *Sources chrétiennes*, 2nd edn. (1970), pp. 168–71 and 184). *Deiformis* is Scotus Eriugena's coinage, to render *theoeides*. The reference to green, obscured in Scotus's translation, emerges in those of Hilduin and Grosseteste (cf. Ph. Chevallier, *Dionysiaca* II, 1023).

10 It is in this context that one traditional meaning ascribed to the gryphon may be important: according to Scotus Eriugena: 'Tantae castitatis ferunt esse gryphum qui, dum semel coniugale consortium perdiderit, semper castitatem suam inviolatam conservat, prioris coniugii memorans. Quod etiam de turture, naturarum inquisitores tradunt' (*Periphyseon* III, 39: P.L. 122, 738c. I am indebted to Edouard Jeauneau for this reference).

Purgatorio XXXII

KENELM FOSTER

The story of the *Comedy* begins in a dark wood and ends in a heavenly city. Midway between is another, very different wood up on the sunlit crest of Mount Purgatory where the central action of the poem takes place. This action, filling the last six cantos of *Purgatorio*, shows Dante confronted by both good and evil, the goodness radiating from Beatrice, the evil located successively in himself and in his world, the world of Western man at the turn of the thirteenth century. And towards each evil he is summoned to assume an appropriate responsibility: as to his own, to repent of it, as to evil in his world, to put it, as a poet, on record. And the summons is effected in appropriately distinct ways, through memory and through vision; Beatrice being involved in both. It is she who in Cantos xxx–xxxi compels Dante to recall the course of his past life, and so elicits his confession of sin, which is, at the same time, his release from it. And it is again she who, in Canto xxxii, having turned his eyes to an enactment in allegory of the degeneration of the Christian world, commands her lover, once returned to that world, to disclose what he has seen, 'in pro del mondo che mal vive' ('for the good of the world that lives ill': 103–8).

This commission is fictitious, of course; but the moment, surely, is one where fiction and autobiography coincide and the writer is revealing his motives, or one of them, for writing. But, if so, isn't it also clear, from the order of events, indeed of the cantos, that Dante is representing moral purification as a prerequisite for his writing *this* poem? Certainly, in the fiction his own purification seems to be completed by the end of Canto xxxi. And a compelling precedent for this way of regarding his task, and one that so biblical a poet can hardly have failed to recall, was chapter

138

6 of Isaiah, describing the prophet's mission to a degenerate Israel. Overwhelmed, here, by a vision of Jahweh, Isaiah cries out in fear and shame: 'Woe is me! . . . I am a man of unclean lips, and I dwell among a people of unclean lips; for my eyes have seen the King, the Lord of hosts!' Whereupon, he says, 'one of the seraphim flew to me with in his hand a live coal . . . and he touched my mouth with it and said: "Lo, this has touched your lips, your sin is removed, your iniquity is purged." ' Purification, then, before prophecy, and above all in this case where the prophet is a Catholic who believes it his duty publicly to castigate the Papacy; and in fact this very passage from Isaiah is cited at the beginning of Book III of the *Monarchia,* Dante's severest critique of the Papacy outside the *Comedy.*

Dante gets his writing-orders, so to call them, at lines 103–5 of our canto and the immediately relevant vision of Church history begins at line 109 and reaches its horrible climax at the canto's close. The Whore enthroned on the Chariot (148–60) is of course an anti-Beatrice, in obvious contrast with Beatrice seated on the bare ground (94) and also, if less obviously, with her unveiled glory at the end of Canto XXXI; the successive cantos being thus set in the strongest possible contrast. And as Dante had to be purified before he could see Beatrice in her glory so, for a different reason, he could not have been permitted to see with mind *un*purified the harlot in her temporary triumph; such a sight, it is clear, would have served no Christian purpose. I stress this theme of purification because it tends, I think, to be under-emphasised – at the cost of a weakened appreciation of the strange religious beauty of these last cantos of *Purgatorio.* One might say that by the end of Canto XXXI the *Comedy* is finished just insofar as it is an account of Dante's personal Christian *metanoia.* Divine grace, through the medium of his memory, has now washed him clean in the will, the moral faculty. True, his intellect, as Beatrice will remark, in Canto XXXIII, is still somewhat clouded, bemused; but that is only a temporary hang-over from past sins – sins no longer even remembered, for has he not drunk of the water of Lethe (XXXI, 100–2)?[1] There will be time enough in *Paradiso* for intellectual illuminations. Here in Purgatory all that remains to be done for him is to flood with new joy his Lethe-emptied memory; which will be the effect of the other sacred stream, Eunoe (XXXIII, 136–45).

Thus the whole action will be concluded that began in Canto
XXVIII with Dante's meeting the radiant nymph Matelda on his
entry into the Earthly Paradise – Matelda the embodiment, as it
were, of this paradise, whose function it is to herald, at some
distance, Beatrice. With hints about her of Eve and
Persephone – not to say Venus – Matelda evokes unfallen human
nature delighting in the Creator's goodness perceived *at a remove*,
in and through the works of his hands. This, it is clear, is why
when Dante meets her she is singing the psalm *Delectasti* (91 in the
Vulgate): 'Thou hast made glad, O Lord, by the works of thy
hands, at the works of thy hands I sing for joy.' This is the Eve
aspect, so to say, of Matelda; but, following a recent study by
Peter Armour, I would also connect her with the female figure for
Wisdom in the Book of Proverbs, the Wisdom that 'played'
before God in the beginning, 'playing in the world' and 'delighting to be with the children of men'.[2] And Matelda is the
forerunner and chief handmaid of Beatrice, herself the handmaid
of Christ. Beatrice has been over-allegorised, but if, as I hold, she
never ceases, in the *Comedy*, to be the young Florentine of the *Vita
Nuova*, her special function now – as a soul now in glory – is to
reflect and transmit to her lover what St Paul called the mystery of
Christ. Hence her very close association, in these cantos of
Purgatorio, with the Church represented by the Chariot, from
which she addressed Dante through Cantos XXX–XXXI, and from
which in our present canto she steps down (36). For the Chariot is
certainly the Church, as the Gryphon who draws it in the sacred
procession is certainly a figure for Christ.[3]

This procession came on the scene, moving westwards, in
Canto XXIX. Its general meaning is the mystery of the Word
incarnate as mediated through holy scripture and the Church
militant on earth. Headed by seven lights, the gifts of the Holy
Spirit, came two groups of white-robed elders representing
respectively the Old Testament and the non-Gospel books of the
New; and between these groups four living creatures symbolising
the Gospels; and in the space between these the Chariot itself
drawn by the Gryphon, eagle-headed and winged with a lion's
body. And at the Chariot's right wheel three women came
dancing, one flame-red, one emerald green, one white as snow,
the colours, respectively, of Charity, Hope and Faith; while at the

left wheel danced four in purple, clearly representing, in some way, the four natural or 'cardinal' virtues.[4] When Beatrice appears in Canto XXX it is stressed that the colours she wears are the three specifically Christian ones: red, green and white. But purple is probably the colour most relevant to the new symbol that will appear in Canto XXXII, as I shall try briefly to show.

This canto opens where XXXI had ended, with Dante gazing entranced at Beatrice, now unveiled. She is still the young woman of the *Vita nuova*, and so vividly indeed as to constitute, for a moment, a temptation to her lover to slip back into the past, oblivious of her present loftier condition (or of its symbolic significance); from which lapse he has to be recalled by one of the Christian, supernatural virtues standing to the right of Beatrice, and therefore leftwards with respect to Dante who is, of course, facing her:

> Tant' eran li occhi miei fissi e attenti
> a disbramarsi la decenne sete,
> che li altri sensi m'eran tutti spenti.
>   Ed essi quinci e quindi avien parete
> di non caler – così lo santo riso
> a sé traéli con l'antica rete! –;
>   quando per forza mi fu vòlto il viso
> ver' la sinistra mia da quelle dee,
> perch' io udi' da loro un 'Troppo fiso!'   (1–9)

(So fixed and intent were my eyes to slake their ten years' thirst that every other sensation ceased; they having on either side a wall of unconcern – so did the holy smile draw them to itself with the old net! – until perforce my face was turned leftwards by those divinities, hearing one of them say, 'Too fixedly!')

Returning to himself Dante then sees that the procession is right-wheeling and counter-marching eastwards whence it had come; and he goes with it (13–33). Presently they all come to a great tree around which they halt in a circle, Beatrice having by now got down from the Chariot. A murmur of 'Adamo' then identifies this tree with that of the knowledge of good and evil which stood 'in medio paradisi' ('in the middle of the garden') (the Vulgate Genesis 2.9), with the Tree, that is, of the Fall. It is bare on every bough (38–9).

After a further terzina (on which more anon) describing the Tree – its great height and curious shape – the main action of the

141

canto unfolds in three scenes: lines 43–69, 70–108, 109 to the end. I shall confine my attention chiefly to the first two scenes, but only touching briefly, to begin with, on scene one.

This opens (43–5) with the company praising the Gryphon for leaving the Tree 'unplucked'; to which he replies – the only words he speaks – that he does so out of reverence for justice: 'Sì si conserva il seme d'ogne giusto' ('Thus is the seed of all justice preserved': 48).[5] Then he attaches the Chariot by its shaft to the Tree, which at once breaks into leaf and flower. I accept the usual view that this shaft ('temo': 49) represents the Cross, the wood of which, according to one legend, came from the Tree of the Fall:

> E vòlto al temo ch'elli avea tirato,
> trasselo al piè de la vedova frasca,
> e quel di lei a lei lasciò legato.
>   Come le nostre piante, quando casca
> giù la gran luce mischiata con quella
> che raggia dietro a la celeste lasca,
>   turgide fansi, e poi si rinovella
> di suo color ciascuna, pria che 'l sole
> giunga li suoi corsier sotto altra stella;
>   men che di rose e più che di vïole
> colore aprendo, s'innovò la pianta,
> che prima avea le ramora sì sole.   (49–60)

(Then turning to the shaft he had pulled, he drew it to the foot of the widowed trunk, and what came from it left bound to it. As our trees, when the great light pours down mingled with that which shines next after the heavenly Fish [the constellation of Pisces], swell with sap and then renew themselves, each in its own colour, before the sun yokes his steeds under other stars; so – disclosing a hue less than of roses and more than of violets – the Tree reflowered, which before had had its boughs so bare.)

The Tree's reflowering is then celebrated by a hymn of ineffable sweetness (cf. Revelation 14.2–3) during which Dante falls asleep (64–9). End of scene one.

We are not told how long Dante's sleep lasted, but when he is awakened by a splendour and a cry (70–2) he finds that the scene has changed. The nature of this change is indicated by a superbly sustained comparison of Dante's return to consciousness with that of the three apostles – in Luke's account – after the Transfiguration of Jesus:

Quali a veder de' fioretti del melo
che del suo pome li angeli fa ghiotti
e perpetüe nozze fa nel cielo,
    Pietro e Giovanni e Iacopo condotti
e vinti, ritornaro a la parola
da la qual furon maggior sonni rotti,
    e videro scemata loro scuola
così di Moïsè come d'Elia,
e al maestro suo cangiata stola;
    tal torna' io . . .   (73–82)

(As Peter and John and James, having been led to see blossoms of the apple-tree that makes the angels greedy for its fruit and an eternal wedding feast in heaven, and having been overwhelmed by the sight, came to themselves at the sound of that voice by which deeper slumbers had been broken, and saw their company diminished by the disappearance of both Moses and Elijah, and their master's vesture changed; so did I come back to myself. . .)

Thus evoked, the Transfiguration scene has a double significance. Immediately, in the narrative, it tells us that as, after the Transfiguration, the apostles, returning to their senses, saw that Moses and Elijah were no longer with Jesus, so Dante, on awaking from *his* sleep, saw that most of the company, including the Gryphon, had departed; and again, that as after the Transfiguration Jesus was no longer visibly glorious, so Beatrice herself – Dante will now see – has undergone a change, in that she is now seated on the bare ground – a posture of humility – under the newly-flowering branches of the Tree. It is Matelda who points her out to the newly-awakened Dante:

Ond' ella: 'Vedi lei sotto la fronda
nova sedere in su la sua radice.
    Vedi la compagnia che la circonda:
li altri dopo 'l grifon sen vanno suso
con più dolce canzone e più profonda' . . .
    Sola sedeasi in su la terra vera.   (86–90, 94)

(And she [Matelda]: 'See her there, under the fresh foliage, seated on its root. See her companions standing round her: the others are following the Gryphon on high, with a song more sweet and sublime' . . . She sat alone on the bare ground.)

But secondly, at a deeper level, the Transfiguration allusion conveys, I think, a clear hint as to the meaning of the Tree. This comes in lines 73–5, which represent the transfigured Jesus as a blossoming apple-tree, an image that would recall for Dante's readers a verse of the Song of Songs (2.3) commonly applied to Christ: 'As an apple tree among the trees of the wood, so is my beloved among young men.' The image beautifully reflects, of course, the picture just given of the reflowering of the Paradise Tree, but it also, I suggest, points to the meaning latent in that Tree. Christ transfigured gave the apostles a transient vision of his 'blossom', but his fruit, the food of the angels – which 'makes the angels greedy and an endless marriage-feast in heaven' (74–5) – is reserved for the eternal life; the blossom being Christ's transfigured humanity, which in turn is both sign and pledge of the apple, his divinity, that is to say of the eternal Logos, the Word and Wisdom of the Father, which is the food desired by every created intellect, and possessed in heaven, as the *Paradiso* will make clear (e.g. at II, 10–12 (cf. *Purg.* XXXI, 128–9); IV, 124–6; XXVIII, 106–11; XXX, 100–2). On these lines, then, I would argue that Dante, in here recalling the Transfiguration, gives us a clue to the meaning of his Tree; and also, by implication, to his theory of the Fall. If the fruit of the Jesus-Tree is divine wisdom, and if the allusion to Jesus as a tree is intended in this context, as I think it is, to throw light on the Paradise Tree, then we can understand why this latter tree is in a very special sense sacred, as reserved to God alone (see Canto XXXIII, 58–60); and this because its fruit is a wisdom properly divine, to which no creature can have access except as a free gift from God, a 'grace' – which none may claim as of right. But Adam and Eve would not have it that way, would not wait for that wisdom-fruit as a gift, but impatiently snatched at it – impatiently and in vain.[6] And their failure, their Fall, is imaged in the withered state of the Tree as Dante first saw it. It follows that the Tree, though its fruit is divine, cannot represent God himself. What I take it to represent I shall try to define before I end, but let me say forthwith that I understand it, in general, as symbolic of an ideal order or relationship holding between God and his rational creature, Man; an order set up in beauty, by divine decree, at the beginning, and then destroyed by sin. Hence the Tree's aridity until restored by the new man, Christ – this being the sense of the reflowering effected by the action of the Gryphon already mentioned. From a slightly different point of view the Tree might be called a symbol of mankind in relation to God, and in particular to God as 'the good of the intellect' (*Inf.* III, 18).

Three important features of the Tree remain to be discussed: its size and shape and the colour of its foliage (40–2, 58–9). To these I shall turn presently.

Meanwhile an interesting question (largely ignored by the commentators) is raised for me by the allusion at lines 64–6 – apropos of Dante's falling asleep – to Ovid's tale about Mercury slaying Argus the hundred-eyed after sending him to sleep with the story of Pan and Syrinx. In Ovid this story is part of a longer one about the nymph Io; how she was loved by Jupiter and then by him turned into a heifer to conceal the fact from jealous Juno; and how Juno gave this Io-heifer to the monster Argus to guard; and how Argus was killed by Mercury, which involved the tale of Pan and Syrinx; and how Io was finally restored to human form and ended as a goddess in Egypt (*Metamorphoses* I, 568–747). Now, of these two interrelated tales only that of Syrinx is directly alluded to in our canto; and the allusion will seem at first merely ornamental. But if we stop to consider the stories, as Ovid tells them, more closely, we shall find, I think, touches in both that are decidedly suggestive of situations arising between *Purgatorio* XXVIII and XXX: compare *Metamorphoses* I, 640–1 with Canto XXX, 76–8, and 694–8 with Canto XXVIII, 49–51, 64–6 (recalling also, of course, *Aeneid* I, 326–9, 402–5) and 703–5 with Canto XXVIII, 69–75. And these coincidences may in turn alert us to the possibility that Dante's Gryphon was connected in his mind with Ovid's figure of Io, and this in respect precisely of Io's eventual transformation *back* from heifer form to human form and her ending up as a goddess (*Metamorphoses* I, 738–47). It seems, in short, possible – I would say indeed probable – that something momentous is left unstated, though hinted at, between lines 82 and 90. At lines 89–90 we have been told that the Christ–Gryphon is in the act of ascending to heaven, followed by 'others' of the company. Notice that the speaker, Matelda, uses the present tense: 'vanno suso' ('they *are* going up'); which is enough surely to connect the 'splendour' that, together with a 'cry', has just awakened Dante, with that ascension –

> e dico ch'un splendor mi squarciò 'l velo
> del sonno, e un chiamar: 'Surgi: che fai?'   (71–2)

(I say that a splendour rent the veil of my sleep, and a cry: 'Arise, what are you doing?')

But what, if not the Gryphon himself, is the likeliest source of that splendour? And isn't it then at least plausible that Dante intended us to imagine the figure ascending as transformed *back* into human form, and precisely into that splendid human form that had been disclosed briefly, to the amazed apostles at the Transfiguration? And that for such an image of re-transformation back from animal form to human form – and to a human form that was also, this time, that of the *true* God – Dante may well have taken his cue from the pagan fable of Io? Such an appropriation of ancient myth would, I think, be characteristic.

At all events, the Gryphon's ascension, however we imagine it, leaves the Chariot – the Church on earth – under the care, though not the control, of Beatrice (on this see C. S. Singleton, *The Divine Comedy, Translated with a Commentary* (3 vols., Princeton University Press, 1970–5), vol. II, part 2, pp. 793–5). The mystery-play is now halfway through. What is to come will be, in fact, an enactment of ruin, almost a second Fall, a swiftly moving allegory of the woes and sins of the historical Church, culminating in the alternate kissing and conflict of the harlot–Papacy and the King of France (148–60). And to all this Dante is now called to bear witness (cf. line 105, echoing Revelation 1.11) and so to prepare for whatever remedy the future may hold. This call, Beatrice's command to her poet, comes and is accepted in lines 103–8. But before the command there is a promise, and before that a moment of pure peace when nothing is said or done, and all we are aware of is Beatrice seated on the ground in queenly humility, with her retinue of the seven virtues, like the wise virgins in the Gospel, bearing the seven lamps of the Spirit, a circle of still figures and motionless flames:

> Sola sedeasi in su la terra vera,
> come guardia lasciata lì del plaustro
> che legar vidi a la biforme fera.
> In cerchio le facevan di sé claustro
> le sette ninfe, con quei lumi in mano
> che son sicuri d'Aquilone e d'Austro.　　　　　(94–9)

(She sat alone on the bare ground, as if left there to guard the car that I had seen the two-formed beast make fast. Around her, forming a cloister, were the seven nymphs with those lamps in their hands that are safe from the north wind and the south.)

Then the promise comes in a terzina of extraordinary simplicity and power, one of the greatest in the *Comedy*. Dante is assured of his personal salvation in an utterance all turning on the archetypal distinction between wild nature and order, the forest and the city:

> 'Qui sarai tu poco tempo silvano;
> e sarai meco sanza fine cive
> di quella Roma onde Cristo è romano' (100–2)

('Here you shall be for a short time a woodsman; and then with me forever a citizen of that Rome whereof Christ is a Roman.')

Note the solemn Latinisms 'silvano' and 'cive'; but especially, in the third line, balanced between 'Roma' and 'Cristo', that the idea of order, already introduced by 'cive', is given *two* referents, a secular and a sacred, firmly combined by the copula 'è'. The natural order is seen as contained by the supernatural, the earthly by the heavenly – by '*that* Rome' of which God's own Son is 'citizen'.

I pass quickly over the last fifty lines of this, the longest canto in the *Comedy*. The grim vision of the historical Church comes in seven scenes involving six figures: an Eagle, a Fox, a Dragon, the Chariot itself, the enthroned Whore, the Giant. The first and the last three of these are easily identified as, respectively, the Roman Empire, the Church itself, the corrupted Papacy and the French monarchy, in particular Philip IV (1285–1314). The first scene and the third show two swoops of the Roman Eagle, down through the Tree to the Chariot and up again (109–17 and 124–9), the first presumably representing the persecution of the Church by the pagan empire, the second quite certainly the so-called Donation of Constantine, by Dante always regarded as a major disaster, though it may, he says here, have been 'sincerely and kindly meant' (137–8). As for the attacks of the Fox (118–23) and the Dragon (lines 130–5), I follow most commentators in identifying them with, respectively, the early Christian heresies and the rise of Islam. The next four terzinas (136–47) then show the Chariot–Church in process of rapid corruption, the 'holy structure' itself (142) now become *actively* corrupt; sprouting out first a load of smothering feathers, then seven bestial heads hideously horned.

The former image, signifying riches, continues that of the second swoop of the Eagle, bearing his fatal gift to the Church of plumage of his own (125–6: 'I saw . . . the eagle come down into the centre of the Chariot and leave it feathered with his own plumage'). But the image of the horned heads introduces, immediately, the appearance of the Whore (148–50); as its evident source in Revelation 17 makes clear:

And [the angel] carried me away in the Spirit into a desert, and I saw a woman sitting on a scarlet beast . . . and it had seven heads and ten horns. The woman was arrayed in purple and scarlet, . . . holding in her hand a golden cup full of abominations . . . and on her forehead was written a name of mystery: 'Babylon the great, mother of harlots and of earth's abominations' (17.3–5).

But Dante's Whore has standing by her a human master, her 'savage lover' the Giant, who proceeds to beat her from head to foot, before dragging her and the now bestialised chariot she rides on off into the wood (151–60). And no doubt this refers, by way of a prophecy *post eventum*, to the establishment of the Holy See at Avignon in 1309; but how trivial, from one point of view, seems that mere transfer of the Curia compared with the colossal audacity of Dante's symbolic scene!

Nowhere else, it seems to me, does Dante *seem* closer to abjuring Catholicism than in the last twenty lines of this canto. But to deal at all adequately with that issue would require another essay. So I will conclude the present one by drawing out more distinctly my interpretation, already adumbrated, of the chief symbolic figure in this canto, the sacred Tree. This has been taken to signify the Empire and I agree that its meaning in some way includes the Empire. There is clearly, I think, a parallel between the lines spoken here in praise of the Gryphon (43–8) and *Mon.* II, x–xi, where Dante insists that Christ lived and died an obedient subject of the Roman Empire, thus clinching the thesis of *Mon.* II, that the Empire was established *de iure*, that is, by the will of God; the truth of this being confirmed by Christ's submission to the imperial authority. The parallel I speak of comes out, for me, in the Gryphon's reply (48) to the praise of him uttered by the company assembled round the Tree: 'Sì si conserva il seme d'ogne giusto' ('So is the seed of all justice preserved'), which I take to be an echo of the Vulgate rendering of Matthew 3.15, where Jesus justifies his reception of baptism from John: 'sic enim decet nos implere omnem iustitiam'. The Son of God's humility in receiving baptism from a mere man would find its counterpart in the Christ–Gryphon's humility with respect to what the Tree signifies. True, there is no reference in the *Monarchia* to the baptism of Jesus, but if one grants that Matthew 3.15 is echoed in line 48 of our canto, then it seems likely that Dante was giving that text a political sense here – as he certainly did in *Epist.* VII, 14 – thus connecting the Gryphon's utterance with *Mon.* II, x–xi. But even so, this would not prove that the Tree's primary meaning was the Empire, but only that obedience to the Empire is involved in whatever the Tree *does* primarily mean. But the simple and sufficient reason why the Empire cannot be what the Tree *primarily* signifies is that whereas in Dante's system the Empire and the Church presuppose the Fall of man (see *Mon.* III, iv, 14), the Tree obviously does not. Having been withered by the first human sin, it must stand for something older than human sin; as the Tree in Genesis existed before Adam's sin.

What then is the Tree's primary meaning? I have suggested that a clue is given in the allusion to the transfiguration, with the image of Jesus as an apple-tree whose fruit is the food of the blessed (73–5), that is, of those whom God feeds with the divine Logos itself, the Wisdom to which no created intellect can have access except as a grace, a free gift. For such a grace neither Lucifer (*Par.* XIX, 46–8) nor Adam (*ibid.* VII, 25–7; cf. *Purg.* XXIX, 23–7) was content to wait. Now this idea of something intrinsically divine, and therefore inaccessible to man *qua* man, is imaged by two features of the Tree, taken in conjunction: its great height and its curious shape – that its branches 'spread ever wider the higher they are' (40–2). Both these properties, Beatrice will affirm in the next canto, have a 'special reason' (XXXIII, 65–6). This she does not explain, but the Tree's loftiness plainly accords with the specially sacred character I ascribe to its fruit; while as to its strange shape, it is clear, I think, that according to the literal sense, this simply signifies that it cannot be climbed. Below, on the circle of gluttons, Dante saw, successively, two trees, of which the first was explicitly said to have the same odd shape as this one in the Earthly Paradise, while of the second he was told that it sprang from the latter's seed (XXII, 123–5; XXIV, 115–17); whence I infer that all three trees had the same shape and that the Paradise Tree was parent of the other two; and that Dante's comment on the shape of the first Tree was meant to apply also to that of the Paradise Tree: 'I think [it so shaped] so that no one should climb it' ('perché persona su non vada': XXII, 135). And the connection with Adam's sin of this image of climbing and failing to climb is fully confirmed by a passage in the great doctrinal canto on the Fall and Redemption, *Par.* VII, 97–100.

The Tree's shape, then, I take to signify a divine ban on human pride, the ban that Beatrice in the next canto (71) will call 'l'interdetto' and expressly relate to the Tree's height and shape:

> Dorme lo 'ngegno tuo, se non estima
> per singular cagione essere eccelsa
> lei tanto e sì travolta ne la cima. (XXXIII, 64–6)

(Your mind is asleep if it judge not that for a special reason it [the Tree] is so lofty and is thus inverted at the top.)

If his mind, she goes on, were not bemused by 'vain thoughts',

> per tante circostanze solamente
> la giustizia di Dio, ne l'interdetto,
> conosceresti a l'arbor moralmente. (XXXIII, 70–2)

(by such circumstances alone you would apprehend, according to the moral sense [of the Tree's height and shape], in the ban the justice of God.)

God's justice, then, which is one with His will (*Mon.* II, ii, 4), is *shown* in this Tree; His justice, that is, precisely as a measure imposed on the activity of man *qua* man, as a creature endowed with reason and free-will, and by nature aware of God, even if 'at a remove' (cf. *Con.* III, ii, 7–9). Primarily, then, the Tree symbolises a basic moral order that ideally contains and measures human knowledge and desire in relation to God.

But it is not a static symbol. We see it at first arid and bare, because of Adam's sin; before which it must have been in sap and flower like the rest of Eden. And then in the scene that follows it reflowers: and then has its bark rent and foliage scattered by the first plunge of the Eagle (112–14). So its significance is certainly historical. But whose history is being enacted? Hardly that of the Empire as such or the Church as such, for, apart from other considerations, each of these institutions has its own separate symbol, respectively the Eagle and the Chariot. The only plausible alternative, it seems to me, is that under its historical aspect the Tree stands, at first, for man or mankind as such, and then, from the moment of the reflowering, for mankind as Christian, at least potentially.

This may well be the answer. Are, then, those many commentators right who have read a specifically Christian sense into the colour of the Tree's new flowers and foliage, taking it as the colour of Christ's blood? For my part I cannot accept this view, but all I can do here is to indicate, very briefly, the lines along which I would continue the argument, on the one hand against the blood-of-Christ view of this colour, and on the other in favour of the only alternative, as it seems to me, namely that the colour is purple, the same as that worn by the four virtues dancing at the Chariot's left wheel – and remembering that, as Edward Moore pointed out long ago (*Studies in Dante* (Oxford, 1896–1917, repr. 1969), vol. III, pp. 184–5, 218–19) in classical and medieval times the terms we render as 'purple' were commonly applied to deep red or crimson.

First, then, the blood-of-Christ interpretation does not, for me, tally with the actual description of the reflowering in lines 52–60, cited above. For me the phrase 'poi si rinovella / di suo color ciascuna' suggests that the Tree originally bore flowers of the same hue as those that broke out afresh – as most readers surely assume anyway. But in that case, according to the view I am criticising, the sin of Adam, by withering the blood-red flowers signifying the sacrifice of Christ, would have symbolically *annulled* that sacrifice which, by the same token, it presupposed; a theological absurdity. Then again, take line 58, the only one that specifies the actual colour of the flowers: 'men che di rose e più che di vïole' is not a description of blood-colour characteristic of Dante, who normally depicts blood as vivid red or vermilion (*Inf.* X, 86; XII, 47; XIV, 134; XVII, 62; XXVIII, 69; *Purg.* IX, 101–2; *Par.* XVI, 154) whereas line 58 suggests bright red dimmed by violet (cf. *Georgics* IV, 274–5) – assuming that the, so to say, typical colour of roses for Dante was bright red, and this on the strength of *Purg.* XXIX, 148–50, where the last figures in the procession are shown as crowned, not with lilies,

> anzi di rose e d'altri fior vermigli;
> giurato avria poco lontano aspetto
> che tutti ardesser di sopra da' cigli.   (xxix, 148–50)

(. . . but rather with roses and other red flowers; seen from a short distance one would have sworn they were all aflame above the eyebrows.)

Not blood-red, then, but purple is the colour of the Tree's foliage: an imperial purple, perhaps, but I prefer to think simply of human nobility, remembering *Dve* ii, i, 5: 'exigit . . . purpura viros nobiles' ('purple befits noble men'). And true nobility consists in virtue (*Mon.* ii, iii, 3–4) or is closely associated with it (*Con.* iv, *passim*). Hence the colour worn by the four dancers at the left of the Chariot. Now the natural virtues represented by these 'handmaidens' of Beatrice must be of a higher order than those possessed by the good pagans in Limbo (see n. 4). So the idea suggests itself that the mixed hue of their apparel may have something to do with that higher dignity of theirs, and that Moore (*Studies*, vol. iii, pp. 184–6) and C. S. Singleton (*Journey to Beatrice*, cited in n. 4, especially pp. 160–2) may well be right in taking that colour as symbolic of natural virtue as enhanced and governed by supernatural charity, traditionally associated with bright or flame red;[7] in short, as what theologians called 'infused' natural virtue (see n. 4).

But more directly relevant to line 58 as a clue to the meaning of the Tree is the four dancers' assertion, in Canto xxxi, 106, that they are 'stars': 'Noi siam qui ninfe e nel ciel siamo stelle' ('Here we are nymphs and in Heaven are stars'); for the reference surely cannot be to anything but the four stars Dante saw in the southern sky over Mount Purgatory, on emerging from the underworld (i, 22–7). Now those stars were reminders of the prelapsarian state of man; as much so as is the Tree itself; so much so that they have never, Dante said, been seen from the inhabited side of the globe since the Fall: 'non viste mai fuor ch'a la prima gente' ('never seen except by the first people') – obviously a reference to Adam and Eve. Inevitably, then, they bring to mind the state or condition called in theology 'original justice', the original prelapsarian state of man in perfect harmony with and under God, and with himself (cf. St Thomas, *Summa Theol.* 1a. 94, 1–4; 95, 1–2; 1a2ae. 82, 3; 85, 3 etc.; Singleton, *Journey*, chapters 9–10, 13). But if the four stars recall that state, then so do the four dancers who are self-identified with them. Therefore the purple of these dancers' apparel must be one of the symbols of that state; and if that is the symbolic sense of purple in their case, so it must be, surely, in the case of the Tree, the colour of whose foliage matches theirs as we have seen. Now Dante's conception of that state of original justice is expressed in *Par.* VII, 67–87, with significant use of the terms 'nobilità' and 'dignità'. If, then, the Tree as withered stands for human nature as once possessed of original justice but now bereft of it, the Tree's reflowering must surely represent the recovery of that state, in some sense, if only by resemblance or analogy; a recovery effected through the Cross and symbolised by the noble purple of the leaves and flowers. That the state recovered, however, is not and cannot be identical with the state that was lost is sound theology, as well as common sense, and it seems to be expressed in the statement quoted above about the four stars; 'never seen except by the first people'. What remains, for me, unclear in the *Comedy* is how that statement – made, according to the fiction, in A.D. 1300! – can be reconciled with the four dancers being present in a procession whose total meaning is the Incarnation: how, in other words, 'original justice' is in one sense irretrievably lost, and in another somehow, in Christ, recovered. But that is a topic for another occasion.

Notes

1 It might be objected that Dante is shown as morally at fault in lines 7–9 of our canto, where he has to be detached from excessive attention to Beatrice's visible beauty. But he receives similar corrections several times in the *Paradiso* (x, 52–63; xviii, 20–1; xxiii, 70–2, etc.), so that if he is sinning here, he would apparently be sinning in Heaven too, which seems absurd. The point, I think, is that such slips or distractions on Dante's part, after *Purg.* xxxi, are mere errors involving as such no *choice* of evil – similar to the self-deception of the little child described in *Purg.* xvi, 91–3; the deception, being involuntary – 'quivi s'inganna' ('there it is beguiled') – is innocent; as Aquinas would say, it occurs only because 'sensus corporis fallitur' ('the bodily senses are deceived': *Summa Theol.* 2a2ae. 10, 2 ad 3).

2 Proverbs 8.31. P. Armour, 'Matelda in Eden: the Teacher and the Apple', *Italian Studies* xxxiv (1979), 2–27. This article demands and deserves close study. In effect Armour presents the Matelda/Beatrice relationship in the *Comedy* as a kind of reworking – with reversal of roles – of the Donna Filosofia/Beatrice relationship in the *Convivio*. This interpretation owes something to Natali and Contini but it has never before, to my knowledge, been worked out so persuasively.

3 For the image of the Church as a chariot, see *Epist.* XI, 5–6. This is the vital text; cf. also *Par.* XII, 106–14. That the Gryphon represents Christ seems clear from *Purg.* XXXI, 80–1, cf. XXXII, 47; as well as from the echo, as it seems to me, at line 48 of the Vulgate Matthew 3.15; a point I shall return to later in this essay (and see n. 5).

4 I insert 'in some way' to avoid the implication that the cardinal virtues, represented by this group of four dancers, only entered the human world with Christianity; which other texts prove was not Dante's opinion; see *Purg.* VII, 34–6; *Par.* XIX, 70–5; *Mon.* III, xv, 8–9. Nevertheless, there can be no doubt that the four dancers both symbolise the cardinal virtues and are very closely associated with Beatrice, to the point of being inseparable from her (*Purg.* XXXI, 107–14; XXXII, 97–9). The best way of meeting this difficulty seems to me to be that proposed by E. Moore and developed by C. S. Singleton – in, respectively, *Studies in Dante* (4 vols., Oxford, 1896–1917, repr. 1969), vol. III, pp. 184–6, and *Journey to Beatrice* (Harvard University Press, 1958), pp. 140–80, 260–70; and cf. F. Mazzoni's commentary on *Purg.* XXXI, in *Lectura Dantis Scaligera* (3 vols., Firenze, 1965–8), vol. II, pp. 1168–72 – namely that the four dancers represent natural virtue precisely as conjoined with and governed by the 'supernatural' Christian virtue of charity; and so as integrated into the life of grace, which even Virgil, of course, did not have. Natural virtue thus 'supernaturalised' was called 'infused' by Aquinas; see *Summa Theol.* 1a2ae. 63, 3–4 and 65, 2. For the thirteenth-century debates on this topic, see O. Lottin, *Psychologie et morale aux XIIe et XIIIe siècles* (3 vols., Gembloux, Belgium, 1942–60), vol. III, pp. 99–252, 459–535.

A further and, to my mind, greater difficulty arises from the four dancers' identifying themselves (*Purg.* XXXI, 106) as, originally, 'stars'; for these can hardly be other than those spoken of at *Purg.* I, 22–7, of which we are told that they have never been seen – presumably, from the inhabited northern hemisphere – since the Fall. What then, we may ask, are the cardinal virtues, even regarded as 'infused', doing in the retinue of the Church Militant? I touch on this difficulty again at the end of this essay, but leave it unresolved; and I only mention it here because the association of the four dancers with the four stars of *Purg.* I, 22–7, will be an important part of my argument about the central symbol of Canto XXXII, the Tree.

5 See n. 3. The rare verb 'discindi' at line 43 may have an echo in *Mon.* III, x, 5: cf., in any case, Matthew 22.21; and for line 45, Revelation 10.9–11.

6 Adam and Eve were created to inherit eternal joy, having already the 'arra' or pledge of it (*Purg.* XXVIII, 91–3). But they would not accept this deferment of perfect beatitude (*ibid.* XXIX, 23–30; *Par.* VII, 25–7) and in this resembled Satan (*Par.* XIX, 46–8). Hence the essence of their sin was disobedience, in overstepping a temporary limitation imposed by God (*Par.* XXVI, 115–17).

7 See C. Spicq, *Agapè dans le Nouveau Testament,* Études Bibliques (2 vols., Paris, 1958–9), vol. I, pp. 51–2; vol. II, p. 146; J. Braun, *Die liturgische Gewandung* (Freiburg, 1907), pp. 729–36.

Paradiso XVII

UBERTO LIMENTANI

It was not by chance, but by design, that the canto that we are about to examine was placed exactly in the centre of the *Paradiso*: in the symmetrical structure of the *Comedy* there is little room for coincidence. Canto XVII is the culmination of one of the most sustained episodes of the whole poem – Dante's encounter with his ancestor Cacciaguida, which, in its turn, takes place in the Heaven that holds the central position among the nine revolving Heavens, that of Mars, described as a 'stella forte' ('mighty star') in line 77, because it represents 'fortitudo', one of the four virtues that are necessary to the active life. The special place occupied by the fifth Heaven by virtue of its position had already been emphasised in the *Convivio* (II, xiii, 20), and adds to the moment-ous significance of the episode within the poem. Clearly, this was the place for Dante to bring together the many strands that he had woven into his vast canvas, these were the cantos in which to embody the quintessence of his conception of man and the universe, and of the purpose of his lifelong work. Yet, on the surface at least, the episode appears to unfold primarily on a personal and historical plane, its bricks and mortar being not so much doctrinal or universal considerations, as the poet's own story and vicissitudes, and a view of the past and present state of Florence, his native city-state. With individual and civic preoccu-pations coming to the fore, philosophical and theological prob-lems seem to have been discarded or, at least, relegated to the background, and the narrative holds the attention on the literal level. Could it be that an interlude occupying a crucial place in the final cantica was purely and simply used to bring us down from Heaven to Earth? This would be a rash conclusion indeed. In actual fact, although many commentators have failed to see it, the

155

narrative proceeds on more than one plane, and there is a deeper meaning and a more exalted purpose behind the story of Dante's meeting with Cacciaguida. In order to pinpoint this meaning and this purpose, a brief summary of the episode is needed.

In Canto XIV the souls of the warrior spirits in the Heaven of Mars form themselves into the pattern of a radiant cross. Soon after the beginning of Canto XV one of them speeds to the foot of the cross like a shooting-star and greets Dante as affectionately as Aeneas's father Anchises had greeted his son in the Infernal Regions, according to the sixth book of the *Aeneid*, which is here explicitly quoted. Then the spirit reveals himself as Cacciaguida, the grandfather of Dante's grandfather, who lived in Florence between the end of the eleventh and the middle of the twelfth century, followed the Emperor Conrad III in the Second Crusade, was knighted by him, and died in about 1147 fighting against the infidel. At the same time, Cacciaguida draws a vivid picture of the simplicity of life in twelfth-century Florence and goes on to contrast it, particularly in Canto XVI, with Florence in Dante's time, which is described as corrupted and polluted by the immigration of greedy and ambitious newcomers. The encounter reaches its climax in Canto XVII, with which we are now concerned. Here, as we shall see, the poet learns from his ancestor that the future holds in store a life of wandering in exile for him.

For this reason, Canto XVII has been described, with some justification, as Dante's own canto *par excellence*. Yet the theme of his political misfortunes and of the hardships that are the consequence of banishment, which had already constantly recurred both in the *Comedy* and in his other works, ought not to be taken in isolation but in its close links with other themes, all of them present here; and, first of all, with the interpretation of Florentine history, which must have been slowly taking shape in Dante's mind during his exile. This interpretation has come to pervade the pages of the *Comedy* more and more and is now spelt out by Cacciaguida: from its pristine, untarnished virtues in the early twelfth century, Florence had sunk to its present depravity and turmoil on account of its rapid growth and the consequent corrupting influx of strangers from the surrounding countryside and townships. It is, of course, an interpretation that no historian would accept as accurate. By 1300 the town had grown beyond recognition, the number of its inhabitants (perhaps about 100,000) was four or five times greater than a century and a half before, and this expansion had brought about problems; but Dante ignores the bright side of the picture: the splendid reality of the city's economic and industrial development, which had made it the most flourishing banking, manufacturing and trading centre in the Western world. This development had caused the increase in the population and, in its turn, was made possible by it. A concomitant to the greater wealth and power of Florence had been the blossoming of painting, sculpture and architecture, not to speak of literature. Dante, however, preferred to focus on the obverse side of the coin. He knew that when he had been exiled he had suffered a great injustice, and he knew that the political upheaval itself that had caused his exile had been brought about by injustice and treachery. In his solitude and isolation, he meditated, naturally enough, upon the causes of the malaise of his town, and formulated this oversimplified and one-sided explanation, which in addition probably owes something to the scorn of an aristocrat and scholar for the mercantile pursuits that were the mainstay of Florentine power and splendour, and to his lack of interest in economic considerations. In fact, he came to feel passionately that the moral decadence he saw was the root of his own, and of his city's, troubles, the two being conceived as indissolubly linked. But, as he evolved that overall design for the welfare of mankind which is so forcefully expounded in the *Monarchia*, he realised that the corruption of Florence was only a facet of the wider corruption that affected the other towns of Italy and, indeed the whole world, owing to the Emperor neglecting to perform the duties that had been assigned to him by God, and to the Pope usurping the Emperor's functions. He says explicitly in Canto XVI (58–60) that the original purity of Florence would have remained undefiled by immigration if the people who were most degenerate (i.e. the clergy) had not been a step-mother, but rather as kind as a mother to Caesar (i.e. to the Empire).

The task that Dante had set himself was nothing less than bringing about a solution to this world-wide disorder – in fact, as he saw it, the one possible solution. Indeed, he believed he had been invested by providence with the mission of making humanity aware of the system ordained by God for its happiness; this, as we shall see, is implied by what Cacciaguida tells Dante in the final lines of Canto XVII. It is clear, then, that the three main themes of the Cacciaguida episode (the poet's exile, the corruption of Florence, which is almost an epitome, or a blueprint, of the corruption of the world, and the mission of salvation, which is the main purpose of the poem) are intimately joined together; only if all this is borne in mind can we see Canto XVII, as well as the two previous cantos, in their proper light. It had been his exile that had lifted Dante (and he was deeply aware of this) from the narrow range of local politics to the wide perspective of a universal monarchy set up for the welfare of all men, and had determined and justified the mission he had undertaken. His exile and his mission, his misfortunes and what had come out of them, his banishment and his poem came, therefore, to be seen in one and the same context as something that had been willed by providence for a higher end. And this went together with a profound belief that the wrongs he had suffered were to be righted, that peace, harmony and virtue were to return to Florence and that the system predisposed by providence was to be established in the world, for it was unthinkable that God would allow injustice to be perpetuated on earth.

Dante's consciousness of being an instrument of providence seems to have become firmer with the progress of the *Comedy*, feeding on the growing extent of his poetic achievement. It is first clearly expressed in the last two cantos of *Purgatorio*. After his confession of personal sin in Canto XXXI, and after being shown, at the end of that canto, a vision of Beatrice's unveiled glory, Dante is conducted to the centre of the Earthly Paradise where he sees the tree of the knowledge of good and evil, now withered and leafless in consequence of the sin of Adam (*Purg.* XXXII, 13–39; cf. Genesis 2.9, 16–17). He then sees the tree renewed through the agency of the gryphon, representing Christ; and then, at the foot of the same tree, sees allegorically enacted the woes and sins of the Christian world, these being represented by a progressive desecration of the chariot, the symbol of the Church, on which Beatrice had first appeared (*ibid.* 49–60 and 109–60). To all this Dante is commanded by Beatrice to bear witness, on his return to the world of mortal men, 'in pro del mondo che mal vive' (103–5). This command is reiterated in Canto XXXIII, and is coupled with a prophecy of a coming reform of the Church, this reform being associated with some future 'heir of the eagle', that is, with an Emperor who will be God's minister on earth (*Purg.* XXXIII, 52–4 and 34–45).

It is that reiterated commission to Dante as both poet and prophet which is now solemnly confirmed by Cacciaguida. In this central section of the *Paradiso*, moreover, with five sixths of his task completed, the moment had come – here where the main stress falls precisely on Dante as a citizen of Florence – for placing his exile in its proper setting, for relating it, that is, to the extraordinary vocation first openly revealed to him by Beatrice. Now he can at last portray himself as being another Aeneas, another Paul, whereas the dismayed pilgrim of *Inf.* II, 32 had said: 'Io non Enea, io non Paolo sono' ('I am not Aeneas, I am not Paul'); and, indeed, the first greeting imparted to him by Cacciaguida contains more than a hint that his journey was no less significant than those of the forefather of the Roman Empire and of the great apostle who had himself described his *raptus* into the third heaven (II Corinthians 12.2–4).

As Aeneas had met his father in Hades, so Dante meets his forebear; it was a happy and poetical stroke of imagination to engineer a kind of family reunion, and to introduce into the poem this figure, almost surrounded by a legendary halo, made glorious by his being a crusader, and a martyr who had fought for his faith, and also made venerable by distance in time as well as by ancient nobility. Who could have been more appropriate to play the part that Cacciaguida plays, of commemorator of a virtuous past, scathing reprover of the evils of present times, unflinching but paternally sympathetic prophet of personal misfortunes and an-nouncer of Dante's sublime appointed task, than an ancestor, so near to the poet, and at the same time so far removed? Not even Beatrice would have been appropriate, as has been pointed out; for she had been instrumental in achieving another goal of Dante's journey, that of purification from sin and attainment of perfection; she had pitilessly rebuked her lover for going astray from the path of virtue and knowledge, and this could hardly have been artistically consistent with a later solemn affirmation of the providential nature of his journey.

Canto XVII can be divided into three sections, the middle one being Cacciaguida's main speech (37–99), and the first one leading up to it.

> Qual venne a Climenè, per accertarsi
> di ciò ch'avëa incontro a sé udito,
> quei ch'ancor fa li padri ai figli scarsi;
>   tal era io, e tal era sentito
> e da Beatrice e da la santa lampa
> che pria per me avea mutato sito.
>   Per che mia donna: 'Manda fuor la vampa
> del tuo disio', mi disse, 'sì ch'ella esca
> segnata bene de la interna stampa:
>   non perché nostra conoscenza cresca
> per tuo parlare, ma perché t'ausi
> a dir la sete, sì che l'uom ti mesca.'   (1–12)

(As was he who came to Clymene to find out the truth of that which he had heard against himself – he who still makes fathers chary with their sons – so was I, and so I was perceived to be by both Beatrice and by the holy lamp that previously had changed its place for me. Wherefore, my lady said: 'Send out the flame of your desire, so that it may issue well marked with the inward stamp; not in order to add to our knowledge by what you say, but that you may accustom yourself to declaring your thirst, so that drink be poured out for you.')

The simile with which the canto opens may be felt to be somewhat laboured: Dante has heard so many grave words (23) about his fate, both in Hell and in Purgatory, in the form of prophecies (prophecies after the event: remember that the fictional date of the journey is 1300, whereas the *Comedy* was written several years later), that his mood is one of uncertainty and curiosity, like that of him who still makes fathers wary with their sons (3); that is, of Phaethon, who in Ovid's version of the story, had heard doubts expressed as to his being a son of Apollo, and went to his mother Clymene to be reassured (1); whereupon he was allowed by his father to drive the chariot of the sun and thus fell to his death. Beatrice encourages Dante to satisfy his thirst for knowledge (7–9), and to ask Cacciaguida, the holy lamp who had previously sped to the foot of the cross for Dante's sake (6). Lines 10–12 explain why Dante has to speak his mind to the blessed spirits, although his words are superfluous, as the souls of Paradise can read his thoughts; of course, one has to remember that, otherwise, his readers would be left in the dark.

'O cara piota mia che sì t'insusi,
che, come veggion le terrene menti
non capere in trïangol due ottusi,
   così vedi le cose contingenti
anzi che sieno in sé, mirando il punto
a cui tutti li tempi son presenti;
   mentre ch'io era a Virgilio congiunto
su per lo monte che l'anime cura
e discendendo nel mondo defunto,
   dette mi fuor di mia vita futura
parole gravi, avvegna ch'io mi senta
ben tetragono ai colpi di ventura;
   per che la voglia mia saria contenta
d'intender qual fortuna mi s'appressa:
ché saetta previsa vien più lenta.'   (13–27)

('Dear stock whence I sprang, and who now soar so high that as it is with minds on earth when they see that no triangle has two obtuse angles, so you, gazing as you do on the point to which all times are present, see contingencies before they exist in themselves – whilst I was with Virgil, climbing the mountain that heals souls and descending into the world of death, things of ill omen were said to me about my future; for which reason, although in myself I feel foursquare against the blows of fortune, I should be glad to hear what chance has in store for me; for an arrow foreseen comes more slowly.')

The question that is asked in lines 13–27 begins with an affectionate form of address; Dante had already called the spirit that had been the seed of his lineage 'padre mio' (my father), the root of the tree from which he was descended; his ancestor too had shown the most tender solicitude for him, and described him as his son. Clearly Cacciaguida is a father-figure in the *Comedy*, another giver of that fatherly affection for which Dante was longing and of which he may have been starved in real life, for in the poem there is no lack of father-figures: from the most obvious of them all, Virgil, to Brunetto Latini, Guido Guinizelli, and now Cacciaguida. A little later on, in line 35, we will find him designated as 'amor paterno'. Seen in this light, he is even more in keeping with his role.

The question itself that Dante asks has the purpose of eliciting from his forebear the prophecy of his exile. Cacciaguida can see future contingent things (16), that is, earthly events, with the same degree of certainty with which human minds can see obvious geometrical truths (14–17) by gazing on the point in

161

which past, present and future are joined (that is on God: 17–18). He is now asked to enlighten Dante concerning the grave words obscurely hinting bleak developments that he had heard from time to time during his journey. Lines 23–7 give a measure of Dante's moral fibre. Line 27, sinewy and direct, is typical of the poet, although its sentiment is not original, but derived from Latin ancient or medieval sources; the word 'tetragono' (24) is of particular interest; like the simile of lines 14–15, it was, of course, borrowed from geometry, the science that had been described in the *Convivio* (II, xiii, 27) as 'sanza macula d'errore e certissima per sé' ('without spot of error and most certain in itself'). It had been used with this meaning before in Aristotle's *Ethics*, but here it is as good as a newly coined adjective, and Dante's authority, as well as its impressive sound, have made it part of the Italian language.

> Così diss' io a quella luce stessa
> che pria m'avea parlato; e come volle
> Beatrice, fu la mia voglia confessa.
>   Né per ambage, in che la gente folle
> già s'inviscava pria che fosse anciso
> l'Agnel di Dio che le peccata tolle,
>   ma per chiare parole e con preciso
> latin rispuose quello amor paterno,
> chiuso e parvente del suo proprio riso.   (28–36)

(Thus did I address the light that first had spoken to me; declaring, as Beatrice wished, all my desire. Nor with dark riddles such as the foolish folk of old were ensnared by, before the Lamb of God who takes sins away was slain, but in clear words and precise speech did that paternal love reply, sheathed and revealed in his own smile.)

Dante's poem is indeed a mosaic of allusions, of well assimilated materials, of concealed and unconcealed quotations; there are two good examples in lines 31 and 33: 'ambage' is meant to recall the 'ambages' of Virgil's Cumaean Sibyl ('horrendas canit ambages' ('she utters her frightening and intricate prophecy'): *Aeneid* VI, 99), whereas line 33 is taken straight from liturgical language. Cacciaguida's speech, solemn though it is, has nothing of the dark sayings used by oracles to ensnare 'la gente folle' (the pagans: 31); its 'preciso latin' (34–5) has aroused some controversy. Did Cacciaguida actually speak in Latin, as he had previously done, or is the term 'latin' used here in the generic sense of 'language', a sense that Dante often gives it? Sound arguments could be mustered in support of both views, but I doubt if our appreciation or understanding of this passage would be much enhanced if we made our choice. I would find it more rewarding to linger for a moment on the next line, expressive of the quiet joyfulness of this blessed spirit, the word 'riso', echoed later by 'rideva' in line 121, seeming to be so apt to the appearance of a spirit in Paradise; it was more than a smile that enveloped and revealed the soul of Cacciaguida as he was about to speak. One might even imagine that it was a glow of pleasure for the heights to which his distant but direct descendant had risen.

> 'La contingenza, che fuor del quaderno
> de la vostra matera non si stende,
>   tutta è dipinta nel cospetto etterno;
>   necessità però quindi non prende
> se non come dal viso in che si specchia
>   nave che per torrente giù discende.
>   Da indi, sì come viene ad orecchia
> dolce armonia da organo, mi viene
>   a vista il tempo che ti s'apparecchia.'   (37–45)

('Contingency, which does not extend outside the volume of your material world, is all depicted in the eternal vision; without, however, being thereby necessitated, any more than is a ship that goes downstream by the eye in which it is mirrored. It is from thence that there comes to my sight, as to the ear sweet harmony from an organ, the times that are in store for you.')

The first nine lines of Cacciaguida's speech have the purpose of stressing the relationship between free-will and predestination. Although, as Dante had already remarked, contingent, or human events are all depicted in God (37–9), it does not follow that free-will is impaired (40); but, whereas philosophical and theological arguments had been used elsewhere in the poem to define the nature of free-will, here a poetic image endowed with singular visual clarity is equally or more effective: the movement of a ship that drops down a stream ('torrente' (42) means a fast-flowing river for Dante) is not determined by the eye in which it is mirrored. The reaffirmation of free-will at this point is not only intended to bring into a central canto a concept that is crucial to the poem, but also to emphasise Dante's free and steadfast acceptance both of a mission assigned to him by God and of its corollary, the misfortunes that involved him in so much suffering. The simile in the next terzina has caused some

eyebrows to be lifted. How could the dire events that are about to
be recited be described as 'sweet harmony' (44)? Its appropriateness, however, is apparent if one bears in mind that Dante wished
to convey the ease and continuity with which the future reveals
itself to Cacciaguida; and that the evils about to be predicted will
lead to a glorious outcome; so much so that at the beginning of the
next canto Dante himself savours 'il dolce' (the sweet) as well as
'l'acerbo' (the bitter) of what he had been told.

> 'Qual si partio Ipolito d'Atene
> per la spietata e perfida noverca,
> tal di Fiorenza partir ti convene.
>   Questo si vuole e questo già si cerca,
> e tosto verrà fatto a chi ciò pensa
> là dove Cristo tutto dì si merca.
>   La colpa seguirà la parte offensa
> in grido, come suol; ma la vendetta
> fia testimonio al ver che la dispensa.'   (46–54)

('As Hippolytus departed from Athens because of his cruel and treacher-
ous step-mother, so must you leave Florence. This is resolved, it is
already being schemed, it will soon be given effect by him who is
plotting it there where Christ is up for sale every day. The blame will, as
the cry goes, be laid as usual on the injured party; but the retribution will
testify to the Truth that deals it out.')

Now the poet, through the vaticination of his ancestor, faces the
recital of his banishment and of what it will mean for him (or,
rather, what it meant). It is one of the most celebrated passages of
the *Comedy*, in its transparently sincere recollection of hardships
and adversity and in its dignified vindication of innocence.
Solitude, deprivation and humiliation were to be his lot, he was to
be the victim of injustices and false accusations, but was to be
proved right in the end, and to rise far above the men and events
that had conspired to bring about his misfortunes. Right from the
beginning of the prophecy, in lines 49–51, his exile is presented
not only as a personal calamity, but as the outcome of a contest in
which he was pitted against the chief culprit of the corruption
affecting the world, Pope Boniface VIII, intent on pursuing his
simoniac transactions rather than his function of shepherd of
mankind. Note how scathingly the Pope is branded in these three
taut lines. It will be recalled that Boniface was already plotting

164

with the Black faction of the Florentine Guelphs in 1300 for the overthrow of the White Guelphs in Florence, which took place at the end of 1301, and in which Dante was involved. The prophecy had begun with characteristic directness in the previous terzina where his banishment is announced. The comparison with the banishment of Hippolytus, driven out by the false accusation of his disappointed step-mother Phaedra (Dante had read the story in Ovid) serves to stress from the outset the injustice of the charges laid against him and casts on Florence too, by implication, the reproach of having been, like Phaedra, a cruel and perfidious step-mother. Although, as usual, public opinion will blame the injured side (52–4), retribution will swiftly be testimony to truth, for it is dispensed by God who is truth – this retribution being a dark hint of the violent deaths of several of those who had been responsible for the upheaval of 1301.

> 'Tu lascerai ogne cosa diletta
> più caramente; e questo è quello strale
> che l'arco de lo essilio pria saetta.
> Tu proverai sì come sa di sale
> lo pane altrui, e come è duro calle
> lo scendere e 'l salir per l'altrui scale.' (55–60)

('You will leave everything you love most dearly; and this is the arrow the bow of exile first lets fly. You will know by experience how salty is the taste of another man's bread, how hard is the way up and down another man's stairs.')

These two terzinas demand little comment. I will only say that they are couched in a plain style, that their vocabulary is simple: ('ogne cosa', 'lo pane altrui', 'l'altrui scale'); one could, I suppose, weigh every syllable in order to try and extract the secret of their extraordinary intensity, point out the hammering effect of the first two words of each terzina ('Tu lascerai', 'Tu proverai') or the repetition of a key word like 'altrui'; but one would not get much nearer explaining how Dante has succeeded in conveying what it really feels like losing everything loved most dearly and climbing up and down another man's stairs; I, for my part, prefer to abandon myself to the subdued and meditative rhythm of a passage that is the distillation of long, cruel experience.

'E quel che più ti graverà le spalle,
sarà la compagnia malvagia e scempia
con la qual tu cadrai in questa valle;
    che tutta ingrata, tutta matta ed empia
si farà contr' a te; ma, poco appresso,
ella, non tu, n'avrà rossa la tempia.
    Di sua bestialitate il suo processo
farà la prova; sì ch'a te fia bello
averti fatta parte per te stesso.'   (61–9)

('And what will weigh most heavily on you will be the evil and senseless
company with which you must go down into this valley – so ungrateful,
so crazy and savage against you will those men prove themselves – but
before long it will be their brows, not yours, that will turn red. Their
conduct will prove their brutish folly, so that it will be to your honour to
have made a party by yourself.')

During the first year or two of his exile, Dante joined forces
with the other White Guelphs who had been banished and,
inevitably, with the Ghibellines, who had by then a far longer
experience of exile; and he played a prominent part in the several
attempts that were mounted to re-enter Florence and to oust the
new regime. Dante's description of his companions as wicked and
senseless (62) may well be coloured by the bitterness of the
disagreements that must have supervened; but there is no gainsay-
ing the fact that they were inefficient and irresolute, as well as
occasionally unlucky, for their attempts failed one after another;
and there are reports of treachery among their ranks. We learn,
moreover, that they became ungrateful and insanely hostile towards Dante (64), although we know little about the details of
these episodes, apart from unverifiable and vague accounts. As for
their brows becoming red (66), this may well refer to shame, but
the opinion is now prevailing that Dante meant 'red with blood',
following a crushing defeat in the summer of 1304. What really
matters is that in lines 68–9 we have his clear-cut and proud
statement that he finally parted company with his fellow exiles
and made a party for himself. As borne out by the *Convivio*, the
Monarchia, the *Comedy* and his epistles, the fact is that by then his
preoccupations were far higher than party politics, than strife
between Guelphs and Ghibellines, or between White and Black
Guelphs. These issues paled into insignificance in comparison
with the scheme intended to establish ideal conditions for the

happiness of humanity, which he saw more and more clearly in his mind. Thus, the moment in which he made a party for himself was a turning-point in his life. From then onwards he could conduct his lone crusade without hindrance from useless and quarrelsome associates and without the distraction of petty local considerations.

> 'Lo primo tuo refugio e 'l primo ostello
> sarà la cortesia del gran Lombardo
> che 'n su la scala porta il santo uccello;
>   ch'in te avrà sì benigno riguardo,
> che del fare e del chieder, tra voi due,
> fia primo quel che tra li altri è più tardo.'   (70–5)

('Your first refuge and first shelter will be the courtesy of the great Lombard who bears on the ladder the sacred bird; who will hold you in such kind regard that as between doing and asking, whether on your side or his, that will precede which with others comes later.')

As for the following years of his exile, spent in many different towns and in various courts, all he tells us here is that he enjoyed the hospitality of the Scala family in Verona. This passage is the only source of information for his early visit to this city, which is likely to have taken place before 1304, if the 'great Lombard' (71) is, as seems probable, Bartolomeo della Scala, who died in that year; the epithet is due to the fact that Verona was largely built on the west bank of the Adige, and therefore in a territory that Dante considered as Lombardy; the imperial eagle was added to the coat of arms of the Scala family (72) when Henry VII invested them with the dignity of vicars of the Empire, although this happened a few years after the death of Bartolomeo. One may wonder at the high praise awarded in the next three lines to Bartolomeo; he is presented as a shining example of liberality, a virtue that is rated among the greatest in the *Convivio* (I, viii), and reaches its perfection when the giver bestows without being asked. One may wonder, I repeat, for not only had Bartolomeo never been mentioned by Dante before, but whenever another member of the Scala family – his father Alberto, his brother Albuino, his half-brother Giuseppe – had previously appeared in the pages of the *Comedy*, disparaging terms were used. My own view is that Bartolomeo is praised not for his sake but retrospectively, so to speak, as a compliment to his younger brother Cangrande, who ruled Verona jointly with Albuino from 1308

167

and then as sole Lord after 1311, for his eulogy follows immediately.

> 'Con lui vedrai colui che 'mpresso fue,
> nascendo, sì da questa stella forte,
> che notabili fier l'opere sue.
>   Non se ne son le genti ancora accorte
> per la novella età, ché pur nove anni
> son queste rote intorno di lui torte;
>   ma pria che 'l Guasco l'alto Arrigo inganni,
> parran faville de la sua virtute
> in non curar d'argento né d'affanni.
>   Le sue magnificenze conosciute
> saranno ancora, sì che ' suoi nemici
> non ne potran tener le lingue mute.
>   A lui t'aspetta e a' suoi benefici;
> per lui fia trasmutata molta gente,
> cambiando condizion ricchi e mendici;
>   e portera'ne scritto ne la mente
> di lui, e nol dirai'; e disse cose
> incredibili a quei che fier presente.   (76–93)

('With him you'll see the one who at birth was so stamped with this mighty star that his deeds will be worthy of note. Not yet, indeed, because of his youth, have they drawn men's attention, for as yet these wheels have gone round him only for nine years; but before the Gascon tricks noble Henry, sparks of his mettle will appear in a disregard for money and fatigue. His large-hearted liberality will be so famous as to force even his enemies to tell of it. Look to him and to his munificence; through him shall the condition of many be transformed, the rich changing place with beggars. And concerning him, bear this inscribed in your memory, but do not reveal it'; and he told me things that shall be incredible even to those who witness them.)

No other living person is spoken of in the whole poem in terms even nearly approaching the tribute that is now paid to him: his military prowess, augured by his birth under the planet Mars (77) and later abundantly displayed, although not yet apparent in 1300, the fictional date of Dante's journey, when Cangrande was only nine years old (79–81); his early promise of magnanimity and valour (83–4), already evident before the time when the Gascon Pope, Clement V, deceived the Emperor Henry VII (82) by first supporting him and undertaking to perform his coronation in Rome, and then backing out and turning against him in 1312; his sense of justice in helping the deserving poor at the expense of the undeserving rich (89–90) – all this is remarkable praise indeed, particularly if one bears in mind that line 90 is almost a paraphrase of the homage to God in the 'Magnificat' (Luke 1.53): 'Esurientes implevit bonis et divites dimisit inanes' ('The hungry he hath filled with good things; and the rich he hath sent empty away'). But far more is to come: in lines 91–3 Cacciaguida prophesies that the Lord of Verona will perform such great things as to be incredible and not to bear repetition at present. Why was Cangrande so singled out among Dante's many hosts? Several commentators have been content with referring to the gratitude felt by the poet for the especial kindness and hospitality received in Verona during the latter years of his life, and possibly while he was writing these lines. This may be part of the story; but Dante was not given to adulation and was not in the habit of stooping to courtly servility. His real reason for conceiving such admiration for Cangrande and for entertaining such great hopes (for the 'incredible things' of lines 92–3 are obviously fondly cherished hopes for the future) must rest on more substantial foundations. And let us also bear in mind that his letter to Cangrande, if indeed it is genuine, is not less explicit in its professions of devotion and esteem, and that it even dedicates the *Paradiso* to him.

A clue to what Cangrande stood for in Dante's eyes is probably in line 82, and in the association of his name with that of 'l'alto Arrigo'. Henry VII, elected in 1308, had been the Emperor who had attempted the revival of the medieval idea of the Empire. Right from the time of his election he had made it clear that, unlike his immediate predecessors, he was determined not only to take the imperial crown in Rome, but also to demand from all men the obedience and subjection that was due to the universal Emperor. In other words, he was earnestly attempting to achieve exactly what Dante had longed for; and the poet had written three epistles in order to support his campaign in Italy and possibly, or even, I would venture to say, probably, had begun to write his political treatise *Monarchia* under the impression of what he had seen and heard in these years. After at first apparently succeeding in his undertaking (1310–11), Henry had encountered stronger and stronger resistance, and had died in 1313 with his task far from completed; but Dante, who had placed all his hopes in him, remained faithful to his memory, so much so that in Canto XXX of the *Paradiso* he reserved a seat in the Empyrean Heaven for 'l'alto Arrigo', as again he calls him. Now, Cangrande too had identified himself with the cause of the Emperor who had appointed him vicar, and had vigorously and effectively supported him in his military campaign in Italy. After the death of Henry, his court had become the rallying-point of the hopes of all Ghibellines. This prince, whose very name had something vaguely mysterious about it, had gained a reputation for political and military skill and resourcefulness, for splendour and generosity, and had inflamed the imaginations of his contemporaries, to whom he seemed the only Italian ruler capable of a stand against papal encroachments. Indeed, he seemed a kind of spiritual heir to Henry VII – all the more so as he coupled his advocacy of the universal Emperor with a devout attitude towards the Church in matters of faith. His position was entirely analogous, then, to that of Dante, who wrote the *Paradiso* after Henry had died and who, in his longing for the realisation of his ideal, must have seen in Cangrande another envoy of providence; with the wisdom of hindsight, we might add against all the odds. This, I believe, is the perspective in which the passage is to be understood.

> Poi giunse: 'Figlio, queste son le chiose
> di quel che ti fu detto; ecco le 'nsidie
> che dietro a pochi giri son nascose.
>   Non vo' però ch'a' tuoi vicini invidie,
> poscia che s'infutura la tua vita
> via più là che 'l punir di lor perfidie.'   (94–9)

(Then he added: 'These, my son, are the glosses with which to interpret what has been said to you; now you know the snares hidden behind a few circlings [of the sun and the stars]. Yet I would not have you envious of your fellow citizens, seeing that your life will far outlast the punishing of their perfidies.')

Cacciaguida's prophecy ends with a glimpse of the timelessness that is promised to Dante's message; the forecast that his life (98–9), that is, the effect of his work, shall far outlast ('s'infutura' – a typically Dantesque word) the punishment of the Florentines serves as an introduction to the final section of the canto.

> Poi che, tacendo, si mostrò spedita
> l'anima santa di metter la trama
> in quella tela ch'io le porsi ordita,

io cominciai, come colui che brama,
dubitando, consiglio da persona
che vede e vuol dirittamente e ama:
    'Ben veggio, padre mio, sì come sprona
lo tempo verso me, per colpo darmi
tal, ch'è più grave a chi più s'abbandona;
    per che di provedenza è buon ch'io m'armi,
sì che, se loco m'è tolto più caro,
io non perdessi li altri per miei carmi.
    Giù per lo mondo sanza fine amaro,
e per lo monte del cui bel cacume
li occhi de la mia donna mi levaro,
    e poscia per lo ciel, di lume in lume,
ho io appreso quel che s'io ridico,
a molti fia sapor di forte agrume;
    e s'io al vero son timido amico,
temo di perder viver tra coloro
che questo tempo chiameranno antico.'   (100–20)

(When by his silence the holy soul showed that he had finished putting
the woof into the warp that I had held out to him, I began like one who,
being perplexed, longs for advice from a person who sees clearly and
wills justly and who loves: 'My father, I see well how time is spurring
towards me to deal me such a blow as falls the heavier on the more
heedless. I shall do well, therefore, to arm myself with foresight, so that
if the place I love most is taken from me, I shall [at least] not lose others
because of my poems. Down through the endlessly bitter world and up
the mountain from whose lovely crest the eyes of my lady lifted me, and
then passing from light to light through heaven, I have learned things
which, repeated, will taste exceedingly bitter to many; while if I'm a
timid friend to truth I fear to lose life among those who will speak of the
present age as of times long past.')

Here Dante, in what is almost an inner soliloquy in the form of
a dialogue, rehearses the doubts and perplexities that must have
assailed him when he started to write the *Comedy*, and, in giving
these doubts a triumphant solution, proclaims the purpose of the
poem: the fearless propagation of truth for the benefit of mankind.
He frames his dilemma as follows: he may be left with nowhere to
shelter in, after his native city is taken from him, if he is not
prudent (108–11), for what he has learnt in Hell, Purgatory and
Paradise will be unwelcome to many, if he repeats it (112–17);
on the other hand, if he is a timid friend to truth, he will not be
remembered by posterity (118–20).

171

La luce in che rideva il mio tesoro
ch'io trovai lì, si fé prima corusca,
quale a raggio di sole specchio d'oro;
    indi rispuose: 'Coscïenza fusca
o de la propria o de l'altrui vergogna
pur sentirà la tua parola brusca.
    Ma nondimen, rimossa ogne menzogna,
tutta tua visïon fa manifesta;
e lascia pur grattar dov' è la rogna.
    Ché se la voce tua sarà molesta
nel primo gusto, vital nodrimento
lascerà poi, quando sarà digesta.
    Questo tuo grido farà come vento,
che le più alte cime più percuote;
e ciò non fa d'onor poco argomento.
    Però ti son mostrate in queste rote,
nel monte e ne la valle dolorosa
pur l'anime che son di fama note,
    che l'animo di quel ch'ode, non posa
né ferma fede per essempro ch'aia
la sua radice incognita e ascosa,
    né per altro argomento che non paia.'   (121–42)

(The light wherein was smiling the treasure I found in heaven [cf.
Matthew 6.21; 19.21] first glowed and flashed like a golden mirror in
sunlight; and then replied: 'To the conscience grown dark with its own
or another's shame, your words will indeed seem harsh; nevertheless,
throwing aside all subterfuge, speak out your total vision clearly; and let
them scratch where they feel the itch! For if at the first taste your
utterance give offence, it will leave vital nourishment once digested. This
cry of yours will be like the wind that strikes hardest the highest
summits; and that is no small honour! This is why there have been
shown you – in these wheels [the heavenly spheres], on the mountain, in
the sorrowful valley – only souls known to fame; for the hearer's mind
does not dwell on, or put faith in, examples whose origin is unknown
and hidden; or any other proof not clearly visible.')

Appropriately, Cacciaguida's light glows brighter as he gives
his stern yet stirring reply: 'Tutta tua visïon fa manifesta' ('Make
all your vision plain': 128) whatever danger might ensue. These
words contain Dante's acceptance of his mission to teach mankind
and to further its redemption, with all that this mission implies:
it is for him to wake up consciences to their sins and to the evils of
the world (124–6); it is for him to nourish mankind with truth,
even though his voice will be grievous at first taste (130–2). The

172

outburst of line 129 has disturbed some commentators as being unseemly in the rarefied atmosphere of the fifth Heaven because of the plebeian coarseness of its language; their squeamishness, however, might be soothed by the reflection that for Dante this was not a matter to be considered with detachment; all his feelings were involved, and if he put it in this way, it is because there was no other way that he knew of putting it more vigorously. Besides, this kind of rough language seems to be in keeping with the character of the speaker, who is almost the symbol of a simple, unpolished way of life; and, above all, it fits into a passage whose masterly concision adds force and elevation to this dignified statement of the purpose of the poem. For here Dante lifts us up to the lofty region of towering summits and powerful winds in which his poem ranges, and which is evoked by lines 133–4, and declares his awareness of his mission, and his determination to pursue it, even when it may be disagreeable to the powerful of the earth. He had been aiming high, in the full knowledge of his strength and of his task. A memorable, powerful claim is put forward in lines 133–4; the statement that follows them, and closes the canto, strikes a more prosaic note but is, nonetheless, worthy of attention. Only famous people have been shown to Dante during his journey, because their example strikes the reader's mind more cogently and teaches more effectively than the example of obscure individuals. There are two points that I would like to make: in the first place, the providential nature of his journey is confirmed here by implication, if God himself has pre-arranged every detail; and, secondly, we have in these lines one of the criteria used for the compilation of the poem, set out by the author himself for us to note.

The dialogue with Cacciaguida continues briefly in the next canto; but what he has to say there is, if such a thing is possible, paradisiac routine. As far as Dante and his mission are concerned, we have reached the climax and the end of the episode. The old crusader has invested his descendant with the insignia of a new crusade.

Paradiso XXVI

JOSEPH CREMONA

Paradiso XXVI forms the third, right-hand panel of a triptych of which XXV is the centre. All three cantos are set in the highest of the physical heavens or celestial spheres – the Heaven of the Fixed Stars. They share a single theme, central to an understanding of the *Comedy*: the examination of Dante's knowledge of the three theological virtues, faith, hope and charity, in preparation for the final vision of God. Each examination is conducted by one of the major apostles, Peter, James and John, the three towards whom Jesus showed most favour ('Iesù . . . fé più carezza': *Par.* XXV, 33). St Peter leads with questions on faith (Canto XXIV), St James asks the questions on hope (Canto XXV) and lastly, in our canto, St John examines the poet on the third and greatest of the virtues, charity. We are thus forced by the structure of the sequence to begin *in medias res* and we shall be unable to discuss many of the aspects that belong to the triptych as a whole. The most important of these omissions is perhaps the significance of the triple examination in the spiritual journey of the pilgrim.

Only the first half of the canto, however, is taken up by the examination on charity. The second is devoted to the encounter with Adam and to the answers Adam gives to a series of questions that their meeting brings to Dante's mind. The two halves are thus diverse in content, and if the canto is among the best known in the *Paradiso*, it is chiefly because of Adam's speech. This constitutes one of the intellectual highlights of the *Comedy*, for it expresses Dante's final view on the nature of human language, a problem that has exercised his mind throughout his career as a writer.

> Mentr' io dubbiava per lo viso spento,
> de la fulgida fiamma che lo spense

174

uscì un spiro che mi fece attento,
    dicendo . . .   (1–4)

(As I stood frightened at having lost my sight, there came a breath from the resplendent flame that had blinded me, arresting my attention by saying . . .)

The canto opens on a relatively sombre note of uncertainty and fear, for Dante is blind. At the end of Canto xxv, St Peter and St James were joined by the Evangelist. Now, a legend current from early Christian times, based on a discredited interpretation of a passage in the fourth Gospel (John 21.21–3), maintained that John did not die an earthly death but was taken up bodily into heaven. Dante the character, wishing to check the truth of the legend, had gazed fixedly at the effulgent vision and his misplaced curiosity and the credulity that it betrayed attracted a rebuke from the saint: 'Why dazzle yourself to see something that has no place here?' (*Par.* xxv, 122–3). The fixed gaze at the saint's radiance brings its own punishment with it: Dante has lost his sight, albeit temporarily, and it will not be restored to him until the end of his examination. The punishment fittingly underlines the contrast between the weakness of the poet's sight and the keenness of the Evangelist's, whose symbol, of course, is the eagle.

With St John's first question comes the reassurance that the blindness is only temporary:

'Intanto che tu ti risense
de la vista che haï in me consunta,
ben è che ragionando la compense.
  Comincia dunque; e dì ove s'appunta
l'anima tua, e fa ragion che sia
la vista in te smarrita e non defunta:
  perché la donna che per questa dia
regïon ti conduce, ha ne lo sguardo
la virtù ch'ebbe la man d'Anania.'   (4–12)

('While you recover the sight you have consumed in me, you will do well to compensate for it with speech. Begin, then, and say upon what aim your soul is set. Be assured that your sight is lost, but not for ever; for the Lady who guides you through this holy region has in her look the power that the hand of Ananias had.')

Setting aside its moral significance, Dante's blindness at this point of the narrative richly enhances the dramatic quality of the scene in the telling of the story. In the *Paradiso* light is paramount and the visionary element supremely important. Being unable to see brings in an element of pathos precious to the story-teller of the journey through the heavens, particularly in this section of the cantica.

The loss of sight on Dante's part has also the advantage of allowing speech to come fully into its own. It allows the attention to be focused upon the questions and answers that are to follow. Focusing the attention on language prepares us for Adam's account of human speech in the second half of the canto and thus helps to bridge the gap between the two halves. The use of the verb *ragionare* (6) is worth noting: an equivalent of *parlare*, it is a cognate of *ragione* 'reason', so that the verb encompasses both the meaning 'to speak' and the meaning 'to reason, to use one's reason'. *Ragionare* then is to compensate for the loss of the physical sense of sight by the use of the intellectual power, of the mind's eye. One further point: Dante's temporary blindness makes more intimate his dependence on Beatrice. It will be her gaze that will remove the film from Dante's eyes, just as in Damascus the hand of Ananias removed the scales from the eyes of Saul (Acts 9.10–18).

> Io dissi: 'Al suo piacere e tosto e tardo
> vegna remedio a li occhi, che fuor porte
> quand' ella entrò col foco ond' io sempr' ardo.'   (13–15)

(I answered: 'Soon or late, at her pleasure, may healing come to these eyes that were open gates when she entered with the fire with which I am still aflame.')

The central role played by Beatrice in the 'examination' cantos is one of the aspects there is no space to develop fully here. Her part is essentially the part of the mediator and the friend. In these lines, however, she is also what she was on earth in Dante's eyes. For Dante, Beatrice is still a woman, the woman he loves. The tone of his words, the reference to her eyes and to the power of her bright gaze are more than reminiscent of the poems in his youthful work, the *Vita Nuova*.

> 'Lo ben che fa contenta questa corte,
> Alfa e O è di quanta scrittura
> mi legge Amore o lievemente o forte.'   (16–18)

('The good that fills this court with contentment is the Alpha and Omega of all the lessons that Love teaches me, whether softly or loudly.')

St John's first question (7–8) receives the shortest of the three answers. The terzina amounts to an almost scholastic definition of charity: quite simply, God is the first and last object of true love. The language, however, is intricate and the syntax verges on ambiguity (only the sense tells us that 'Amore' is subject and not object of 'mi legge'). The metaphors, prompted by the biblical 'Alfa e O' ('beginning and end': Italian medieval scholars rarely distinguished between omega and omicron), are drawn from the language of the school: *Amore* is personified as a teacher, *leggere* is 'to teach' and *scrittura* 'what is taught, the lesson'.

The answer to the second question is the longest. Who was it, asks St John, who directed the poet's bow on the target of true love? Dante's answer is in two parts, summarised in the first terzina:

> 'Per filosofici argomenti
> e per autorità che quinci scende
> cotale amor convien che in me si 'mprenti . . .'   (25–7)

('Such love must of necessity imprint itself in me by philosophical arguments and the authority that descends from here . . .')

Each means of knowing is then expanded into a set of three terzinas. First, the argument of reason, given in syllogistic form:

> 'ché 'l bene, in quanto ben, come s'intende,
> così accende amore, e tanto maggio
> quanto più di bontate in sé comprende.
>   Dunque a l'essenza ov' è tanto avvantaggio,
> che ciascun ben che fuor di lei si trova
> altro non è ch'un lume di suo raggio,
>   più che in altra convien che si mova
> la mente, amando, di ciascun che cerne
> il vero in che si fonda questa prova.'   (28–36)

('For goodness, as soon as it is known for what it is, kindles love for itself, and this love is greater the greater the amount of goodness it contains. Therefore that Essence which so abounds in goodness that every good outside it is but a reflection of its radiance must necessarily attract most love in the mind of anyone who sees the truth on which this reasoning rests.')

The syllogism ('prova': 36) reads as follows: (*a*) good attracts love (28–9); (*b*) the greater the good, the greater the love (29–30);

(c) therefore God, the greatest good, attracts the greatest love (31–6).

The rational grounds Dante has given for aiming his bow at the true target are now followed by those provided by authority, classical and scriptural:

> 'Tal vero a l'intelletto mïo sterne
> colui che mi dimostra il primo amore
> di tutte le sustanze sempiterne.
> Sternel la voce del verace autore
> che dice a Moïsè, di sé parlando:
> "Io ti farò vedere ogne valore."
> Sternilmi tu ancora, incominciando
> l'alto preconio che grida l'arcano
> di qui là giù sovra ogne altro bando.'   (37–45)

('The man who shows me the first love of all eternal beings proclaims this truth to my understanding. The voice of the truthful Author proclaims it when He says to Moses, speaking of Himself: "I will make you see every goodness." You also proclaim it to me, when you begin the lofty announcement that heralds the mystery of this place down below louder than any other.')

The man referred to in the first of the three terzinas (38) is probably a classical philosopher. The vagueness of the reference has led to some debate as to his identity, but most agree that the reference is to Aristotle, and some scholars find the closest parallels in the neo-Platonist *Liber de causis*, which, until Aquinas, was often attributed to Aristotle. The *Liber de causis* is explicitly quoted in this context by Dante in two distinct passages of the *Convivio* (III, ii, 4 and III, vii, 2). The second and third authorities are biblical: one from the Old Testament (Exodus 33.19: note the 'Io ti farò vedere' in the context of Dante's blindness); the other a passage by St John himself, in all probability the first verses of his Gospel (John 1.1–14). In these lines, the language becomes sonorous and rises in tone to reach prophetic heights. The terzinas are symmetrical, with one citation each for the classical authority, the Old Testament and the New, in true Dantean fashion. They are full of Latinisms: 'sempiterne' (39), 'preconio' and 'arcano' (44); the unusual *sternere* 'to show' is repeated three times at measured intervals. Nevertheless, the syntax is simple and direct and the language sounds more spontaneous than that of the other two answers. Especially fine is the paratactic 'di qui là giù' ('from [up] here [to] down there'), which conveys in just four syllables the sense of the distance, physical and moral, between the outermost heavens and the earth.

Before coming to his last question, St John recapitulates approvingly the gist of Dante's answer. The third question is couched in a language that sounds strange in this context to modern ears:

> 'Ma dì ancor se tu senti altre corde
> tirarti verso lui, sì che tu suone
> con quanti denti questo amor ti morde.'   (49–51)

('But say further if you feel any other cords draw you to Him, and so declare how many are the teeth with which this love bites you.')

The strong, dramatic metaphors in the mouth of St John pull us away from the abstract language used so far and place us firmly in the physical world that is to permeate the substance of Dante's last answer.

It is time we said something on St John and his role in the *Paradiso*. The effulgent appearance of the saint – 'l'aguglia di Cristo' ('Christ's eagle') as Dante calls him (53) – takes place in Canto XXV and was, as we have seen, the indirect cause of Dante's blindness. The saint's brightness is insisted upon repeatedly. The words used to describe him include 'lume' ('light': XXV, 100), 'schiarato splendore' ('bright splendour': 106), 'foco ('fire': 121) and 'fulgida fiamma' ('resplendent flame': *Par.* XXVI, 2). Light and brightness are to be considered the distinctive qualifiers of charity, just as love is associated with heat (fire, ardour, burning). Dante's blindness comes as an almost ironic consequence of the meeting, for it is clear that, of the three apostles, John is the favourite. His role in the action is to be the champion of charity, as Peter was of faith and James of hope, and we know that 'the greatest of these is charity' (St Paul, I Corinthians 13.13). All three saints were especially close to Christ: they were present at the transfiguration and at the agony in the garden. But it was to John that Christ entrusted His mother at the Cross, and it was John who leant his head against the breast of the redeemer at the last supper. For long St John had been the object of special veneration: this may explain the legend regarding his bodily assumption into heaven on a par

179

with Christ Himself and Mary His mother. Dante shared this veneration and the signs of it are many. It is said that he called his three sons John, James and Peter, in that order. The *Convivio* has a number of direct, almost literal quotations from the writings of the saint. In this canto, there is a direct reference to the Gospel of St John ('alto preconio': 44) and a number of indirect ones: 'Alfa e O' (line 17: see Revelation 1.8; 21.6; 22.13), the reference, still to come, to the incarnation (line 59: see 1 John 4.9), the reference to God as the 'eternal husbandman' or 'gardener' (line 65: see John 15.1 and 20.15) and finally perhaps even the 'holy, holy, holy!' of line 69 (Revelation 4.8).

The metaphors used by St John in his third question are taken up in Dante's answers:

> Però ricominciai: 'Tutti quei morsi
> che posson far lo cor volgere a Dio,
> a la mia caritate son concorsi:
> ché l'essere del mondo e l'esser mio,
> la morte ch'el sostenne perch' io viva,
> e quel che spera ogne fedel com' io,
> con la predetta conoscenza viva,
> tratto m'hanno del mar de l'amor torto,
> e del diritto m'han posto a la riva.
> Le fronde onde s'infronda tutto l'orto
> de l'ortolano etterno, am' io cotanto
> quanto da lui a lor di bene è porto.'   (55–66)

(So I began again: 'All the bites that can make one's heart turn to God have come together in my charity. The world's existence and my own, the death that He endured that I might live, and that which all believers hope for as I do, together with the living knowledge of which I have already spoken, all have pulled me out of the sea of twisted love and brought me to the shore of the love that is straight. As for the boughs that embower the orchard of the eternal Gardener, I love them in proportion to the good He has bestowed upon them.')

'The teeth of the love that bites him' are listed in three marvellously succinct lines (58–60), of which only the last needs to be glossed: 'quel che spera ogne fedel' is the promise of eternal life in the sight of God. All four of the motives adduced by Dante were commonplaces in the theological and devotional literature of the time, and all concern love for the self. As the examination progresses, Dante deals with the principal objects of charity in the order in which they were set out in traditional Christian theology: the love for God (in the first two answers), love for the self (in the first part of his third answer) and, finally, love for one's neighbour. This last aspect is developed in the last terzina where humanity is likened to the leaves of the trees in the orchard of 'l'ortolano etterno' (65), in lines memorable for the near repetition, in close succession, of two words: 'fronde'–'infronda' and 'orto'–'ortolano' (note too the assonance 'fronde'–'onde'–'infronda').

The examination is at an end. Dante the character has satisfied his examiner by answering all three questions on charity in accordance with the teachings of the Church, modelling himself closely on the formulations of St Thomas. It is difficult to go further, within the limits of a *lectura*, into the significance of charity in the *Comedy* and particularly into the subtle distinction between charity and love (*agapê* and *eros*). The canto itself gives little clue on the nature of the distinction: the word 'carità', for instance, occurs once only (57), whereas 'amore' is repeated seven times in the first sixty-six lines.

We can, on the other hand, say something about the tone and pace of the language in which Dante's answers are presented. Several critics have commented on the measured scholastic treatment of this third examination (the phrases introducing direct speech, for instance, are present at every appropriate place). This in contrast with the rapid pace and the warmth of the passages devoted to faith and charity in the earlier cantos. Commentators have also noted the brief amount of space devoted to the passage dealing with the love we should bear our neighbours, a central tenet of the Christian faith: it receives a mere three lines out of a total of thirty-six. Others have stressed the measured way in which love towards one's neighbours is apportioned in proportion to the good bestowed upon each individual, a reasoning that follows logically from the statement that the greater good attracts the greater love (29–30). It also follows closely the teaching of St Thomas (cf. *Summa Theol.* 2a 2ae, 25 and 26).

The language too has been found to be cold, scholastic, intellectual, lacking the fire and fervour that might have been expected in the treatment of such a theme. Characteristically enough, the only passage that gives the feeling of warmth and spontaneity is the one devoted to the teachers of classical and biblical antiquity (37–45): Dante's *pietas* in these lines is unmistakable. The feeling of unspontaneity has made one critic write that Dante cannot get away from his intellectualism, that he does not know the words of mystical exaltation.[1] For another, Dante is unable to communicate St Paul's conviction of the primacy of charity. Let us remember, however, with Pier Vincenzo Mengaldo, that Dante's treatment is deliberately anti-mystical and intellectual, that his attention is turned not to the emotional aspects of his theme but to the rational possession of a truth, the 'vero in che si fonda questa prova' of line 36. The theme is not fire, but light.

As the examination ends, a hymn of praise resounds through Heaven, the thanksgiving of the blessed to God for the successful outcome of the test.

> Sì com' io tacqui, un dolcissimo canto
> risonò per lo cielo, e la mia donna
> dicea con li altri: 'Santo, santo, santo!' (67–9)

(As I fell silent, the sweetest song resounded through heaven, and my Lady was singing with the others: 'Holy, holy, holy!')

A perceptive critic has pointed out the fine parallelism between the visual and the aural in this scene. On each of the two sensual planes, an element in the foreground ('la mia donna', 'Santo, santo, santo!') stands out against its background ('lo cielo', 'un dolcissimo canto').

At this point, the exact middle of the canto, Dante recovers his sight. As foretold by St John, Beatrice removes with her gaze the scales that had blinded the poet. A strange simile (70–81) likens this moment to that of a man being suddenly awakened from sleep by a bright light. The description is highly technical, with an account of the physiology of sight as then understood, and of the reaction of the waking man unconsciously shrinking away until the internal sense then called 'estimation' (*aestimativa*) comes to his rescue. When the poet is able to see again, he discovers that, as on an earlier occasion in the *Paradiso*, his eyes can better endure the dazzling lights around him. The symbolism behind the loss of sight and its recovery through the agency of Beatrice's gaze is complex and even a little obscure. An allusion is perhaps being made to Dante's past life, but there is also an indication of the role played by theology, in some sense personified by Beatrice, in the personal salvation of the poet and of mankind.

We now come to the encounter with Adam. As the poet is able to see again, he is amazed to find that a fourth light has appeared among the three saints. Beatrice answers his unformulated question:

> 'Dentro da quei rai
> vagheggia il suo fattor l'anima prima
> che la prima virtù creasse mai.'
> Come la fronda che flette la cima
> nel transito del vento, e poi si leva
> per la propria virtù che la soblima,
> fec' io in tanto in quant' ella diceva,
> stupendo, e poi mi rifece sicuro
> un disio di parlare ond' ïo ardeva.
> E cominciai: 'O pomo che maturo
> solo prodotto fosti, o padre antico
> a cui ciascuna sposa è figlia e nuro,
> divoto quanto posso a te supplìco
> perché mi parli: tu vedi mia voglia,
> e per udirti tosto non la dico.'   (82–96)

('Within those rays, the first soul ever created by the First Power is gazing lovingly upon his Maker.' As the bough bends its top at a passing gust of wind and then springs back with natural resilience, so did I bend with amazement as she spoke, till the burning desire I had to speak restored my confidence. So I began: 'O fruit, the only fruit that was born fully ripe, O ancient father to whom every bride is both daughter and daughter-in-law, I beg you as devoutly as I can to speak to me. You see what it is I want to know: to hear you quickly, I shall not put it into words.')

The likening of the pilgrim to a bough is the second reference to a tree in the canto. This time it is a reference with literary antecedents, for it is one we find in Statius (*Thebaid* vi, 854). At this place in the poem, the simile is particularly forceful, for besides its literary function, that of conveying the poet's natural awe at his encounter with the first man, it suggests something of the stature acquired by Dante the character towards the end of his journey, confident in his powers, with a confidence quickened by the thirst for knowledge, the knowledge Adam can impart.

It is not easy for the modern mind to grasp the significance that the figure of Adam must have had for the medieval. For us he is the legendary first man, but in a purely genealogical sense. For them he was much more: he was the ideal man, the archetype of man. Created fully grown, he was the incarnation of God's idea of human nature, a perfect image. It is not by chance that Dante the poet makes him the first human being to meet Dante the character after his examination. Adam was created as the ideal whole man, perfect in nature and in grace, with the wholeness to which Dante may aspire, he now being in a state of grace, as is symbolised by his restored vision.

Dante has several questions to put to Adam, but he does not formulate them himself. As Adam will explain at the beginning of his speech, he can see the unformulated questions mirrored in God's mind in perfect reflection. Dante knows this, and his speech is limited to the opening address and the request to speak. Adam stirs with pleasure and joy as he hears Dante's request, and this movement makes the halo of light that surrounds him ripple and vibrate. With an extraordinary desire for precision, Dante likens Adam's motion and that of the light around him to the movement of an animal stirring under a covering. It is an unexpected simile, with no apparent literary antecedent. Its unexpectedness has given trouble to the commentators who, for once, are clearly at a loss. Someone has suggested a caparisoned horse, others the quivering of an animal's skin.

Adam now speaks. He explains why he has no need to be told the questions in Dante's mind and, to prove the point, outlines them briefly:

> 'Tu vuogli udir quant' è che Dio mi puose
> ne l'eccelso giardino, ove costei
> a così lunga scala ti dispuose,
>   e quanto fu diletto a li occhi miei,
> e la propria cagion del gran disdegno,
> e l'idioma ch'usai e che fei.'   (109–14)

('You want to know how much time has passed since God placed me in that highest of gardens, where this Lady prepared you for the long ascent; and how long the delight lasted in my eyes; and the real cause of God's great wrath; and what language I used and fashioned.')

There is marvellous economy of words in these six lines. There is economy too in the incorporation of questions and answers into one speech. After the triple set earlier in the canto, the narrative technique had to be different.

Four questions: the first two concern time, the next the real nature of original sin, while the last deals with the nature of the language Adam spoke on earth. Adam answers the third question first:

> 'Or, figliuol mio, non il gustar del legno
> fu per sé la cagion di tanto essilio,
> ma solamente il trapassar del segno.'   (115–17)

('Now, my son, it was not the actual tasting of the tree that was the cause of such great banishment, but only overstepping the mark.')

The banishment, of course, refers both to Adam's 'essilio' and to that of all humanity until the death on the Cross. The original sin, then, did not consist in the curiosity that made Adam and Eve taste of the forbidden fruit, but in the disobedient pride, the conscious going beyond the limit set by God. The parallel with Ulysses' 'folle volo', his 'mad flight', told in the *Inferno* (also in a twenty-sixth canto, at line 125), is clear: like Adam's, Ulysses' sin was not the spirit of curiosity, however worthy, that made him sail beyond the bounds set by Hercules, but the defying of the god's command.

If we look now at the re-ordering of Dante's questions by Adam in his answer, we can see that Adam is answering the most important question first. Of the four, it is the only one with a moral content. Now, is the order in which the questions were put to Dante the character the one in which Adam saw them in his mind? If it was, and I have reasons for believing it was, then we may read in the re-ordering of Dante's answers an unspoken rebuke on Adam's part. For the non-theological questions are there, in a sense, to satisfy Dante's intellectual curiosity: they concern the lifespan of Adam and of the world, and the nature of man's first language. Only the third question affects the essential relation between man and God. There is then, in Adam's re-ordering, a rebuke to the expression of Dante's eager but uncritical curiosity, similar to (though not so serious as) the curiosity that led him to peer too closely at the figure of St John. Taken together with what Adam says on original sin – that it was not the

185

tasting of the tree in Eden in itself ('per sé': 116) that was important – we can see that there is, running through the canto, a minor theme, the condemnation of curiosity, not in itself, but because it can blind man to what really matters, the proper ordering of one's values.

The second answer relates to the first question:

> 'Quindi onde mosse tua donna Virgilio,
> quattromilia trecento e due volumi
> di sol desiderai questo concilio;
>   e vidi lui tornare a tutt' i lumi
> de la sua strada novecento trenta
> fïate, mentre ch'ïo in terra fu'mi.' (118–23)

('At the place from which your Lady moved Virgil, I longed for this assembly during four thousand three hundred and two revolutions of the sun. During my life on earth, I saw the sun review all the stars on its course nine hundred and thirty times.')

Adam had spent 4,302 years in Limbo, the place from which Beatrice had summoned Virgil to come to Dante's rescue. This figure represents the time between Adam's death and the Harrowing of Hell. If we add to it the 930 years of Adam's life and the 1,266 elapsed since Christ's death on the Cross, we have a total of 6,498, the figure Dante the character had originally asked for.

Adam now answers Dante's fourth question:

> 'La lingua ch'io parlai fu tutta spenta
> innanzi che a l'ovra inconsummabile
> fosse la gente di Nembròt attenta:
>   ché nullo effetto mai razïonabile,
> per lo piacere uman che rinovella
> seguendo il cielo, sempre fu durabile.
>   Opera naturale è ch'uom favella;
> ma così o così, natura lascia
> poi fare a voi secondo che v'abbella.
>   Pria ch'i' scendessi a l'infernale ambascia,
> I s'appellava in terra il sommo bene
> onde vien la letizia che mi fascia;
>   e El si chiamò poi: e ciò convene,
> ché l'uso d'i mortali è come fronda
> in ramo, che sen va e altra vene.' (124–38)

('The language that I spoke was quite extinct by the time Nimrod's people undertook the task that could never be accomplished. No product of human reason lasts for long, for man's pleasure keeps changing with the heavens. That man should speak is part of his nature, but whether in this way or that, nature then leaves you to follow your own pleasure. Before my journey down to the anguish of Hell, *I* was the name given on earth to the Supreme Good, from whom comes the joy that enfolds me; later He was called *El*. And this is as it should be, for the customs of mortals are like leaves upon a branch: one goes and another takes its place.')

The origin and nature of human language were questions that had occupied many minds before Dante's, but no other author, certainly no other creative author, had displayed such intense and personal interest in them as Dante did. The theme recurs in his writings throughout his life, but its fullest treatment occurs in an unfinished book on the art of writing in the vernacular, the *De vulgari eloquentia*. In Adam's speech, the passage on language is by far the longest, to the extent that some have seen it as being out of place in this part of the *Comedy*. We shall see that it is not: for one thing, Dante expresses in these lines a rethinking of earlier ideas whose consequences are far-reaching. It required the authority conferred through its being uttered by Adam himself.

As expressed in the *De vulgari eloquentia*, Dante's views on the nature of language are briefly the following. Language was a gift of God to man: at his creation, Adam had received not just the faculty of speech, but the actual structures and forms of the language he spoke – in other words, language was handed to him ready-made. This pristine Adamitic language which Dante called 'the language of grace' was of course Hebrew, and it remained unchanged after the Fall until the catastrophe of Babel. After Babel, it was retained unchanged only by the children of Heber, the Hebrews, who had taken no part in the building of the Tower. All other peoples spoke 'languages of confusion', different from each other, changing with time and place, corruptible.

These notions undergo a profound change in the passage spoken by Adam. In the new version, it is only the faculty of language that God has given man. In Adam's words, it is natural for man to speak (130). *What* he speaks is left to him (131–2). The linguistic forms used by Adam were thus Adam's own (114). Languages, then, are the product of man's mind. In his book on language, Dante tells us that man is a most unstable and variable animal: 'homo . . . instabilissimum atque variabilissimum animal'

187

(*Dve* I, ix, 6) and here we are told that no product of man's mind lasts for long since man's pleasure is governed by the shifting influence of the stars (127–9). Like all other human institutions, languages must change with time and place. Adam's language was no exception to this rule: it was dead (124) at the time of the building of Babel, the unaccomplishable task of Nimrod's people (125–6). To illustrate his point, and to show that mutability was a feature of language from the very beginning, Adam gives Dante a brief history of the first word thought to have been pronounced by his lips, the word for God: in his days it was *I*, the first sound of the name Yahweh; later it was *El*, the Hebrew name for God (133–6). Adam ends this part of his speech with a lovely analogy, reworked from Horace (*Ars Poetica* 60–2), where mankind changing its customs is compared to a tree changing its leaves.

What led to this change of opinion? Since the answer to this question throws light on the meaning of the canto as a whole, it is worth spending a little time on it even in a short *lectura*. There is first a passage in Genesis that appears to contradict the view that God had given Adam a fully-formed language: 'And out of the ground the LORD God formed every beast of the field, and every fowl of the air; and brought them unto Adam to see what he would call them: and whatsoever Adam called every living creature, that was the name thereof' (Genesis 2.19). But there is a deeper reason. Dante's original theory had in it the germ of self-contradiction.

By the time Dante came to write the *De vulgari eloquentia*, he had become convinced that of the two languages that concerned him most, Latin and the Italian vernacular, it was the vernacular that was the nobler of the two, despite its impermanence and variability. The superiority of the vernacular came from, among other things, its spontaneity, its naturalness; whereas Latin was an orderly *grammatica*, an artifact fashioned by man. Now Hebrew too was a *grammatica*, but one that, according to Dante's first theory, had been fashioned by God. It was difficult, therefore, to maintain the superiority of a vernacular over a *grammatica* without indirectly impugning the God-given status of Hebrew. By demoting Hebrew to the status of a *grammatica* fashioned by man, on a par with Latin, all threat is removed from the argument that the vernacular is nobler than Latin. Furthermore, there is no longer the taint of corruption to disparage the vernacular: since language was changing from the time of creation, the linguistic significance of Babel is reduced and it becomes no longer possible to oppose one incorruptible 'language of grace' to many corruptible 'languages of confusion'. By following his thought to the end, Dante is here buttressing intellectually what he always knew to be the case, the primacy and validity of his own vernacular over Latin for the Italy of his time.

Adam closes his speech with his answer to the second question:

> 'Nel monte che si leva più da l'onda,
> fu' io, con vita pura e disonesta,
> da la prim' ora a quella che seconda,
> come 'l sol muta quadra, l'ora sesta.'   (139–42)

('I lived on the mountain that rises highest from the sea, in innocent and sinful life, from the first hour to the hour that follows the sixth, when the sun changes quadrant.')

The time spent in Eden, at the top of Mount Purgatory, before and after the Fall, was seven hours, from 6 a.m. to 1 p.m. With this precise but rueful and suggestive note, the canto ends.

Let me conclude by returning to the question of the structure of the canto, the question I raised at the beginning. The content of the two halves is certainly diverse, but the canto does not fall apart, for a number of links bind them together. The language, for instance, is uniform in tone and style: the vocabulary of both sections is intellectual with a high density of Latinisms, for the most part philosophical and scientific terms. The metaphors have the same ring about them. The most noticeable is the recurring theme of the tree and its boughs: the word 'fronda' occurs three times across the canto (64, 85, 137), to which we could add 'legno', the forbidden tree of line 115. The themes too repeat each other: I have already mentioned the theme of curiosity and the way it underlies the canto as a whole. The theme of speech, so prominent in the half devoted to Adam, is first announced by St John, when he calls upon Dante to compensate for the loss of vision with speech.

The deepest bond, however, concerns the function of the two halves considered in relation to the objective of the *Comedy* as a whole. In Adam's speech Dante has finally justified his choice of the vernacular as the medium for his message. He has made Adam himself sanction its use (notice the 'lascia . . . fare a voi' of lines 131–2: it is equivalent to 'it's up to you'). It will no longer be possible to say, on any ground, that his is an inadequate, ignoble language, unfit for the sacred poem he conceived. At the same time the canto serves to vindicate the content of his message. His examination over, he has received the blessing of the celestial court, of the Church triumphant. More fully than ever before he is now in a state of grace, fit to receive the explicit invitation to speak out his message on his return to earth from St Peter himself, in the following canto. He is now fully the poet and the prophet.

Note

1 E. Donadoni (in *Letture dantesche: Paradiso*, ed. G. Getto (Firenze, 1961), pp. 527–48). I have been particularly helped by the following works in preparing this *lectura*: G. Getto, 'Canto XXVI', in *Lectura Dantis Scaligera: Paradiso* (Firenze, 1968), pp. 931–55; Pier Vincenzo Mengaldo, 'Appunti sul canto XXVI del "Paradiso" ', in *Linguistica e retorica di Dante* (Pisa, 1978), pp. 223–46; N. Sapegno's edition of the *Comedy* (Firenze, 1957); and the relevant articles in the *Enciclopedia dantesca*.

Paradiso XXX

PRUDENCE SHAW

With Canto XXX of the *Paradiso* we are at the beginning of the end of the *Comedy*. The last four cantos of the poem form a unit: they describe Dante's experience when he reaches the Empyrean – Heaven itself as distinct from the heavens through which he has been travelling in the previous twenty-nine cantos – where he enjoys first the vision of the heavenly hosts, and then, in the final canto, the vision of God. Canto XXX is then both an end and a beginning. It marks the end of the physical journey, the moment of arrival at the goal towards which the pilgrim has been striving since he lost his way in the dark wood. From this point on, his progress is measured purely in terms of his ability to see and his ability to understand. He travels forward in the intellectual sense only. But equally it marks a beginning: the beginning of Dante the character's final great effort, as a living man, to penetrate and comprehend the mystery of beatitude and of God; and the beginning of Dante the poet's final great effort, as an artist, to describe the visionary experience in which his journey culminates.

For in this canto Dante emerges from the world of time and space into eternity, a world beyond time and beyond space. This final experience of eternity unfolds as a single episode over four cantos, as Dante moves from understanding God through his angels and the blessed to understanding God directly, without the need of an intervening medium. Inevitably, in reading Canto XXX divorced from those that follow it, we lose a great deal. It is a canto of initiation and acclimatisation into a completely new world; it is the first stage in a magnificent crescendo of light, joy and ecstatic fervour, whose true climax is in the final lines of the poem, where Dante's power to see and understand embraces the whole of creation through the creator.

The shape of the canto reflects in microcosm the shape of the

191

whole poem. The movement is from lesser to greater light, from lesser to greater understanding. But in this canto a qualitative change occurs in Dante's mode of apprehension. His power to see is transformed, and as a result of this transformation he begins to be able to experience the mystery of beatitude directly, instead of apprehending it imperfectly through his limited human faculties. Following on this transformation, which is the central event of the canto, he perceives a series of visions of mounting splendour and radiance. Each stage in the action is followed by a short speech from Beatrice, who explains what is happening, what the vision signifies, and in what way Dante's sight is still defective. The pattern of the canto is vision followed by explanation, seeing followed by understanding, image followed by doctrine: and it contains some of the most dazzlingly beautiful images and some of the most pregnant theological statements in the whole poem.

The canto opens, appropriately enough, with a light image. The first nine lines describe the coming of dawn, personified as the 'chiarissima ancella' (7), the 'brightest handmaiden' of the sun. As dawn advances, the stars become gradually invisible one by one to an observer down here on earth, until finally even the brightest star in the heavens is outshone by the dawning splendour in the east.

> Forse semilia miglia di lontano
> ci ferve l'ora sesta, e questo mondo
> china già l'ombra quasi al letto piano,
>   quando 'l mezzo del cielo, a noi profondo,
> comincia a farsi tal, ch'alcuna stella
> perde il parere infino a questo fondo;
>   e come vien la chiarissima ancella
> del sol più oltre, così 'l ciel si chiude
> di vista in vista infino a la più bella.   (1–9)

(Perhaps six thousand miles away the sixth hour [noon] blazes, and this world already inclines its shadow almost to the level bed [of the horizon], when the atmosphere deep above us begins to change so that some stars are no longer visible down here on earth; and as the brightest handmaiden of the sun advances, so one by one the stars fade from the sky, until even the loveliest one has gone.)

The immediate point of the image is to describe what Dante sees. In Canto XXVII Dante and Beatrice had risen to the *Primum Mobile*, the ninth and largest of the spheres circling the earth, in which the whole of the created world is contained. At the beginning of Canto XXVIII Dante had his first direct experience of God. He saw a point of light so infinitesimally small that a star in comparison with it would seem as big as the moon, and yet a point so bright that anyone who gazed at it would be forced to shut his eyes. This point of light is surrounded by a spinning circle of fire, which in its turn is surrounded by another fiery circle, and so on. In all there are nine of these concentric circles, the ninth one enclosing all the others. Beatrice, in response to an unspoken question of Dante's had explained in a brief but magnificently resonant phrase, echoing Aristotle (*Metaphysics* XII, 7, 1072*b*): 'Da quel punto / depende il cielo e tutta la natura' ('From that point hang the heavens and all nature'). The point is God, the circles are the hierarchies of the angels, each one responsible for the motion of one of the heavenly spheres circling the earth. The point appears to be surrounded, but in reality it surrounds or encloses the circles and the whole universe – the familiar paradox will recur in our canto in line 12.

The point and the fiery circles – yet another prefiguring, in a form accessible to human understanding, of what he is to see in its true nature at the end of his journey – remain visible to Dante throughout Canto XXIX, in which Beatrice delivers a long lecture on the creation of the angels, the rebellious angels, and human and angelic faculties, leading to a passionate outburst against bad philosophers and preachers. At the beginning of Canto XXX the vision fades. Now at last in line 10 the point of the opening image becomes clear.

> Non altrimenti il trïunfo che lude
> sempre dintorno al punto che mi vinse,
> parendo inchiuso da quel ch'elli 'nchiude,
>   a poco a poco al mio veder si stinse:
> per che tornar con li occhi a Bëatrice
> nulla vedere e amor mi costrinse.   (10–15)

(In just this way the triumph that rejoices eternally around the point that overcame me, seeming to be enclosed by that which it encloses, gradually faded from my sight; so that seeing nothing and love constrained me to return with my eyes to Beatrice.)

The rejoicing throng surrounding the point faded from sight as the stars do when dawn approaches. When Dante turns back to look at Beatrice, as he does in lines 14–15, with the daring zeugma, 'nulla vedere e amor' (*'seeing nothing and love* constrained me to return with my eyes to Beatrice') he finds that she is shining with a new resplendence. By now Dante can assume that the reader is familiar with the process by which travel takes place in the *Paradiso*: it is an instantaneous transposition, signalled only by the increased brilliance of Beatrice's light. Her new radiance, reflecting her increased closeness to God, is a sign that the travellers have emerged into the Empyrean, just as it has signalled their arrival in each new sphere. But this is something that Dante the character, and the reader with him, only learns in line 38. Characteristically, the event precedes the explanation. Less characteristically, as we shall see, it is separated from it by a long digression.

Quite apart from its intrinsic beauty as a description of the fading of the circles, it seems clear that Dante has opened with this extended astronomical image for a number of reasons that bear on the overall structure of the canto. First, it marks a pause in the narrative flow, a moment of quiet absorption, in contrast with which the accelerating tempo of the visions at the centre of the canto will seem all the more striking. Secondly, at a point in the journey where we might have become blasé about the notion of interstellar travel, it serves to remind us of the immensity of the heavens, of the distance from earth to the stars, and of how far Dante has already travelled – and this is something we are re-minded of in different ways and with increasing frequency as we approach the end of the poem. Finally, the dawn image enables Dante to provide a satisfying example of narrative symmetry and balance. As we read these lines, we have our feet firmly on the ground and are looking up into space, we are at the centre of Dante's universe looking out; at the end of the canto we will look down from Heaven to earth, not just to the earth's crust or surface, but down inside it to Hell for our last glimpse of the corrupt Popes. So the opening image not only has an obvious beauty and visual appropriateness, it also has a wider function in terms of the shaping of the whole episode.

In line 15 Dante turns to Beatrice, and in line 38 she tells him that they have reached the Empyrean. The intervening lines constitute a digression celebrating her beauty and Dante's inability to do her justice in his words – the last major statement on this theme in the poem. Although Beatrice is still Dante's guide and close by him till the end of this canto, and although she is still working on his behalf right to the end of the *Paradiso*, it is here that Dante as poet pays his final tribute to her,[1] reminding us that she has been the centre of his life since he was nine years old. The first lines of the digression emphasise the continuity of Dante's experience back beyond the *Comedy*: if everything he had ever said of Beatrice were to be compressed into a single *loda*, a single expression of praise, it would fall far short of what was required here. The youthful *Vita Nuova* had recorded how Dante discovered a style to praise Beatrice – the *stilo de la loda*. Seen in this perspective, the *Comedy* becomes an extension of the *Vita Nuova*, the fulfilment of the promise made at the end of that work that he would say of Beatrice 'quello che mai non fu detto d'alcuna' ('that which was never said of any woman'). Beatrice's beauty has now transcended the human, for on entering the Empyrean she at last reflects her full glory as a blessed soul; in fact Dante claims with daring hyperbole that it transcends not only human experience but that of the angelic intelligences as well: only Beatrice's maker, only God, can fully enjoy her beauty – 'solo il suo fattor tutta la goda'.

> Se quanto infino a qui di lei si dice
> fosse conchiuso tutto in una loda,
> poca sarebbe a fornir questa vice.
> La bellezza ch'io vidi si trasmoda
> non pur di là da noi, ma certo io credo
> che solo il suo fattor tutta la goda.
> Da questo passo vinto mi concedo
> più che già mai da punto di suo tema
> soprato fosse comico o tragedo:
> ché, come sole in viso che più trema,
> così lo rimembrar del dolce riso
> la mente mia da me medesmo scema.
> Dal primo giorno ch'i' vidi il suo viso
> in questa vita, infino a questa vista,
> non m'è il seguire al mio cantar preciso;
> ma or convien che mio seguir desista
> più dietro a sua bellezza, poetando,
> come a l'ultimo suo ciascuno artista.   (16–33)

(If all that has been said of her up to this point were gathered into a single expression of praise, it would fall short of what was needed here. The beauty I saw is not only beyond our human measure, but I truly believe that only her maker fully enjoys it. I acknowledge myself defeated by this passage more than comic or tragic poet was ever overwhelmed by any point in his theme, for, like sunlight striking very sensitive eyes,[2] so the memory of her sweet smile severs my mental powers from my self. From the first day I saw her face in this life, up to this sight of her, the pursuit has not been cut off in my song; but now I must cease pursuing her beauty further in my poetry, as every artist must when he reaches the limit of his powers.)

Dante's protestation that his powers are unequal to the task is far from unselfconscious – such a declaration was a commonplace of medieval rhetoric. The writer declares that what he is about to describe can never be expressed in human speech: his very protestation of the inadequacy of his words serves to enhance the person or incident that is said to be indescribable. In Dante the device is more complicated than in most medieval poets, for whom it tended to be no more than a conventional way of paying a compliment to the greatness of a prince or the generosity of a patron. There is a chain of inadequacy in Dante because of the visionary nature of the experience he is describing. The mind cannot fully grasp what it experiences, because this transcends the human capacity for understanding; the memory cannot now recall even that which the mind did grasp at the time; and finally, the poet's words cannot do justice even to what he *can* recall to mind. The poet's words are three stages removed from what he is attempting to represent.

Dante concentrates on different links in the chain at different points in the poem. In the early stages it tends to be his linguistic resources as a writer that cannot do justice to something that he understood at the time and now remembers quite clearly. But towards the end of the *Comedy*, it is on the first and second links in the chain that the emphasis falls. The opening lines of the *Paradiso* state the theme; and it is perhaps not surprising that it should be restated with particular insistence at the beginning of Canto XXX, the canto where Dante is initiated into eternity, and at the end of Canto XXXIII, where the disparity between what he saw and what he remembers, and then again what he remembers and what he can put into words, is so great that he simply stops writing. The whole of the final section of the poem is framed by these two statements of inexpressibility, the first in relation to Beatrice, the second in relation to God.[3]

Beatrice's smile is Dante's first experience of the light of beatitude, and it is the memory of its intensity that prompts him to the digression, which emphasises every step separating his words from the vision itself. Her beauty is such that only God himself can fully enjoy it (19–21); Dante's memory of her smile, that is of what he as a human being was able to experience of it, is so overwhelming that his mental faculties are unable to operate (25–7) – the emphatic alliteration underlines the devastating effect: 'la mente mia da me medesmo scema'; this is the point at which he must stop writing about her, as his words are not equal to the task (31–3). He has reached 'l'ultimo suo', the limits of his expressive powers. These are the three key terzinas in which the links in the chain of ineffability are made clear.[4] Each is followed by a terzina that elaborates on the theme. Lines 22–4 point out that the difficulty Dante faces here is greater than that faced by any poet before him, whether comic or tragic – no earlier writer had ever attempted so taxing a theme. Lines 28–30 emphasise Dante's constancy to his theme up to this point. In the lovely lines 'Dal primo giorno ch'i' vidi il suo viso / in questa vita, infino a questa vista' – once again there is a very high degree of formal patterning with the alliteration of 'vidi'–'viso'–'vita'–'vista' – Dante reminds us that from the first day he ever saw Beatrice he has allowed no obstacle to deter him. It is not that he is easily deflected from his course, but that this is the point at which he *must* renounce the attempt. And in lines 34–6, which conclude the digression and link it up to the action that follows, Dante entrusts her praise to a 'maggior bando / che quel de la mia tuba', to a greater poetic talent than his own.[5] The emphasis here is placed clearly on his own limitations as a poet, not on the limitations of human speech as such.

The whole digression shows us the complete revitalisation of a hackneyed theme, of what in earlier writers was almost an automatic gesture; a revitalisation that is entirely characteristic of Dante's art, which is so deeply-rooted in medieval rhetorical traditions and yet so extraordinarily vital and original. All the scattered passages about his inability to do Beatrice justice reach their triumphant culmination in this formal leave-taking, the careful placing of which at this point in the narrative shows Dante's skill in orchestrating his themes. The action will build in intensity in an uninterrupted series of images and speeches right through the remaining cantos – digression at a later point would have destroyed that effect. In terms of narrative pace and shape the digression functions as an extension of the opening image, a further device for postponing the action till the centre of the canto, and it enables Dante to achieve one of his most striking effects, that of the contrast between Dante *poeta's* sense of fatigue as he nears the end of *his* task, and Beatrice's sense of release as she nears the end of hers. Just as lines 28–9 caused us to look back and embrace almost the whole of Dante's life in a glance, as though it were a single entity whose meaning was contained in itself and was now clearly discernible, so now Dante reminds us explicitly that he is nearing the end of his task. The effortfulness of 'deduce / l'ardüa sua matera terminando' – the verb gives an almost physical sense of the labour of moulding, drawing-out and shaping a resisting material – contrasts strikingly with Beatrice's 'atto e voce di spedito duce'. The authority and decisiveness of her words introduce a marked change in mood and tempo.

> Cotal qual io la lascio a maggior bando
> che quel de la mia tuba, che deduce
> l'ardüa sua matera terminando,
> con atto e voce di spedito duce
> ricominciò: 'Noi siamo usciti fore
> del maggior corpo al ciel ch'è pura luce . . .'   (34–9)

(Such as I leave her to a greater heralding than that of my trumpet, which draws out the difficult matter as the end approaches, with the manner and voice of a guide whose task is complete, she began again: 'We have emerged from the largest body to the heaven that is pure light . . .')

The 'maggior corpo' is the *Primum Mobile*, the largest of the spheres, within which the whole of the created universe is contained; the 'ciel ch'è pura luce' is the Empyrean. The distinction between 'corpo' and 'luce' is a vital one, and the transition from one to the other is a crucial step in Dante's journey. Up till now, through all the many stages in his progress towards God, he has been travelling in a world of matter; through all the varied descriptions and images involving light in the *Paradiso*, we have always been dealing with light as we know it from our own experience, physical, sensible light emitted by material bodies, which may be of a brightness and splendour that is difficult to comprehend because it so exceeds our everyday experience, but is not qualitatively different from light as we know it. Now he leaves the world of matter behind and enters a world made of *pure* light, and pure light *is* qualitatively different from sensible light.

The concept of pure light was a commonplace of medieval theology. It can be traced back to Plato, who says in the *Republic* (507–9) that, just as for an act of seeing to take place, there must be an organ of sight, the eye, an object to be seen, and light, the medium that makes the act possible; so for an act of understanding, of seeing in the intellectual sense, three things are necessary: the organ of understanding, the mind; the truth to be understood; and the medium that makes the act possible. Medieval theologians called this medium 'pure' or 'intellectual' or 'spiritual' light and debated whether God Himself could be called 'light' literally or only metaphorically. Where Dante as philosopher stands on this issue is not entirely clear; as poet, he used the notion of pure light to represent what would otherwise be unrepresentable. In the final cantos of the *Comedy*, Heaven and God Himself are shown as being made of this pure light; or, to be more exact, God is shown as its source and Heaven as its reflection.

The definition that Beatrice offers of this pure light in lines 40–2 is a definition in terms of the interplay of its properties. Light, love and joy, the key words in Dante's conception of the Empyrean, are woven into a series of interlocking phrases that reflect the endless ecstatic fervour of the beatific experience:

> 'luce intellettüal, piena d'amore;
> amor di vero ben, pien di letizia;
> letizia che trascende ogne dolzore.
>   Qui vederai l'una e l'altra milizia
> di paradiso, e l'una in quelli aspetti
> che tu vedrai a l'ultima giustizia.'   (40–5)

('intellectual light, full of love; love of true good, full of joy; joy that transcends every sweetness. Here you will see both hosts of Paradise, one of them in that form that you will see at the Last Judgement.')

Lines 40–2 give us the first definition in the canto of the light of which the Empyrean is made. Much later in the canto, in lines 100–2, we are offered another definition, when we are told that it is the light that makes the creator visible to the creature: it enables man to know God. These two doctrinal statements frame the central experience of the canto, and are in turn almost equidistant from its beginning and end – yet another example of Dante's delight in symmetry and pattern-making. The central experience is Dante the character's initiation into this new world of light. In order to apprehend it at all, his sight must be purified and elevated beyond its normal human capacities. He must stop seeing with the eye of the body and see with the eye of the soul.

It is true that Dante began to *trasumanar,* to go beyond or transcend the human condition, in Canto I of the *Paradiso.* In order to understand the decisive transformation that he now undergoes it is helpful to bear in mind a distinction made by medieval theologians between the three kinds of light that enable man to know God: *lumen naturale intellectus*, the natural light of reason; *lumen fidei*, the light of faith; and, after death, *lumen gloriae*, the light of glory. All men share the natural light of reason; some are given the light of faith; only the most exceptional – the example usually adduced was the *raptus* of St Paul (II Corinthians 12.3–4) – may be granted a vision of the light of glory while they are still alive, for the light of glory is the light by which the blessed in Heaven perceive God. To have seen by the *lumen gloriae* is to have seen God in His essence, an experience that is beyond mortals as mortals, in which they temporarily transcend their human limitations and are raised to participation in the beatific vision.

It has been persuasively argued by an eminent Dante scholar[6] that these three kinds of light correspond to the three stages in Dante's journey – not to the obvious stages, Hell, Purgatory and Paradise, but to the stages of the journey as symbolised by his guides: the journey with Virgil, from Hell to the Earthly Paradise, undertaken by the natural light of reason; the journey with Beatrice, from the Earthly Paradise to the Empyrean, undertaken by the light of faith; and the journey with St Bernard, undertaken by the light of glory. (St Bernard is Dante's companion in the last three cantos of the poem, when Beatrice has left him.) The definitive transformation Dante undergoes in the Empyrean can be seen as the passage from *lumen fidei* to *lumen gloriae*. Once he is initiated into *lumen gloriae* he is potentially able to see God; the rest

200

of the canto, indeed the rest of the poem, shows the actualisation of this potentiality as his new powers are exercised and gain strength, and he gradually becomes more and more able to absorb the reality that is before him, to penetrate it deeper and deeper.

The central section of our canto then describes the process of initiation and its first result, which is Dante's vision of the heavenly host. In lines 43–5, just after the first definition of pure light, Beatrice explains to Dante that he is about to see both hosts of heaven, one being the host of angels and the other being the host of saved souls. In lines 95–6, just before the second definition of pure light, Dante will at last have seen them, 'ambo le corti del ciel manifeste' ('both courts of heaven revealed'). There are four steps in the process that takes him from the prediction to the reality.

The first is the initiation, which is described in lines 46–60. Once again, the experience precedes the explanation. In lines 46–51 Dante says he was suddenly surrounded by a living light, which, just as a flash of lightning temporarily blinds us, left him unable to see anything. He is left swathed in a veil of brightness.

> Come sùbito lampo che discetti
> li spiriti visivi, sì che priva
> da l'atto l'occhio di più forti obietti,
>   così mi circunfulse luce viva,
> e lasciommi fasciato di tal velo
> del suo fulgor, che nulla m'appariva.   (46–51)

(Like a sudden flash of lightning that scatters the spirits in the optic nerve so that it deprives the eye of its function and its power to see even the clearest objects, so a living light shone around me, and left me enfolded in such a veil of its brightness that nothing was visible to me.)

There can be no doubt that Dante expects us at this point to think of Saul on the road to Damascus. He too was suddenly surrounded by a flash of light that blinded him and led to his conversion and change of name. The account of his experience in the Acts of the Apostles is echoed even in the use of the Latinate verb 'circunfulse': 'subito de coelo *circumfulsit* me lux copiosa; cum non viderem prae claritate luminis illius . . .' ('Suddenly there shone from heaven a great light around me; when I could not see for the glory of that light . . .': 22.6).

The unmistakable parallel here established between Dante and

St Paul confirms the relevance of the notion of *lumen gloriae* to this last section of the *Paradiso* – it was precisely St Paul, we remember, whose experience was commonly cited in this connection. It carries us back too to the lines in Canto II of the *Inferno*, where Dante had protested that he was not worthy to be singled out for the privilege of visiting the other world: 'Io non Enea, io non Paolo sono' ('I am not Aeneas, I am not Paul'). His very protestation had established a connection in our minds: that connection is now reinforced beyond any possibility of doubt. Just as the encounter with Cacciaguida in *Par.* XV–XVII had reaffirmed the parallel with Aeneas – Dante is a new Aeneas – so these crucial lines confirm that Dante is a new St Paul, and in a way that goes far beyond their shared and divinely ordained role of teachers to a corrupted humanity.[7]

Beatrice tells Dante (52–4) that each new soul who arrives in heaven is greeted in this way: 'con sì fatta salute'. Dante is a candle whose wax must be prepared to receive the flame. As soon as he hears Beatrice's explanation, he realises that his powers are increasing, he feels that he is transcending the limitations of his human self. In line 58, perhaps the key line in the canto, he is kindled with a new power to see, a 'novella vista', so strong that nothing could ever dazzle or overpower it.

> 'Sempre l'amor che queta questo cielo
> accoglie in sé con sì fatta salute,
> per far disposto a sua fiamma il candelo.'
> Non fur più tosto dentro a me venute
> queste parole brievi, ch'io compresi
> me sormontar di sopr' a mia virtute;
> e di novella vista mi raccesi
> tale, che nulla luce è tanto mera,
> che li occhi miei non si fosser difesi . . .   (52–60)

('Always the love that keeps this heaven motionless welcomes a soul into itself with a salutation of this kind, in order to prepare the candle for the flame.' No sooner had these brief words entered my being than I understood that I was rising above my own powers; and I was kindled with a new sight of such a kind that no light is so bright that my eyes could not have withstood it . . .)

As a direct result of this transformation of his vision, he can see something that he could not see before. It had been there all along, but Dante was simply unable to perceive it in his earlier state.

What Dante sees is a great river of light flowing between two banks covered with flowers. From the river shoot forth living sparks, which settle on the flowers and then plunge back into the river, so that there is a ceaseless coming and going between water and bank.

> e vidi lume in forma di rivera
> fulvido di fulgore, intra due rive
> dipinte di mirabil primavera.
>   Di tal fiumana uscian faville vive,
> e d'ogne parte si mettien ne' fiori,
> quasi rubin che oro circunscrive;
>   poi, come inebrïate da li odori,
> riprofondavan sé nel miro gurge,
> e s'una intrava, un'altra n'uscia fori.   (61–9)

(And I saw light in the form of a river radiant with brightness, between two banks painted with marvellous spring. Living sparks issued from the flood and on either side they settled in the flowers, like rubies set in gold. Then, as though intoxicated with the perfumes, they plunged back into the wondrous waters, and as one went in, another emerged.)

The river of light is the first of Dante's images for Paradise. It is a traditional image, rich in connotations for the medieval Christian. We have only to think of the Revelation of St John, with its description of 'a river of living water, bright as crystal, which flowed from the seat of God' ('Et ostendit mihi fluvium aquae vivae, splendidum tamquam cristallum, procedentem de sede Dei': 22.1). Furthermore there was a wealth of medieval commentary showing its appropriateness as an image of eternal glory, such as St Bonaventure's: 'The river of eternal glory is the river of God . . . Eternal glory is called a river, because of its abundance; of living water, because of its unfailing nature; bright, because of its purity; as crystal, because of its transparency.'[8]

In choosing the image of the river of light, then, Dante is not being original; but the way in which he integrates the traditional image into the poem is entirely so. In lines 70–4 Beatrice anticipates Dante's question as to what the spectacle means, explaining that he must drink the water of the river before his thirst to know can be satisfied.

> 'L'alto disio che mo t'infiamma e urge,
> d'aver notizia di ciò che tu vei,
> tanto mi piace più quanto più turge;

> ma di quest' acqua convien che tu bei
> prima che tanta sete in te si sazi':
> così mi disse il sol de li occhi miei. (70–5)

('The lofty desire that now inflames and impels you to learn about what you see, pleases me the more it grows; but you must drink of this water before you can quench such great thirst'; thus spoke the sun of my eyes.)

One of the linking images that has recurred right through the poem is that of the desire for God expressed as a thirst that can be quenched only by the water of divine grace. These lines echo earlier passages in which Dante has spoken of this water (most notably in Canto XXI of the *Purgatorio*, whose opening lines speak of 'the natural thirst, which is never satisfied except with the water that the woman of Samaria asked for' – that is, the water of divine grace). On the naturalistic level the image of the river is splendidly appropriate – Dante has at last reached the water that can slake his thirst.

But the river of light is not the true form of Paradise. Beatrice explains in line 78, using one of those marvellously evocative Latinisms that contribute so powerfully to the poetic force of the canto and so characteristically fall in the rhyme position, that the river, the sparks and the flowers 'son di lor vero umbriferi prefazi'. They are 'foreshadowings' or 'prefigurings' of their true selves; they appear to Dante in this form because his eyesight is not yet strong enough to perceive them as they really are. We are not dealing here with another qualitative change. It is simply that Dante's eyes discern imperfectly as yet, because, we might almost say, he is not looking hard enough.

> Anche soggiunse: 'Il fiume e li topazi
> ch'entrano ed escono e 'l rider de l'erbe
> son di lor vero umbriferi prefazi.
> Non che da sé sian queste cose acerbe;
> ma è difetto da la parte tua,
> che non hai viste ancor tanto superbe.' (76–81)

(She added too: 'The river and the topazes that go in and out and the joy of the plants are shadowy prefigurings of their true selves. Not that these things are defective in themselves; it is a failing on your part, for your eyes are not yet strong enough.')

Dante acts immediately on Beatrice's suggestion that he must drink of this water, although, of course, the drinking is only metaphorical. Just as the infant who wakes up later than his normal feeding-time turns eagerly to the milk, so Dante eagerly bends to the water. Some critics have found this image ill-judged: we are brought back with a jolt from the sublime to the mundane reality of babies and their needs. Momigliano, for example, describes it as *meschina*, 'mean' or 'poor'. But its use here *is* effective, because it continues the thirst theme and emphasises the naturalness and instinctiveness of wanting to satisfy this thirst. It also enables Dante to make a telling contrast with the later image of an infant behaving unnaturally and self-destructively in lines 139–41.[9]

Dante bends eagerly to the water, in order to see better. As he gazes, the vision has changed shape. It has turned from being a river into being a circle.

> Non è fantin che sì sùbito rua
> col volto verso il latte, se si svegli
> molto tardato da l'usanza sua,
>   come fec' io, per far migliori spegli
> ancor de li occhi, chinandomi a l'onda
> che si deriva perché vi s'immegli;
>   e sì come di lei bevve la gronda
> de le palpebre mie, così mi parve
> di sua lunghezza divenuta tonda. (82–90)

(No baby waking up much later than usual thrusts its face so impetuously towards the milk as I did, to make still better mirrors of my eyes, bending to the water that flows forth for our betterment; and as the eaves of my eyelids drank it in, so it seemed to me that from its length it had become round.)

The circle is a traditional image for eternity – it has no beginning and no end, and its simplicity and perfection were thought to reflect the unity, simplicity and perfection of the Creator. It too had a long history in medieval literature and art. Just as the river is the culmination of all the thirst imagery in the poem, so the circle represents the culmination of all its circle imagery. The change from length to circularity – from time to eternity, in effect – is the third stage in the process. The fourth follows immediately. Just as a masked person appears in his true guise when he removes his mask, so now the flowers and the sparks are revealed in their true identity as the heavenly hosts. The flowers are the souls of the blessed, the sparks are the angels who hover over them.

> Poi, come gente stata sotto larve,
> che pare altro che prima, se si sveste
> la sembianza non süa in che disparve,
>   così mi si cambiaro in maggior feste
> li fiori e le faville, sì ch'io vidi
> ambo le corti del ciel manifeste.
>   O isplendor di Dio, per cu' io vidi
> l'alto trïunfo del regno verace,
> dammi virtù a dir com' ïo il vidi!   (91–9)

(Then, just as people who have been wearing masks look different from before, if they remove the alien appearance that had concealed them, so the flowers and the sparks changed before me into greater rejoicing, so that I saw both courts of Heaven revealed. O splendour of God, through which I saw the lofty triumph of the true kingdom, give me the power to tell it as I saw it.)

That Dante should have been able to produce a description of such extraordinary power from what are essentially stereotyped elements is remarkable. Each stage in the central progression – the blinding light, the river, the circle, the blessed and the angels – is beautifully depicted, and yet each achieves its full impact only as part of a progression, a crescendo of light and joy and astonishment as Dante is able to see more and more clearly what is before him in its true nature. It is this sense of excitement, this thrill of expectation as Dante feels himself transcend his human limitations, that generates the narrative energy we feel running so powerfully through this central section of the canto. It reaches its climax in line 96, when Dante at last sees the heavenly hosts as they really are. At this point he is so overcome that he calls on God's light to help him describe what he saw, an invocation whose directness, simplicity and urgency are startling when compared with the elaborate rhetorical invocations to the Muses with which we have become familiar in the course of the poem: 'dammi virtù a dir com'io il vidi' ('give me the power to tell it as I saw it').

In terms of the narrative structure of the canto, these lines mark the second important change in direction. The *non*-rhyme of lines 95, 97, and 99 signals this clearly. One advantage of the *terza rima* as a metrical form for a narrative poem is its inexorable forward drive: the unrhymed middle line of each terzina propels us forward to the next terzina whose first and last lines provide its natural fulfilment. On the very few occasions when Dante chooses deliberately to ignore the demands of the rhyme scheme and repeat the same word three times, he always does so with some precise rhetorical effect in mind. We all know that the word *Cristo* is 'rhymed' only with itself, because no other word is worthy to rhyme with the name of Christ. This reverence for the holy name probably makes amends for the fact that Dante as a young man had rhymed the word in a highly irreverent, if not actually blasphemous, context (*Rime* LXXVII, 11). In *Purg.* XX, 65–9 the words 'per ammenda' are 'rhymed' together, and the rhetorical effect is one of savage irony as successive outrages are described as making amends for earlier ones. Here when 'vidi' is 'rhymed' with itself the failure to provide a rhyme is an arresting device for changing the pace and mood of the canto. It makes simultaneously a climax (the exclamatory repetition), and a pause (the failure to move forward). Dante has at last reached the point where he can see the heavenly host in its true nature. He now pauses, takes a breath, so to speak, and tries to take in the full significance of what he can see.

In choosing to put the word 'vidi' in this position Dante is being very daring. One cannot fail to notice even on a first reading of this canto, how some form of the verb 'to see' occurs every few lines, with an insistence and reiteration that might well in the hands of a lesser poet have become monotonous and clumsy. There are two threads running through the canto, seeing and light, and the richness and variety and seeming inexhaustibility of the vocabulary associated with light is contrasted with the insistence on the simple verb 'to see' used over and over again. Very rarely do we get a more indirect or elegant variation on the idea. Here Dante is consciously drawing attention to the verb, by a bold stroke turning what might have seemed a weakness into a technical *tour de force*.[10]

The change in direction is immediately apparent in the lines that follow. As Dante the character takes in the details of the incredible spectacle he is gazing upon, Dante the poet explains to us, in a doctrinal formulation of magisterial incisiveness and energy, what this light is. It is the light that makes the creator visible to the creature; it is circular in shape, and the circle is so vast that it is wider than the sun's circumference; the pool of light is formed by a ray reflected from the convex surface of the *Primum Mobile* – convex because we are now outside the outermost of the heavenly spheres; it is from this ray that the *Primum Mobile* receives its very being and its power.

> Lume è là sù che visibile face
> lo creatore a quella creatura
> che solo in lui vedere ha la sua pace.
>   E' si distende in circular figura,
> in tanto che la sua circunferenza
> sarebbe al sol troppo larga cintura.
>   Fassi di raggio tutta sua parvenza
> reflesso al sommo del mobile primo,
> che prende quindi vivere e potenza.   (100–8)

(There is a light on high that makes the creator visible to those of His creatures whose only peace lies in seeing Him. It spreads in the form of a circle, so far that its circumference would be too wide a girdle for the sun. All its visible extent is made of a ray reflected from the surface of the *Primum Mobile*, which takes life and power from that ray.)

Having told us that the Empyrean is nothing other than this sphere of radiance, Dante now describes the company of the blessed in terms of an image, or rather a series of images that describe the same visual effect. We return to Dante the character and the emphatic 'vidi' in line 113.

All these new images represent an elaboration on the basic idea of the circle. It is the way Dante elaborates on the image, rather than his choice of it in the first instance, that is strikingly original. The first image is of a sloping hillside; the next of an amphitheatre; the third of a rose. All are attempting to suggest the relationship of the hosts of heaven to the circular pool of light. The hosts slope upwards and away from the pool of light just as a hillside does from a lake at its feet in whose waters it is reflected; they surround the pool like the seats in an amphitheatre, ascending 'in più di mille soglie' ('in more than a thousand tiers'); they are like the petals around the centre of a rose.

> E come clivo in acqua di suo imo
> si specchia, quasi per vedersi addorno,
> quando è nel verde e ne' fioretti opimo,
>   sì, soprastando al lume intorno intorno,
> vidi specchiarsi in più di mille soglie
> quanto di noi là sù fatto ha ritorno.

E se l'infimo grado in sé raccoglie
sì grande lume, quanta è la larghezza
di questa rosa ne l'estreme foglie!   (109–17)

(And as a sloping hillside is mirrored in water at its foot, as though to see itself in its beauty when it is luxuriant in green and flowers, so, rising above and around the light, in more than a thousand tiers I saw mirrored all those of us who have returned up there. And if the lowest tier encloses within itself so great a light, how great is the width of this rose in its outermost petals!)

The slope turns into an amphitheatre and the amphitheatre into a rose almost without our noticing it, as though the poet is searching for an image adequate to the reality he is describing. The earlier changes in images (from river to circle) reflected a real change in the appearance of the object as Dante was able to perceive it. Here the progression is quite different. The chain of images reflects the onlooker's increasing grasp on the sight he beholds. First a section of the circle (slope with water at its feet); then the whole circle (amphitheatre); then the circle grasped as a whole (rose).

The image of the rose for Paradise is Dante's final choice, and its elaboration provides the basis of the next two cantos. Unlike the river of light and the circle of eternity, it has no obvious counterpart in scriptural sources or medieval religious literature. It has been variously suggested that Dante may have taken the idea from the rose-windows of Gothic cathedrals; from pictorial representations of the blessed around God which show them ranked in tiers; or from the more limited scriptural use of the image in association with the passion of Christ, with the blood of the martyrs, and with the Virgin Mary – in Canto XXIII of the *Paradiso*, for example, she was referred to as a rose. Although all these associations enrich the image, none of them offers a very convincing explanation of its derivation.[11]

Dante's choice of the rose is all the more remarkable when we consider the medieval associations of the flower with the courtly literature of love and romance. The most famous long poem in medieval literature, completed only decades earlier and enormously successful, was the *Roman de la Rose*; it can hardly have been fortuitous that Dante should choose to finish the *Comedy* with the very image that is central to the earlier secular poem.

Apart from its visual and sensual appositeness, which enables him to keep the shape of Paradise in his reader's mind, and simultaneously exploit all the associations of perfume, gladness and spring – as most brilliantly in lines 125–6 – it is almost as if in choosing the image he is responding to a challenge. In the French poem the rose is the symbol of sexual love, and the poem tells how the young poet attempts to pluck the flower in spite of the protection of her loyal supporters. In the *Comedy* the rose is no longer a symbol, it is the reality of the blessed in heaven, the reality of divine love. Both poems tell how the rose is won. That Dante intended a conscious contrast seems beyond doubt.

Indeed, it may well be that we have here another case of the mature poet making amends for the aberrations of his youthful self. There is a late thirteenth-century Florentine version of the *Roman* called *Il fiore* ('The Flower'). Although its attribution is debated, close stylistic analysis of the text reveals striking affinities with Dante's verse, and many scholars now accept his authorship.[12] So just as the rhyme of *Cristo* only with itself makes amends for the irreligious sonnet of his youth, here the rose of Paradise makes amends for a similar youthful indiscretion, the adaptation of a poem whose celebration of sensual love can only have seemed to the mature poet, in the light of his Christian convictions, sinful.

The remainder of the canto shows Dante gazing at the rose, helped by a final commentary from Beatrice. The paradoxical contrast between the size of the rose and Dante's ability to see it in every minute detail is emphasised. His faculty of sight is strong enough not to *smarrirsi*, not to lose itself; and in the Empyrean sight is not affected by distance, for here where God governs directly the laws of physics do not operate.

> La vista mia ne l'ampio e ne l'altezza
> non si smarriva, ma tutto prendeva
> il quanto e 'l quale di quella allegrezza.
> Presso e lontano, lì, né pon né leva:
> ché dove Dio sanza mezzo governa,
> la legge natural nulla rileva. (118–23)

(My sight did not become lost in the breadth and the height, but took in all the extent and the quality of that rejoicing. Near and far, there, neither add nor take away; for where God governs without intermediary natural law has no force.)

Beatrice draws Dante into the yellow of the rose, the centre of the amphitheatre. The canto ends with her words. They are to be her last words in the poem, but neither Dante nor the reader knows this, just as the words spoken by Virgil at the end of *Purgatorio* XXVII were, unknown to Dante the character and the reader, to be *his* last – another example of narrative symmetry, but this time working from one cantica to the next. Beatrice too emphasises the size of the rose. Three sentences all begin with imperatives: 'Mira', 'Vedi', 'vedi'. She points out that there are few seats still unoccupied, her words reflecting the contemporary belief, evidently shared by Dante, that the world was close to its end.

> Nel giallo de la rosa sempiterna,
> che si digrada e dilata e redole
> odor di lode al sol che sempre verna,
>   qual è colui che tace e dicer vole,
> mi trasse Bëatrice, e disse: 'Mira
> quanto è 'l convento de le bianche stole!
>   Vedi nostra città quant' ella gira;
> vedi li nostri scanni sì ripieni,
> che poca gente più ci si disira.' (124–32)

(Into the yellow of the eternal rose, which unfolds and opens and breathes forth perfume of praise to the Sun that makes perpetual spring, Beatrice drew me – I was like someone who wishes to speak yet is silent – and she said: 'Look how great is the assembly of the white robes! See our city, how wide a space it encircles; see our seats, so full that few people are still wanting here.')

But most of her speech is devoted yet once more to the problem of politics on earth, to the issue of Papacy and Empire. She sees Dante gazing at one empty seat over which a crown is set, and explains that it is waiting for Henry VII, the man who was elected Emperor eight years after the fictional date of the *Comedy*, and on whom Dante had based his hopes for a universal empire. But the world is not ready for him. Men are led astray by 'cieca cupidigia' ('blind greed') – and after all the light imagery in the canto the adjective 'blind' stands out with a new force. The last seven lines refer to the hypocrisy of the Pope, Clement V, who pretended to support Henry but secretly plotted against him. Beatrice predicts bitterly that he too will take his place in the circle of the simoniacs

211

in Hell – note the peculiar violence of the Latinism 'detruso', again in the rhyme position – where he will cause his predecessor Boniface VIII to sink even deeper into the rock. The dismissive periphrastic identification of Boniface – 'quel d'Alagna' ('that man from Anagni', perhaps even 'that man who was at the centre of the shameful episode of the kidnapping of Christ's vicar at Anagni' – conveys a fine contempt.

> 'E 'n quel gran seggio a che tu li occhi tieni
> per la corona che già v'è sù posta,
> prima che tu a queste nozze ceni,
>   sederà l'alma, che fia giù agosta,
> de l'alto Arrigo, ch'a drizzare Italia
> verrà in prima ch'ella sia disposta.
>   La cieca cupidigia che v'ammalia
> simili fatti v'ha al fantolino
> che muor per fame e caccia via la balia.
>   E fia prefetto nel foro divino
> allora tal, che palese e coverto
> non anderà con lui per un cammino.
>   Ma poco poi sarà da Dio sofferto
> nel santo officio: ch'el sarà detruso
> là dove Simon mago è per suo merto,
> e farà quel d'Alagna intrar più giuso.'   (133–48)

('And in that great seat on which you fix your eyes because of the crown set over it, there shall sit, before you take your seat at the wedding feast, the soul of the great Harry, Emperor on earth, who will come to set Italy on the right path before she is ready. The blind greed that casts its spell on you has made you like a baby dying of hunger who pushes away his wet-nurse. And the Prefect in the forum of God will at that time be one who will take one course towards him openly and another covertly. But God will suffer him only a short while in the holy office; for he will be thrust down where Simon Magus is deservedly punished, making that man from Anagni go deeper still.')

These lines may seem an abrupt switch in mood and theme; they may even on a first reading seem something of an anticlimax after the splendours of Paradise we have encountered in the course of the canto. But, as we noted at the outset, this canto loses a great deal if it is divorced from those that follow it. The exploration of the rose continues in Cantos XXXI and XXXII, and Beatrice's words can be seen in perspective as a bitter parting shot in which, for the only time in the Empyrean, Heaven and Hell are deliberately juxtaposed. We are reminded, for the last time in the canto, and by Beatrice herself, of just how far Dante the pilgrim has travelled.

Notes

1 Dante the character will pay his final tribute in *Par.* xxxi, 79–90.
2 This comparison with the effect of sunlight on weak eyesight seems a deliberate echo of the end of the *Vita Nuova* (xLI, 6).
3 In relation to Beatrice, the theme had been repeated, but much more briefly, at three points in the journey through the heavens: *Par.* xiv, 79–81; *Par.* xviii, 8–12; *Par.* xxiii, 22–4.
4 Interestingly, the points are made in precisely the reverse order in *Par.* i, again one to a terzina: the inadequacy of human language (4–6); the failure of memory (7–9); the limitations of the human mind (10–12).
5 The possibility that a greater poet may follow him also echoes a theme first stated in *Par.* i (35–6).
6 C. S. Singleton, 'The Three Lights' in *Journey to Beatrice* (Harvard University Press, 1958), pp. 15–38.
7 On Dante's Pauline role, see K. Foster, *The Two Dantes* (London, 1977), pp. 70–3.
8 Quoted by N. Sapegno in his commentary *ad loc.*
9 The baby image will recur in *Par.* xxxiii (106–8), where it will be directly linked with the theme of the inadequacy of Dante's words: 'Omai sarà più corta mia favella, / pur a quel ch'io ricordo, che d'un fante / che bagni ancor la lingua a la mammella.' A mother–son relationship had been established between Beatrice and Dante at the beginning of the *Paradiso* (i, 101–2): 'li occhi drizzò ver' me con quel sembiante / che madre fa sovra figlio deliro' (cf. also *Purg.* xxx, 79). Thus the major divisions of the cantica – the beginning (i), the new beginning in the Empyrean (xxx), and the end (xxxiii) – are marked by the recurrence of the child-baby image as well as the inexpressibility theme. There is of course an implicit connection with the idea of being born again, of spiritual rebirth: 'You are children new born, and all your craving must be for the pure milk of the word, that will nurture you unto salvation' (i Peter 2.2).
10 Note that Beatrice in *Par.* xxviii (109–11 and 139–40) had insisted on the primacy of seeing–understanding in the beatific experience: it precedes and generates love.
11 P. Dronke, in *Medieval Latin and the Rise of European Love Lyric* (2 vols., O.U.P., 1966), vol. i, p. 75, makes an interesting connection with a different literary tradition. Others connect the rose with oriental *mandala*: see especially the diagrams (figs. xv, xvi and xx) in the volume *Lectura Dantis mystica* (Firenze, 1969).
12 The case for Dante's authorship is argued cogently by G. Contini in a series of articles: 'La questione del fiore' in *Cultura e Scuola* (1965), pp. 768–73; 'Il fiore' in *Enciclopedia dantesca,* vol. ii, pp. 895–901; 'Un nodo della cultura medievale: la serie "Roman de la Rose" – "Fiore" – "Divina Commedia" ' in *Un'idea di Dante* (Torino, 1976), pp. 245–83.